THE MOVIE LOVERS' CLUB

Other Books by Cathleen Rountree, Ph.D.

The Writer's Mentor: A Guide to Putting Passion on Paper
On Women Turning 30: Making Choices, Finding Meaning
On Women Turning 70: Honoring the Voices of Wisdom
On Women Turning 60: Embracing the Age of Fulfillment
The Heart of Marriage: Discovering the Secrets of Enduring Love
50 Ways to Meet Your Lover: Following Cupid's Arrow
Fifty Ways to Meet Your Lover
On Women Turning 50: Celebrating Midlife Discoveries
On Women Turning 40: Coming into Our Fullness

THE MOVIE LOVERS' CLUB

How to Start Your Own Film Group

CATHLEEN ROUNTREE

INNER OCEAN PUBLISHING
Maui · San Francisco

Inner Ocean Publishing, Inc.
P.O. Box 1239
Makawao, Maui, HI 96768-1239
www.innerocean.com

Cover design by Gia Giasullo
Book design by Suzanne Albertson

PUBLISHER CATALOGING-IN-PUBLICATION DATA
Rountree, Cathleen.
   The movie lovers' club : how to start your own film group / Cathleen Rountree. —
Maui : Inner Ocean, 2006.
     p. ; cm.
   ISBN-13: 978-1-930722-52-1 (pbk.)
   ISBN-10: 1-930722-52-4 (pbk.)
   Includes a year's worth of monthly suggestions for classic, contemporary, independent,
and foreign films, plus discussion questions.
   Includes indexes. 1. Motion pictures—Plots, themes, etc. 2. Motion pictures—
Philosophy. 3. Motion pictures—Appreciation. 4. Forums (Discussion and debate)—
Handbooks, manuals, etc. I. Title. II. How to start your own film group.
   PN1995 .R68 2006
   791.43/01—dc22   0605

Printed in the United States of America
05 06 07 08 09 10 DATA 10 9 8 7 6 5 4 3 2 1

DISTRIBUTED BY PUBLISHER'S GROUP WEST
For information on promotions, bulk purchases, premiums, or educational use, please
contact: 866.731.2216 or sales@innerocean.com.

☆ DEDICATION ☆

For my mother, the original Movie Lover

For my son, my favorite Movie Lover

For Movie Lovers everywhere

And for Pauline Kael, the most erudite and passionate
Movie Lover of all

☆ CONTENTS ☆

PART 1

Starting Your Own Movie Lovers' Club

Being able to talk about movies with someone,
to share the giddy, high excitement you feel
—that is enough for a friendship.

—PAULINE KAEL

Welcome to
The Movie Lovers' Club

This book is for every movie lover who values compelling films, good friends, and engaging conversations. If you enjoy occasionally inviting friends over for hot fudge brownie sundaes and a movie, creating a movie club that uses this book as your group's guide will heighten your movie-viewing experience. For starters, after the closing credits roll, you'll have an abundance of thought-provoking and entertaining discussion questions to choose from, smoothly navigating you past the same-old "I liked it/didn't like it" post-movie conversation. By the end of each delightful evening, you'll have a deeper understanding of the film, yourself, and your film-watching friends.

In addition, *The Movie Lovers' Club* also gives you the inside scoop about the films you're watching: pithy quotes from actors, directors, and critics; social and cultural background that directly informs the film; and behind-the-scenes insider information. You'll learn scores of insightful movie facts; for instance, *Annie Hall* was originally titled *Anhedonia*, which means the inability to enjoy anything—a fair description of the misanthropic protagonist Alvy Singer, but perhaps not as catchy on a marquee. All of these tidbits will enhance your movie-watching experience and illuminate your after-film discussions.

The Movie Lovers' Club is your ultimate companion and guide, providing everything you need to know to set up and sustain your movie club for years, including tips on selecting members, movies, and munchies.

There's more to be gained from participating in a movie club than just a pleasant diversion (though fun is certainly part of the equation). Movies help us connect and empathize with others, both fellow viewers and movie characters alike. Watching movies together can provide a sense of connection that may be missing from our lives, by presenting shared cultural touchstones. For instance, just the mention of a particular movie, such as *Breakfast at Tiffany's*, evokes the

3

notion of "small town girl makes good in the big city." And anyone who has seen the film will instantly understand what you're getting at if you say, "I felt like Holly Golightly floating down Fifth Avenue."

During the past 100 years the cinema has both mirrored and shaped our internal and external lives: what we think and feel, how we dress, the cars we drive, to whom we are sexually attracted, and so on. The movies we love and identify with throughout our lives have real power to shape who we are and who we aspire to become. Because films have such a capability to transform us, it's inherently and deeply satisfying to talk with friends and family about how the movies we watch relate to our lives.

Discovering and Enjoying the Multiple Benefits of a Movie Lovers' Club

I started my first movie club in 1994 during a time when I was watching one or two films a day as part of my research for a series of books I was writing about women's lives. I found these films to be a source of inspiration in my work and of enrichment in my life. Although I belonged to two book clubs at the time, I knew of no movie clubs. On a whim, I invited several girlfriends to join me in watching movies about women in various life stages, and within a couple of weeks a dozen of us, ages ranging between 30 and 65, began to meet biweekly. I was immediately able to share my insights with others and benefit from theirs.

The group met at my place, which was small enough that some of us had to sit on the floor on cushions. Still, I had a state-of-the-art (for that time) Sony Trinitron, and as a former pastry chef, I happily provided dessert. The other women alternately supplied refreshments, and we took our treats seriously, deriving great delight in serving a spicy mango tea with a fresh boysenberry tart. Once I even prepared homemade espresso ice cream with chocolate-rum truffles. I know, this sounds like a cross between *Big Night* and *Babette's Feast*, but, just as often, I'd serve a cheese board or slices of succulent melon or, the old reliable, hot-buttered popcorn and Cokes. The food, after all, was secondary to the featured event: watching a film with friends. After a few weeks, we began to share recipes and became excited about designing a meal or snack that would perfectly complement the genre, country, or theme of our future films.

We were a sundry assortment of married and single, employed and retired, gay and straight. A few of us still had children at home, and we all shared a combined passion for travel and movies. We called our movie club "In Full Flower: A Closer Look at Women in the Movies," and we met regularly that year. Occasionally a fresh face joined the group and one of them, Katherine, soon became my new best friend.

I compiled a rather exhaustive list of possible film choices, and at each meeting we selected our next feature. The movies spanned from the campy but depressing classic *Sunset Boulevard,* to the madcap *The Summer House*, starring, with palpable panache, the *éternele* Jeanne Moreau. Our first film was the playful *Shirley Valentine*, about a middle-aged, middle-class British housewife who is so far gone she's begun to talk to walls. But Shirley regains her Aphroditic sensuality on a trip (sans husband) to Greece, where she declares, "Sex for breakfast, sex for dinner, sex for tea, and sex for supper." Now, that's my kind of woman. A few months later, with Shirley in mind, we each created our own dream vacation.

By the end of the year, several of us resolved to continue our movie club, but this time we decided to focus on movies about marriage and committed relationships. Those of us who had existing liaisons invited our partners to join the group. Our motto was based on a line from a Marianne Moore poem: "I wonder what Adam and Eve think of it now?" It was de rigueur to watch Bergman's *Scenes from a Marriage*, but we balanced the torturous with the hilarious by including films like the Tracy/Hepburn gem *Adam's Rib*, in which Spence and Kate play married lawyers who find themselves on opposite sides of a criminal trial and nearly divorce each other as a result (see July: Independent Spirits). Luckily, love triumphed, and, like the film's characters, we all went home happy that night. During our gatherings, the opportunity to hear the male perspective on issues of gender, marriage, and men's and women's concerns proved fascinating and often enlightening. One newcomer, Brad, the fiancé of my friend Lori, was especially grateful to be part of the movie club because, as he said, "In addition to providing Lori and me a chance to discuss some topics that were important, I also got to meet and make friends with Lori's buddies, and I got to see and appreciate her through their eyes." Needless to say, we were all invited to Brad and Lori's wedding later that year.

This group met at one couple's house, which provided more comfortable accommodations, but, alas, an inferior television, once again proving you don't need the perfect setup to watch quality films. Shifting the theme and the membership revivified our movie club and introduced an entirely new set of benefits: refreshed curiosity and attentiveness, and novel points of view. Although our group dynamics had been transformed, we continued to learn from one another and the films, and to have a grand time in the process.

Since the days of those early movie clubs, I've started or participated in perhaps a dozen others. And I've loved each of them. Several friends who participated in that first one have gone on to organize their own clubs. One even relocated to Paris, where she started a movie club for American expatriates! Movies are the great equalizer, and all anybody needs to start a movie club are twin passions for good movies and conversation with friends.

Building a Momentous and Close-Knit Community

There's something especially rewarding about watching movies with someone and having a quality conversation afterward. A movie club provides more than simple entertainment, it offers a unique venue for starting, building, or strengthening your relationships, along with a chance to get to know yourself and others better.

A Movie Lovers' Club can consist of as few as two people or as many as your living room or community hall will hold. A couple may decide to create a "club" that is really just an excuse for a weekly movie date. Someone visiting family members or friends may decide to take along this book, watch a few of the movies it highlights, and take advantage of the subsequent conversation as an opportunity to reconnect.

You may want to form your Movie Lovers' Club as a way of connecting with a certain demographic. It's fine to limit your group to single people over 50, or women of all ages, or couples in committed relationships—especially if there's a lack of such connections in your life. This is your group, and you can use it to build the type of community you crave most. Some common types of groups are women-only or men-only, singles, couples, or extended families; parents (including new parents); students; teachers; therapists and counselors; religious leaders and congregants; coworkers; sports groups or recreational center members; environmental or political groups; retirement communities; hospitals or health care groups; recovery, hospice, or grief counseling centers; and prison, alcohol, or drug rehab centers.

The purpose of a group is to bring family and friends together or extend your community by making connections with new people. Think in terms of commonalities of interests. There might be people you know through your hobbies, work, congregation, or volunteering, with whom you have tried to get together, but lacked the appropriate occasion. Movie Lovers' Clubs can help fill specific unmet social needs for conversation about relevant issues and simultaneously enhance your developing community. Movie Clubs are also useful models for youth and the elderly—two demographics for whom movies are a natural enticement for engaging in conversation.

Just as we named one of my movie clubs for women the Femme Film Club, you might want to create a fitting name for yours. Deciding on a name for your group may also help maintain cohesion among the members, as well as help decide on which demographic your club will exemplify. You may find just the right adaptation for your club among the following suggestions, but feel free to devise your own. A natural title for a couples gathering, Scenes from Marriages, is, of course, a twist on the Ingmar Bergman film. Or use another movie-related title, such as Single, Multicultural, Female or You Go, Girl: Chutzpah Unlimited, to represent a club for single women. A cluster of therapists could call themselves The Analyze These Bunch. Or The Mall Alternative Crowd could describe a club for teens. The Mentors as Models Club would suit a team of teachers, while one called Mommies Without "Me" Morning, could bring a much-needed few hours of adult companionship to new mothers, as it deflects or alleviates postpartum depression.

Coming Together for Memorable Movie Moments

One reason we watch certain films repeatedly is because they have unforgettable "movie moments" that cause us to hold our breath, laugh aloud, or shed sympathetic tears—reawakening personal recollections and animating our connection to others. For example, no matter how many times we might watch *Casablanca*, the moment Bogey altruistically sends Bergman to safety on a flight with the husband she doesn't love, we can't help but urgently ask the question, Is he making the right decision or is true love just as worthy of fighting for as world democracy?

Regardless of our answer (and often our answer will change depending on our age and life condition at that particular viewing), we still *feel* something when he reminds her, "We'll always have Paris." Because so will we. The movies we watch become part of our lives and our memories.

Think I'm overstating the power of these movie moments? Just consider how you feel when you recall some of these most memorable scenes:

☆ Rhett Butler racing up a double staircase to sweep an unyielding Scarlett O'Hara into his bracing arms.

☆ The glance between Thelma and Louise on the brink of the Grand Canyon—and the threshold of eternity.

☆ The inimitable Bette Davis in *All About Eve*, telling everyone within earshot at her party to "Fasten your seatbelts. It's going to be a bumpy night."

☆ A youthful Jean-Paul Belmondo and Jean Seberg in Goddard's *A bout de soufflé/Breathless* driving their boat of an American convertible to an inevitable disaster.

☆ Carrie, the prom queen, dripping with pig's blood and ready to inflict carnage on her classmates in the high school gym.

☆ Russell Crowe in the middle of the gladiators' coliseum: "Are you not entertained? Are you *not* entertained?" (Uh, yeah.)

☆ Elevator sex in *Fatal Attraction*.

☆ Juliette Binoche, in the *English Patient*, swaying on a suspended rope as she views, by the light of lit flares, Renaissance frescoes on the ceiling of a Tuscan church.

☆ Fireworks on the Riviera coinciding with Grace Kelly and Cary Grant's first kiss in *To Catch a Thief*.

As intoxicating as these movie moments are when you're watching them alone, there's nothing like sharing these unforgettable scenes with others, especially when you go over them in delicious detail after the closing credits. A postmovie conversation, particularly with a group of intriguing people, can be alternately dynamic, heated, provocative, and illuminating.

A Movie Lovers' Club is the perfect setup for pure pleasure: watching terrific films in the company of other film lovers and eating delicious food. You get to enjoy rich and lively conversations that probe the puzzles of plot, even as you connect cinematic characters' experiences to your own. You get a unique opportunity to go deeper into the meaning of movies, learning about life while having a great time socializing. Pauline Kael, arguably the greatest film critic of all time, appreciated the fact that sharing the "giddy, high excitement you feel" about movies is all you need to create and cement friendships. Which is why you may want to consider starting a movie club of your own, ASAP.

Starting Your First (or Fifth) Movie Lovers' Club

Choosing the Theme

With increasing frequency movie groups are forming, in large cities or provincial towns and villages. One such group decided to focus on American films of the 1970s. Their list included, *Klute*, with Jane Fonda; Coppola's *Apocalypse Now*; Steve McQueen and Ali MacGraw in *The Getaway*; Mel Brooks's *Young Frankenstein*; and one of the very first Hollywood blockbusters, *Star Wars*.

Another movie club consisting of a group of women have been meeting monthly for five years and focus their group solely on documentary films—from *Surfing for Life* to *Waco: The Rules of Engagement* to *The Life and Times of Harvey Milk.*

The Movie Lovers' Club offers various ways to approach the theme of your own film group: by category (choosing to watch only classic, contemporary, independent, or foreign films every month for a year), by monthly theme (selecting one of the four films that interests you most that month, regardless of category), or simply by whichever of the four dozen films highlighted in this book suits your fancy for each particular gathering.

Whatever time of year you start your club or however you choose to use the films in this book, there are abundant film suggestions waiting for you. Depending on how often your group meets (monthly, biweekly, or weekly), there are enough movies and discussion topics for one to four years. However you approach it, your movie group is bound to be a hugely entertaining and enlightening experience.

Choosing Members

So how do you go about finding members? First, decide what you are looking for in terms of tone: Do you want light, fun evenings that focus just as much on the food as the movies? Do you want to intellectually delve into the political, social, or psychological aspects of the film? Do you want to come together with others who use movies as a venue for self-reflection and personal growth? Being clear about what *you* want will help immensely when inviting or screening potential members.

Then ask yourself what you're looking for in terms of size. Generally, anywhere between six and twelve members seems to operate best (though you and your best friend getting together might be just what you're looking for, and that's great, too). It's inevitable that at least one member may miss every other meeting or so, so it's important to have enough remaining voices for an engaging conversation.

Once you are clear about your needs and parameters, it's time to cast the net. If you want to spend time with particular family members and friends, just give them a call and see if they're interested. If you are starting a group specifically to extend your social circle, you can try a few different routes. For friends of friends, put the word out to anyone you know who fits your particular criteria for a good movie club member, and have them do the same (providing them with your guidelines for the kind of group you are starting). Either let your friends choose whom to invite, or ask that anyone you've never met email or call you for a brief conversation to make sure they're a good fit. To meet completely new people, place an ad on a local listserve, in a community paper, or favorite café, explaining the kind of group you're starting as specifically as possible, and asking them to email you regarding their interest (open an anonymous free email account for this). Ask them a few questions about themselves, as well as why they're interested in the group. Use their answers as a gauge for whether to invite them to join or not.

Deciding on the Basics

Before your first meeting, you may want to decide some of the basics about the new film flock, such as, where to meet, how long, and how often. Again, as the person starting the group, you can design it to meet your needs.

Most clubs will probably meet at someone's home or, perhaps, on a rotating basis, at different people's homes. If yours is an organization-based club (teachers, congregation, therapists, or retirement community) there may be a common facility that is suitable for gatherings and that you can get permission to use, either for little or no cost.

Your biggest battle will be deciding on a time that accommodates every member. Most people seem to prefer to have their groups meet in the evenings on a weeknight. But holding your group on a Sunday late afternoon or early evening could be a lovely way to spend the day and an invigorating way to begin the week, with thoughts about both inner and external considerations— personal and world events—on your mind. In terms of the duration of your movie club meetings, since the average length of a movie falls somewhere between 90 and 120 minutes, it makes sense that groups would meet for a minimum of three hours. Of course, depending on whether you serve baguettes and Brie for a showing of *Amèlie*, a baked Alaska (*The Call of the Wild*, anyone?), or a six-course dinner inspired by *Eat, Drink, Man, Woman*, you can adjust the time of your encounter accordingly.

Keep in mind the needs of the group. If you meet on a weeknight, take everyone's schedules into account: who must drive 50 miles to work and arrive by six the next morning; who has a colicky two-year-old at home with whom they will probably be up half the night; who meditates at five o'clock every morning, no matter what; who works at home and answers to no external timetable? As much as possible, keep the group decisions flexible and reasonable for every need. And, naturally, there is always the democratic consensus.

Assembling Your Cast and Crew

For an amusing way of organizing your club, think about the following "movie production roles" that members can assume and exchange each month, each quarter, or at six-month intervals. These are meant to be a whimsical way to structure your club and keep it operating smoothly. Obviously, your group may have too few members to carry out the roles that are listed here, just as other clubs may have too many members to utilize this model. Still, be mindful of the benefits of having specific people serve as a Producer, Director, Caterer, Publicist, Musical Arranger, and Postproduction Crew. Don't try to do everything yourself. It's just too much work, and besides, this is your chance to wear that hat of a publicist or cinematographer that you've been secretly coveting for years.

Some clubs may consider several of the following roles as too minor or peripheral to the needs of their group—or just plain too much trouble; others may enthusiastically designate each role to a specific member. Take a consensus and use as many (or few) of the suggested roles as befits the particulars of your club. You may wish to assign the following roles to group members, have them select the title they will assume, or have them choose a role by pulling a card that lists the function out of a hat. Also, more than one role may be assigned to an individual. The goal is to keep it enjoyable for everyone!

The Executive Producer

As the principal organizer, you have the option of producing your dream club. Where will the gatherings be held? (You may decide it's awfully nice to be able to walk to bed after everyone departs, instead of having to brave the elements on the drive home, or you may relish the opportunity to get out of the house for the evening.) How many members would work best? Should there be a facilitator or a more casual conversation? What types of films will your group watch? How will food be handled (BYO snacks or elaborate feasts)? As Executive Producer, you can be the sole decision maker or you can collaborate with a good friend. Once you've got the blueprint for how the group will be structured, you can start to enlist others. The first thing you'll need is members.

The Casting Director takes responsibility for finding members. (See the preceding section: "Choosing Members" for specific suggestions.)

The Location Director provides a comfortable environment, whether it is a member's home or a community center or church.

The Director

A superlative film director can spin a less-than-brilliant screenplay, and actors with below-A-list status, into box-office gold. So, too, a skillful movie club director (aka Facilitator) can be the foundation for a congenial and long-lived group. The group may select one individual to serve in this role or decide to rotate leadership. Either way, one of the most important functions of good facilitating is the ability to assure that everyone's voice is heard by inviting the more reserved, unassuming members into the discussion—for often these members contribute the most insightful comments. The Director may also read the film description, possibly the accompanying questions, and, perhaps, any extra material, such as interviews with the director or actors, or reviews provided in *The Movie Lovers' Club*.

The Publicist sends out announcements and keeps up the correspondence among group members (who will be absent, who will be the Host for the next gathering—and their address and directions, who will be the Caterer, and so on). It's up to the Publicist to announce, via email or telephone, where the next meeting will be held and who will be (or not be) in attendance.

The Caterer provides the meal, snacks, drinks, and so on, or organizes the other members for potluck contributions. This is a big one, especially for those clubs focusing on fare and libations. The food factor also includes money. Therefore, pooling funds to cover the expenses is probably the way to go. As the participants in these film clubs view their movies, they may be sipping a glass of chardonnay and gobbling up a bowlful of wasabi-covered peanuts. Others may design elaborate theme dinners, such as a potluck Greek feast—fluffy phyllo pastry pillows (cheese *tiropetes*), grape leaves stuffed with rice, currants, and toasted pine nuts (*dolmades*), a custardy eggplant *moussaka*, roast lamb with artichokes, and yogurt/walnut cake, butter cookies (*kourabiedes*), and baklava—while watching *Zorba, the Greek*. Be as simple or elaborate as your collective tastes desire. But, whether one person remains the Caterer for the endurance of the club's lifespan or members alternate this role, it is important to keep the fare fair.

The Cinematographer records the food at theme parties and the lively discussion groups. For those among you who love taking photographs, here is your opportunity to document your club's activities. Thinking ahead, this could also provide material for a club photo album.

The Postproduction Crew is in charge of cleanup after the get-together. This is pretty self-evident: *No one likes to be stuck with a messy house after a party*. Assigning this component of the "cast" makes sure that you aren't! However, the host may prefer to do their own cleanup, in which case, they may simply wish to make the helpful suggestion that each member clear away their own dishes and other such contributions before they leave.

A few additional roles that members might find fun are:
The Set Designer, who arranges for the decorations and/or party-theme ideas.

The Musical Arranger, who decides which CDs will best accompany a particular evening's film and theme activities. Perhaps the film's soundtrack?

The Props Manager, who is responsible for renting or buying the DVD or videocassette (with the club funds) and making sure it is available for the evening's viewing. (Note: It is advisable to purchase the DVD. For an extra benefit, after the meeting the DVD can be raffled off to one of the members.)

The Researcher, who brings extra information connected to the film showing that night: an interview with the actor or director, a film review, a documentary about "The Making of . . ." or about one of the stars, a print article about the movie's time period, a poster, or an autobiography or biography of the director or stars that another member may wish to borrow.

The Scriptwriter compiles a brief sketch of the evening's highlights and emails them to the members. This person could also work closely with The Cinematographer, so that the occasion becomes a concrete happening, not just a lovely, lingering memory.

Before the Show Begins

The *Movie Lovers' Club* will serve as your handbook to establishing a new type of community. As you read earlier in Part 1, this book includes everything you need to know to start and facilitate lively and meaningful movie discussion groups in the comfort of your own home or at a community center.

In Part 2 you will find the *Movie Lovers'* film selections, which are categorized by themes that loosely follow the 12 months of the year, such as, New Beginnings in January, Independent Spirits in July, Working Stiffs in September, and Political Passions in November. The beauty of this cyclical system is that whatever time of year you start your club—summer, autumn, winter, or spring—the film suggestions are waiting for you. You'll never miss anything or feel behind, because you can always catch the film on the next go-round. And if the club members decide on a hiatus or holiday, when you return, you just begin again in the appropriate month.

The 48 films presented in Part 2 provide the basis from which to select your monthly, biweekly, or weekly viewing pleasure. Depending on how often your group meets, there are enough movies and discussion topics for one, two, or as many as four years. Each month features four categories, or genres, of films from which to make your viewing selection: Classic, Contemporary, Independent, and World Cinema. Your club may prefer to watch all the films in one genre— say, all twelve classics for the first year—and then proceed to all the foreign films during the second year (or perhaps in a subsequent or concurrent club). The special features that end/follow each film provide additional material that will enhance your understanding and enjoyment of each movie you watch and discuss. In addition, each selection has a two-part discussion questions section. Of course, you have the option to read the questions, or not, as you prefer prior to viewing the film. Most of the questions are devised in such a way as to avoid spoiling the secrets, but you might wish to watch the movies with a clear mind. The first section, "Reading the Movie" includes four questions concerning the general *mise en scene* and technical aspects (setting, actors, costumes, music, camera angle, and so on) of each film. The second section, "Finding the Meaning," includes six questions, which cover all other areas of discussion, such as character and plot development and relevance between a movie's content and your personal experience. Many films also have a "Bonus Question." These questions have a broader context and deal with either a specific director or actor's body of work or some cultural/political/aesthetic theme. They provide an opportunity to extend your discussion of a film into a wider arena and wander into your own life and store of wisdom for answers. In addition, for a deeper analysis of specific scenes, films' chapter numbers and scene markers are included.

Once you have your club organized, your group of movie lovers ready for action, and your food and drink at hand . . . you are ready to let the show begin!

PART II

Monthly Themes and Films

PAULINE KAEL: In front of the screen, I'm still a kid. Movie love is abiding throughout life . . . we're lovers who are let down all the time, and go on loving.

INTERVIEWER: When I'm at the movies, I feel like I'm swept up, lost.

PAULINE KAEL: I feel as if I'm found.

—A 1998 INTERVIEW

January: New Beginnings

★ ★ ★ ★

The ending is only the beginning.

The Human Comedy, 1943
DIR. CLARENCE BROWN

CLASSIC MOTION PICTURE: *Truly, Madly, Deeply*

CONTEMPORARY MOVIE: *About Schmidt*

INDEPENDENT FILM: *In America*

WORLD CINEMA FEATURE: *After Life*

PREVIEWS

☆ The comedy *Truly, Madly, Deeply* is a *Ghost* for thinking people. The protagonist, Nina, mourns her recently deceased partner, Jamie. When he returns in the flesh, she is overjoyed . . . until his annoying habits (that, in her grief, she had forgotten) begin to resurface. Does she remain in limbo with Jamie, or does Nina move on and commit to a new life with potential beau Mark?

☆ The social satire *About Schmidt* is the best role to come along for Jack Nicholson in years. His portrayal of Warren Schmidt, the saddest of all sad sacks, is nuanced and tempered. We see Schmidt retire from his deadening 9-5 job and encounter life's surprising losses. But in those defeats, he discovers that there may be enough time left to build a life worth living.

☆ *In America* presents the plight of immigrants in a sentimental, yet endearing light. An Irish couple hopes to begin a new life in the United States after the accidental death of their five-year-old son. The story is told through the eyes of their young daughters, Christy and Ariel. The wrenching moments in this movie are balanced by indomitable hope, humor, and generosity of spirit.

☆ The Japanese film *After Life* poses venerable and worthy hypothetical questions: What is heaven and what happens there? And what was the most significant experience in your life? *After Life* is a gem of a film, one that persuades us to contemplate our own memories with gratitude.

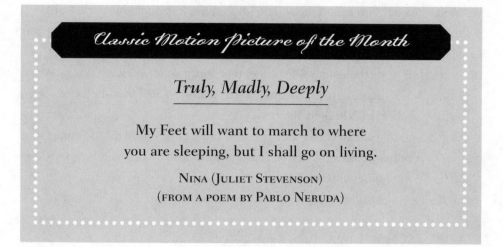

Classic Motion Picture of the Month

Truly, Madly, Deeply

My Feet will want to march to where
you are sleeping, but I shall go on living.

Nina (Juliet Stevenson)
(from a poem by Pablo Neruda)

THE DETAILS

England, 1991, 106M/C; NR; DVD. **Director/Screenwriter:** Anthony Minghella. **Cinematographer:** Remi Adefarasin. **Awards:** Australian Film Institute: Best Foreign Film. BAFTA Awards (Britain): Best Original Screenplay. London Critics Circle Film Awards: British Actor of the Year, Alan Rickman. Seattle International Film Festival: Best Actor, Alan Rickman.

THE SETTING

Late 1980s; England: Bristol, London, Highgate, South Bank.

THE STORY

Forget *Ghost*. Although *Truly, Madly, Deeply* tells a similar tale—the spirit of a grieving woman's dead lover revisits the material realm—it stays away from the gushy emotions, special effects visitations from demons, and obligatory Hollywood action climax portrayed in *Ghost*. Instead, it deals with the sorrow people experience when they lose their most beloved and try to learn how to move forward in their lives—or not. "I want the world to go away," the bereaved Nina (Juliet Stevenson), an accomplished interpreter, tells a friend. Then, one evening as she forlornly plays the piano and imagines that her dead lover Jamie (Alan Rickman), a cellist, is once again playing a duet with her, she slowly turns and is stunned to see him in the flesh. The impossible has happened, what bliss . . . until Nina begins to understand that in her sorrow she may have forgotten aspects of what life was really like with the hypochondriacal, opinionated, sometimes imposing, but nevertheless lovable Jamie. Be careful what you wish for. . . . When he brings home his fellow ghost-buddies to watch videos of old classics from Chaplin to Fellini in Nina's living room ("What *dead* friends?" she asks, incredulously, when he tells her), she may have to put her foot down. The veracity of Stevenson's portrayal is, well, dead on as she flip-flops between genuine bereavement and comical bewilderment. And Alan Rickman's "supernatural" performance makes you wonder why he has yet to become a romantic lead in movies.

READING THE MOVIE

1. A number of miracles transpire in the film. What are they and what place do they hold in the story? What are the aftereffects of these miracles?

2. The working title of *Truly, Madly, Deeply* was *Clouds*. What was the significance of clouds in the film? Which title do you think best represents the film?

3. The cello plays a significant role in the film. What are its symbolic references? How does Nina's flat reflect her state of mind and heart?

4. There is a leitmotif of the issue of immigrants' difficult lives in England during the Thatcher years. How does Anthony Minghella, the director, make his views on this subject clear?

FINDING THE MEANING

5. Is Jamie real or a figment of Nina's imagination? What are the indications that Nina might be hallucinating? What is the specific clue that Jamie and his friends are real? How important is it to you as a viewer to know whether or not Jamie is "real"? What are the qualities that Nina seems drawn to in Mark? What are the similarities and differences between Jamie and Mark? What qualities does each man bring out in Nina?

6. Nina admits to Jamie that she had hidden away parts of her personality or, in the words of Minghella, "surrendered [her] judgment," just as she had put away certain of her possessions that Jamie had been averse to, in order to please him. (#15, 1:29:35) What effect can this subjugation of one's self have on an individual and, ultimately, on a relationship?

7. Jamie tells Nina, "I forgot you could be that way," and reminds her that things are "just like old times." (#11, 1:01:10) Later she asks him, "Were we like this before?" What do they mean? How does this indicate that their life together might not have been as wonderful as Nina has remembered it? What were some of the issues between them?

8. The notion that the dead can return in order to comfort the living is not new, but the absurdity of these two characters actually having a conversation about the geography of heaven and the logistics of being dead (hot water bottles and rats) is wonderfully whimsical. (#14, 1:19) What narrative techniques does the director use to make this situation seem completely plausible, and what impact does it have on your experience of the film?

9. In the end, Jamie seems almost determined that Nina push him out of her life. (#15, 1:25:15) Do you think Jamie had planned this all along in order to release and heal Nina by enhancing her desire to move on? (#15, 1:30:45) Or are you more inclined to think he just realizes that the life/death barrier between them is simply too much to overcome?

10. Over the years many psychologists and therapists have used *Truly, Madly, Deeply* as a vehicle for discussing issues of loss through death and divorce. In what ways do you think this film could console a grieving person and why? Would you recommend it to someone going through a loss? How effective do you think a film can be in helping people through difficult life stages?

MEMORABLE QUOTES

Jamie: The capacity that people have to love … Where does it go?

Nina: I can't believe I have a bunch of dead people watching videos in my living room.

DID YOU KNOW...?

- According to the DVD director's commentary, Anthony Minghella wrote the screenplay specifically for Juliet Stevenson. They had already worked together in nine previous radio, stage, and television productions.
- This was Minghella's first motion picture (made for BBC). He would go on to direct *The English Patient*, 1996 (which won nine Oscars in 1997, including Best Picture and Director), *The Talented Mr. Ripley*, 1999, and *Cold Mountain*, 2003.

CRITICALLY SPEAKING

Mark Duguid, British Film Institute, www.screenonline.uk.org

The film is ostensibly a story of love surviving beyond the grave, in a mini-genre which includes *Here Comes Mr Jordan* (US, 1941), *The Ghost Goes West* (d. René Clair, 1935) and *Ghost* (US, 1990). But Minghella's story, in which a young translator is so overcome by the death of her lover that he comes back, is really a metaphor for the grieving process (although it is just as effective if taken literally).

MORE CLASSIC MOTION PICTURE FAVORITES

The Graduate, Groundhog Day, It's a Wonderful Life,
The Philadelphia Story, Shirley Valentine

Contemporary Movie of the Month

About Schmidt

Helen, what did you really think of me, deep in your heart? Was I really the man you wanted to be with? Was I? Or were you disappointed and too nice to show it?

WARREN SCHMIDT (JACK NICHOLSON)

THE DETAILS

US 2002, 124M/C; R; DVD. **DIRECTOR:** Alexander Payne. **SCREENWRITERS:** Alexander Payne and Jim Taylor (from the novel by Louis Begley). **CINEMATOGRAPHER:** James Glennon. **AWARDS:** Golden Globes: Best Actor, Jack Nicholson; Best Adapted Screenplay. National Board of Review: Best Supporting Actress, Kathy Bates. Kansas City Film Critics Circle Awards: Best Film. London Critics Circle Film Awards: Film of the Year. Los Angeles Film Critics Association Awards: Best Actor, Jack Nicholson (tied with Daniel Day-Lewis for *Gangs of New York*). Best Picture. Best Screenplay.

THE SETTING

Contemporary Colorado: Denver, Boulder; Nebraska: Dundee, Kearney, Ogallala, Omaha (Woodmen Life Assurance Company Building), Great Platte River Road Archway Monument, Pioneer Village, University of Nebraska, Lincoln, University of Kansas, Lawrence.

THE STORY

Sixty-six-year-old Warren Schmidt (Jack Nicholson) is being forced to retire from his work-a-day world as a contracted Omaha insurance executive. Without his duties as an employee to revolve around, this failed Babbitt—along with Helen (June Squibb), his wife of 42 years, who has as much disdain for Warren ("Don't dillydally," she drills him), as he has for her ("Why does everything about her annoy me?")—is adrift on an ice floe of unnamed unhappiness. But after Helen's sudden death, Warren takes a road trip to Denver in his brand new Winnebago, to attend the wedding of his only daughter Jeannie (Hope Davis) to Randall (Dermot Mulroney), a dim-witted waterbed salesman. Along the way, Warren visits his birth home (now a tire store); his alma mater, the University of Kansas; and a monument to pioneers. He makes a nervous pass at a married woman in a trailer park, discovers the pleasures of a hot tub and the dangers of a waterbed, gets loaded on Percodan, and is chased by Randall's aging hippie mom Roberta (Kathy Bates, at her naked best). Along the way, the director uses the device of letter writing to give us access to Warren's self-absorbed interior rantings. The letters are to Ndugu, a six-year-old Tanzanian orphan he has "adopted" for $22 a month. I've never been a full-on Nicholson fan, but as Schmidt he had me at "Dear Ndugu". . . and for the remainder of the film. This is not the over-the-top Jack of "Heeeeere's Johnny" fame from *The Shining*, or the smarmy Harry Sanborn in *Something's Gotta Give*, or the misanthropic Melvin Udall in *As Good as It Gets*. No, Warren is closer to the post lobotomized Randle Patrick McMurphy in *One Flew Over the Cuckoo's Nest*. In fact, it appears that Warren Schmidt has been brain-dead for decades: something to do with living in a loveless marriage and performing mindless work for 40-odd years. That'll do it, all right. Like Warren's Winnebago is for him, this bleak comedy is the perfect vehicle for Jack at his best.

READING THE MOVIE

1. What is the prominent color scheme in the first half of the film, and what does it suggest about Schmidt the character? How does it affect you emotionally when the color scheme changes?

2. What is the significance of the name The Woodmen Life Assurance Company? Why does the film conclude on this image?

3. When Roberta Hertzel, Randall's mother, starts telling Warren Schmidt about her own and (worse) Jeannie and Randall's sex lives, he is

appalled and becomes self-conscious. (scene #20, 1:34) What do you think about the character of Roberta and how she's portrayed? How does her presence in the film affect Schmidt's evolution as a character?

4. Warren Schmidt thinks he's doing the right thing when he tells his daughter not to marry Randall Hertzel. He even goes so far as to share a nightmare he had about Hertzel: "It was very real. Your mother was there and you were there and your Aunt Estelle. And there was a . . . well, it wasn't really a spaceship, it was more like a blimp or an orb of some kind. And then a bunch of weird creatures came out and started trying to take you away, and you wanna know what? They all looked like Randall. Do you understand? And I was jumping up and down to save you." Was Warren right to try to dissuade his daughter from marrying her fiancé? How would you handle a similar situation in your own life and why?

FINDING THE MEANING

5. Warren Schmidt is portrayed as a middle-aged Midwestern "Everyman." He says, "I know we're all pretty small in the big scheme of things, and I suppose the most you can hope for is to make some kind of difference, but what kind of difference have I made? What in the world is better because of me?" Do you agree with his view of his life? Do people have to "make a difference" in order to have lived a valuable life, or does someone have inherent value even if they don't seem to make a valuable contribution to the world?

6. What he writes to Ndugu is alternately touching (because it gives us access to Warren Schmidt's inner life) and maddening (because Schmidt clearly hasn't a clue about 6-year-old Ndugu's kind of existence in Africa). In many instances, including this one, it seems that Schmidt has no comprehension of anyone else's reality or needs. How does that make you feel about him as a character? Have you had experience with people like this in your own life, and if so how have you responded?

7. Jeannie Schmidt tells her dad, "All of a sudden you're taking an interest in what I do? You have an opinion about my life 'now'?" (#18, 1:27) What does this dialogue indicate about her childhood and about her father? As she continues on and puts him in his place, did you empathize with Jeannie or Warren? What do you think this says about your view of the parent–child relationship?

8. At the climax of *About Schmidt*, the title character rises to make a toast to the marriage of his only daughter to a man he regards (accurately) as a nincompoop. (#24, 1:48) Do his words seem genuine? How did this scene affect you emotionally, and what do you think its impact was on the film's overall message?

9. How do you think the action of the film continues after the closing credits? Does Warren Schmidt become a different person or remain the same? (#26, 1:57)

10. What statement is the film making about American culture?

BONUS QUESTION

Jack Nicholson has created a wide range of memorable characters, in addition to the films already listed, such as Jerry Black in *The Pledge*; Will Randall in *Wolf*; Col. Nathan R. Jessep in *A Few Good Men*; Daryl Van Horne in *The Witches of Eastwick*; Garrett Breedlove in *Terms of Endearment*; Eugene O'Neill in *Reds*; Frank Chambers in *The Postman Always Rings Twice*; Jake "J. J." Gittes in *Chinatown*; Billy "Bad Ass" Buddusky in *The Last Detail*; Jonathan Fuerst in *Carnal Knowledge*; Robert Eroica Dupea in *Five Easy Pieces*; and George Hanson in *Easy Rider*. How does his performance as Warren Schmidt compare with these or others that you remember? What was it like to see Nicholson playing an older, less glamorous character? Was his performance believable and affecting, or did you find yourself not being able to forget about Nicholson the actor and believe him as Schmidt?

MEMORABLE QUOTES

[Lying underneath the stars one night, atop his Winnebago, Warren speaks to his dead wife's spirit.]

Warren Schmidt: I forgive you for Ray. I forgive you. That was a long time ago, and I know I wasn't always the king of kings. I let you down. I'm sorry, Helen. Can you forgive me? Can you forgive me?

[A star falls in apparent response.]

DID YOU KNOW...?

"The word 'Ndugu' means brother literally in Kiswahili (same as Swahili). It is also used as slang for 'friend' as in the US." (imdb.com)

ABOUT THE DIRECTOR

Director Alexander Payne was born in Omaha, Nebraska, the location for *About Schmidt*. His other films include *Sideways* (2004); *Election* (1999); and *Citizen Ruth* (1996).

CRITICALLY SPEAKING

Stephen Holden, *New York Times*, 27 September 2002

Warren may be the least colorful character Mr. Nicholson has ever played on the screen, and the role inspires this great actor's least flamboyant performance. The Mephistophelean eyebrows remain at half-staff, and the ferocious bad-boy grin that has illuminated many of his most famous roles with jagged lightning is stifled.

Instead of flash, what Mr. Nicholson brings to his role is a sorrowful awareness of human complexity whose emotional depth matches anything he has done in the movies before.

David Edelstein, *Slate*, 12 December 2002

A Nicholson who doesn't unleash the full force of his libidinous counterculture energy is a Nicholson unrealized. ... *About Schmidt* is flat, depressed, and at times—given this director's talent—disappointingly curdled; it needs every

quivering molecule of Nicholson's repressed rage to keep it alive and humming. . . . And yet the movie holds you. Its characters are one-dimensional, but there is real emotion in its aura of hopelessness. And Nicholson is capacious in his stillness. He will always be the world's most mythically bedraggled rich guy.

MORE CONTEMPORARY MOVIE FAVORITES

Avalon, Closer, The Door in the Floor, Good Will Hunting

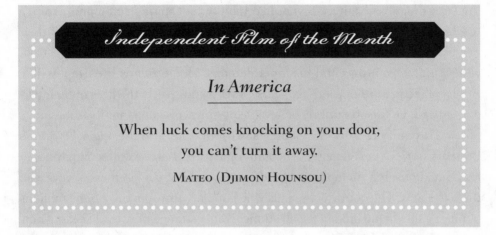

Independent Film of the Month

In America

When luck comes knocking on your door,
you can't turn it away.

MATEO (DJIMON HOUNSOU)

THE DETAILS

2002, 105M/C; PG-13; DVD. **DIRECTOR:** Jim Sheridan. **SCREENWRITER:** Jim
Sheridan, Naomi Sheridan, Kirsten Sheridan. **CINEMATOGRAPHER:** Declan
Quinn. **AWARDS:** AFI Fest: Audience Award, Best Feature Film. Independent
Spirit Awards: Best Supporting Male, Djimon Hounsou; Best Cinematography.
National Board of Review: Best Original Screenplay. Bangkok International Film
Festival: Best Director. Academy Award Nominations: Best Actress, Samantha
Morton; Best Supporting Actor, Djimon Hounsou; Best Original Screenplay.

THE SETTING

Early to mid-1980s; New York City.

THE STORY

Irish emigrants Johnny (Paddy Considine) and Sarah (Samantha Morton), along
with their two daughters, ten-year-old Christy and five-year-old Ariel (played by
real life sisters Sarah and Emma Bolger), drive their 1970s-era station wagon
over the border from Canada. The family is as much running from something—
debilitating grief over the death a few years earlier of their son/brother Frankie—
as they are toward something—the promise of the American dream. In a garbage-
and junkie-ridden section of New York City, the family settles into what should
be a condemned building, but is instead home to a cross-cultural assortment of

the struggling disadvantaged who, like Johnny, an aspiring actor, and Sarah, a teacher, do their best to cope in the face of prejudice and poverty. One of their neighbors is Mateo (Djimon Hounsou), a regal but lonely Nigerian artist struggling with his paintings and his inner demons. He befriends the irrepressible Ariel and the mature-beyond-her-years Christy, and affects the lives of their parents as well. Hounsou's utterly believable portrayal of magnanimity is rare in its purity. There may be fairy tale elements in this movie: as in the original Grimm's Brothers stories, the characters encounter plenty of scary, even seemingly hopeless, situations, but metaphoric breadcrumbs and human kindness always lead them to safety. The courageous souls who populate this film invoke the millions of immigrants living among us, all strangers in a strange new land seeking new beginnings. On the soundtrack, in his classic tune, John Sebastian of the Lovin' Spoonful asks us, "Do you believe in magic?" You will after seeing *In America*.

READING THE MOVIE

1. *In America* embraces an Irish form of magical realism, as exemplified by the magic-wish motif and the trinity of intercut scenes comprised of thunder and lightning, human conception, and Mateo painting with his own blood. How do these details enhance or detract from the film's believability for you?

2. In Hebrew, the name Ariel means "lion of God." It also has significance in English literature. Authors including Shakespeare, (*The Tempest*), Milton (*Paradise Lost*), Pope (*Rape of the Lock*), and Sylvia Plath ("Ariel"), have also used this name prominently. What might be some of the shared characteristics between the literary uses of this name and the film's child named Ariel?

3. At one point, Sarah speaks directly into the camera, as if challenging the suspension of disbelief necessary for a viewer to immerse herself/himself in the story. (#16, 1:03:30) Did it feel like a distraction from the film or did it somehow enhance the emotional power of that moment? How might this scene have played differently if she hadn't directly addressed the viewer in this way?

4. Mateo seems to represent Johnny's alter ego, as if he were the spiritual father to Johnny's despairing parent. What is the process of Johnny's reintegration as a restored, intact father? (#25, 1:29:30)

FINDING THE MEANING

5. Christy says, "We heard Manhattan before we ever saw it, a thousand strange voices coming from everywhere. And you're not going to believe this, but we had to go under the water to get to the city. And we lost contact with everything; it was like we were on another planet." What are other indications in the film of the family's "alien" status? Have you ever had an experience where you felt this different or alien from your surroundings?

6. One of the most unnerving scenes is when Johnny bets the family's next month's rent money to win a doll for Ariel. (#8, :21:20) How did this scene make you feel? What were the underlying circumstances of this desperate gamble? Do you think Johnny's actions were an act of good or poor parenting?

7. What are the qualities that make Mateo so compelling to the other characters? How do your feelings about him change over the course of the film, and what do you think is the purpose of including him so prominently in this story?

8. In the scene where Johnny is watching the movie *The Grapes of Wrath*, what parallels might the filmmakers have been drawing between this family of immigrants (who, in some way, symbolize all immigrants) and the Depression-era migrant workers who are the subject of *The Grapes of Wrath*? What might be the similarities and differences between being an immigrant and being a migrant worker in your native country?

9. Because Halloween derives from a pre-Christian, pagan festival, there is an irony in this exchange between Mateo and Ariel:

Mateo: You the kids from upstairs?

Christy: Yeah.

Mateo: Is this Halloween?

Christy: Yeah.

Mateo: Hm. Where you from?

Christy: Ireland.

Mateo: You came all the way to America to trick or treat?

In the film, Halloween represents a psychological state of mind. What are the issues around which it is a focal point?

10. Sarah tells Johnny, "If you can't touch something you've created, how can you create something that touches people?" What does she mean by this? Do you agree with her statement? (#14, :55:55)

CULTURAL REFERENCES

- Although the disease is never mentioned by name (because it had not yet been identified), we know that Mateo is dying of AIDS when we see his refrigerator filled with drugs and witness the physical symptoms, such as weight loss and sarcoma lesions, that lead to his eventual demise.

- During the time Johnny and Sarah emigrate from Ireland, there is a full-blown war in Northern Ireland, and the unemployment rate was at 17 percent. (DVD director's commentary)

HE SAID/SHE SAID

Mateo: I'm an alien, like E.T., from a different planet. My skin is too sensitive for this Earth. The air is too hard for me.

Ariel: Are you going home like E.T.?

Mateo: I suppose I'm going home.

DID YOU KNOW...?

- The semiautobiographical *In America* is based on events from director Jim Sheridan's life. "Frankie" —the son and brother in the film—was the name of Sheridan's own brother, who died when he was ten. The film is also dedicated to "Frankie Sheridan." (*Script* magazine, November/December 2003)

- The working title for *In America* was *East of Harlem*. Ewan McGregor and Kate Winslet were originally approached to play Johnny and Sarah in the film's early stages of production. (imdb.com)

MOVIE HISTORY

- Steven Spielberg's 1982 film *E.T.: The Extra-Terrestrial* plays prominently in *In America*. Although we are not told specifically when the action of *In America* takes place, we are safe to assume it is the summer of 1982, when the Irish family, in order to escape their economic and emotional woes and the sweltering New York City heat, escape to an air-conditioned movie theater showing *E.T.* Of course, the film mirrors the "alien" theme of the story, and it is also an E.T. doll that Johnny (finally) wins at the street fair.

- *In America* "quotes" an image from Akira Kurosawa's 1952 film *Ikiru*, which is about a Japanese clerk who learns he is dying from cancer and, in order to give something back to the world, decides to build a children's playground. The two scenes of Mateo sitting on a swing are mirror images of the *Ikiru* clerk. (#18, 1:10; #27, 1:37:35) Still, even though interviewers repeatedly brought this to his attention, Jim Sheridan says that he was unaware of the allusion. (DVD director's commentary)

MORE INDEPENDENT FILM FAVORITES

The Cooler, El Norte, The Good Girl, Monster's Ball, The Piano, The Snapper, Waking Life

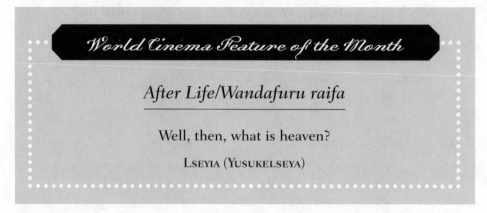

World Cinema Feature of the Month

After Life/Wandafuru raifa

Well, then, what is heaven?

LSEYIA (YUSUKELSEYA)

THE DETAILS

Japan, 1998, 118M/C; NR; DVD. **DIRECTOR/SCREENWRITER:** Kore-eda Hirokazu. **CINEMATOGRAPHERS:** Yutaka Yamazaki and Masayoshi Sukita. **AWARDS:** Mainichi Film Concours (Japan): Best Art Direction, Toshihiro Isomi and Hideo Gunji. Buenos Aires International Festival of Independent Cinema: Best Film. San Sebastián International Film Festival: FIPRESCI Prize: Best Director.

THE SETTING

An abandoned school turned barracks-like way station that resembles a movie studio.

THE STORY

The literal translation of the Japanese title *Wandafuru raifu* is "Wonderful Life" (à la Frank Capra), which fits its universal theme, its empathy for nostalgia, and its homage to cinema. The film begins as 22 recently deceased people arrive in what turns out to be a limbo way station. But this is not the *Purgatorio* of Dante. The staff or counselors in this abandoned schoolhouse–cum–film studio, have only beneficent intentions: to help each individual select, in three days, the "most meaningful or precious memory" from their lives. For most of them, this proves to be a decidedly fettered task. One young man flat-out refuses to make a choice, another prefers his dreams to any actual experience, a teenager at first chooses a trip to Disneyland, and a gregarious man focuses on his sexual memories. The reinterpreted and filmed memory becomes more important than the original memory. *After Life* depicts the art of filmmaking as much as it portrays the concept of heaven. Movies do, after all, help shape our memories as faithfully as the madeleines served Proust. The refreshing absence of religious implication keeps the focus on the characters and their memories, and the stark lack of music prevents sentimentalizing the process. Kore-eda also offers some inventive ideas and themes on the conundrum, What happens after we die?

READING THE MOVIE

1. What elements (editing, setting, dialogue, and so on) are repeated to emphasize a point or perception? What props does the film utilize to evoke a metaphysical awareness?

2. How does the setting affect the story? What is the ultimate emotional impact the setting has on you, and do you think it works for or against the ultimate success of the film?

3. If this film had been made as a Hollywood movie, how do you think it would be different in terms of story, characters, actors, emotional impact, setting, music, and so on? How would some of those possible differences enhance or detract from your experience of this film?

4. Which scenes were the most moving for you and why? Which characters did you most relate to? Which scenes resonated the most for you, in terms of your own life? What impact did the filmic techniques have on your viewing of the movie?

FINDING THE MEANING

5. According to Emily Dickinson, "Such good things can happen to people who learn to remember." The gift of this film is that it invites us to reflect on our own most precious memories. What is the cherished memory that you would take with you to eternity?

6. Why do you think the filmmakers decided to emphasize the importance of a single positive memory? If, in fact, this were the reality of

the afterlife, how might you decide to live your life differently?

7. Our memories are not static or fixed. They are dynamic, reflecting selves that are constantly changing. The director Kore-eda Hirokazu believes that "human emotions are the sparks that fly when 'truth' and 'fiction' collide." *After Life* is his attempt to "explore the consequences of such collision by investigating the uncertain areas between 'objective record' and 'recollection.'" Have certain of your own remembrances changed during the course of your lifetime, or been affected by subsequent experiences?

8. One of the characters says, "Ultimately, we end up turning memories into our own images." (#5, :55) What does he mean by this, and how is the idea supported or contradicted in specific moments throughout the film? Is *After Life* an analogy for or an homage to cinema?

9. When Isyea hears the truth about what happens after death, he says, "So everyone ends up here? You mean, whether you were good or bad or whatever; all that stuff about going to hell if you're bad . . . not true? Everyone's here?" (#1, :08) What effect does this have on him? How does this film differ or overlap with your view of the afterlife? How did your similarities or differences in views affect your overall feeling about the movie?

10. The more you can relate to a film and understand it in terms of your own life, the more satisfying the experience. Is there a coherent message in this film, something that the director wants you to understand or a way in which he wants to change you? If so, what do you think that might be?

BEHIND THE SCENES

The director "researched" *After Life* with 500 videotaped interviews, and then chose 10 nonactors to speak about their own lives, intercutting them with actors playing from the script.

DID YOU KNOW...?

Richard Linklater's film *Waking Life* (2001) references *After Life*.

ABOUT THE DIRECTOR

- When Kore-eda was six years old, his grandfather became increasingly senile. He began to lose his way in the streets. "One day," says the director, "he could no longer recognize our faces. Finally, he could not recognize his own." Kore-eda has remained fascinated with the concept of memories and the role they play in a person's sense of self. (DVD director's commentary)

- Kore-eda's first script was based on a "sci-fi film about a submarine trip through the human bloodstream." It originated from his remembrance that his beloved grandfather died of Alzheimer's disease when he was a child and his desire to "enter my grandfather's brain and restore his lost memories." (*Film Quarterly*, Jonathan Ellis, Volume 57, Number 1, Fall 2003)

CRITICALLY SPEAKING

Tony Rayns, *Sight and Sound*, October 1999

The tangle of emotional and cinematic issues here is almost mystical, but the film's simplicity and transparent sincerity make it easy to accept. Kore-eda's unique achievement is that he has turned a deeply personal and private problematic into a mirror for every viewer's own fears, desires and memories. "Masterpiece" seems not too strong a word.

Edward Guthmann, *San Francisco Chronicle*, 23 July 1999

He never indulges in schmaltz or melodrama, as most American filmmakers do when approaching this theme—think of *It's a Wonderful Life* or the awful *What*

Dreams May Come—but delivers a delicate meditation rich with emotion. . . . That said. . . . The second half drags, and scenes in which the guides reenact and videotape the memories of the dead—thereby embossing them in the passenger's mind—are anticlimactic.

MORE WORLD CINEMA FAVORITES
Blue, Under the Sand

February: Unconventional Loves

★ ★ ★ ★

Love is most complex emotion. Human beings unpredictable.
No logic to emotion. Where there is no logic, there is no
rational thought. Where there is no rational thought, there
can be much romance, but much suffering.

Dr. Yang (Keye Luke) to Alice (Mia Farrow)
Alice, 1990
Dir. Woody Allen

 *Featuring*

CLASSIC MOTION PICTURE: *Annie Hall*

CONTEMPORARY MOVIE: *Eternal Sunshine of the Spotless Mind*

INDEPENDENT FILM: *Secretary*

WORLD CINEMA FEATURE: *Talk to Her*

PREVIEWS

☆ *Annie Hall* is Woody Allen's valentine to the pandemonium of romantic love, and stars former real-life companion, Diane Keaton, as the title character. This wistful comedy comments on love, family, the artistic process, staying true to oneself, and East Coast versus West Coast sensibilities.

☆ *Eternal Sunshine of the Spotless Mind* raises the question, When memories of love are too painful to bear, why not try erasing them? Sounds logical, although this visually arresting, psychologically labyrinthine film is anything but. Still, it provides great fun, if occasional confusion, for viewing and discussion.

☆ *Secretary* is the story of two misfits who discover that their unique sexual proclivities equals a faithful yin/yang fit. The provocative undercurrent of sadomasochism manages to be alternately sobering and hilarious. Strangely compelling, one doesn't know whether to giggle or blush while viewing this brilliantly acted love story.

☆ *Talk to Her* addresses many issues, including why men just don't understand women, and it links true love to an ability to communicate fully. But this dark dreamscape of the heart is slightly disturbing and challenges us on both emotional and intellectual levels as we watch two unlikely men become friends as they care for comatose women. This is Almodóvar at his humanist best with an ending representative of a cinematic Lourdes.

Classic Motion Picture of the Month

Annie Hall

Love is too weak a word for the way I feel—
I lurve you, I loave you, I luff you.

ALVY SINGER (WOODY ALLEN) TO ANNIE HALL (DIANE KEATON)

THE DETAILS

1977, 94m/C; PG; DVD. **DIRECTOR:** Woody Allen. **SCREENPLAY:** Woody Allen and Marshall Brickman. **CINEMATOGRAPHER:** Gordon Willis. **AWARDS:** 1978 Oscars: Picture, Director, Screenplay, Actress. BAFTA (Britain): Film, Direction, Screenplay, Editing, Actress. Directors Guild of America: Director. Golden Globes: Actress. New York Film Critics: Film, Director, Screenplay, Actress.

THE SETTING

Late 1970s; New York City and Los Angeles.

THE STORY

As *Annie Hall* begins, the on-again, off-again affair between Annie and Alvy is already history, and Alvy, in crisis, is reflecting on what went wrong. A neurotic and pessimistic comedian and comedy writer, Alvy lives in Manhattan and, with two divorces behind him, is looking for a new woman he can mold to his specifications. Annie is an equally neurotic transplant from the Midwest. Fun-loving and creative as a photographer and a budding singer, she seeks self-improvement. The story, told with penetrating observation and intuitive dialogue, unfolds in a series of alternately hilarious and poignant flashbacks, showing pivotal moments in both the flowering and demise of their relationship. The running conversation between Alvy and Annie brings a real humanity to this film. Although it is often uproariously funny, the overall tone is thoughtful, reflective, and earnest, and provides much material to ponder.

READING THE MOVIE

1. How is it apparent that Alvy carries baggage from his childhood? What are the ways in which he remains in the grip of events from his childhood?

2. In flashback, we see Alvy in a variety of relationships with women. What are some of the things we learn about him through this montage? Are there components that carry over to his relationship with Annie? If so, what are they?

3. Why does Alvy encourage Annie to go back to school? How does this affect their relationship?

4. The "Battle of the Sexes" issue occupies a great deal of time in movies. In what ways is Annie and Alvy's relationship an extension of this "conflict"?

FINDING THE MEANING

5. Can men and women be just friends? What does it take for them to build and sustain a friendship after they've already been lovers? What do you think the film's message is on this matter?

6. Annie and Alvy have very different perspectives and philosophies on just about everything in life: friends, books, movies, family, commitment, and so on. How did they respond to their differences, and how did that ultimately afect their relationship? What are some ways that people can adapt to their partner's preferences and needs yet remain true to their own core values?

7. How is Alvy and Annie's on-again off-again, relationship like the norm? How does it differ? Why did they have so much trouble breaking up? Have you had relationships in which you stayed too long? Was the awareness of the situation mutual or one-sided? In hindsight, what

were the reasons you stayed? How did you finally extricate yourself from the alliance?

8. *Annie Hall* is wonderfully visually inventive. Allen used flashback, split-screen, animation, instant replay, subtitles, double exposure, and splintered realism in which Alvy or other characters address the audience. Which are your favorites, which are the most successful? What do they contribute to the film? Do they ever distract or detract from your connection to the film and its characters?

9. One of the most humorous scenes in the film has Annie taking Alvy home to meet her Chippewa Falls, Wisconsin, family. We already know that Alvy is paranoid about anti-Semitism, but while he's eating his ham during dinner, Grammy Hall comes right out with, "You're a real Jew, aren't you." This makes our skin crawl, just as Alvy's must. How do the differences between Annie and Alvy's cultures affect their relationship? (#23, :47)

10. On their flight home from Los Angeles, Annie and Alvy privately reflect on their increasing dissatisfaction with the relationship. He describes their relationship as a "dead shark." What does he mean? (#41, 1:18)

BONUS QUESTION

Woody Allen's films often evoke his Brooklyn childhood, when the concept of family was absolute. In *Annie Hall* we see him at Coney Island, in the classroom, and at the Passover dinner table. What other earlier Allen films also portray concurrently loving and exasperated images of his childhood?

CULTURAL REFERENCES

Allen's references range from Honore de Balzac, the nineteenth-century French novelist, who wrote 80 novels (after his first orgasm with Annie, Alvy chirps, "As Balzac said, there goes another novel"); to Trigger, cowboy Roy Rogers's horse (when Tony Lacey recounts the list of previous celebrity owners of his Beverly Hills house, Alvy sarcastically mutters, "Yeah, and probably Trigger lived here, too"); and many other in between, including, Ingmar Bergman, Dick Cavett, Federico

Fellini (see May, 8½), Billie Holiday, Franz Kafka, Henry Kissinger, and Frank Sinatra. But perhaps most notably, Allen produces Marshall McLuhan, the Canadian theorist specializing in communications, who coined the phrase "the medium is the message," outside a movie theater to refute a noxious academic who misrepresents McLuhan's theories. (*Annie Hall*. Peter Cowie. London: British Film Institute, 1996.)

HE SAID/SHE SAID

[Alvy and Annie are seeing their therapists at the same time on a split screen.]
Alvy Singer's therapist: How often do you sleep together?
Annie Hall's therapist: Do you have sex often?
Alvy Singer: Hardly ever. Maybe three times a week.
Annie Hall: Constantly. I'd say three times a week. (imdb.com)

BEHIND THE SCENES

- In one of the many cases in Allen's films where art mirrors life, during the making of *Annie Hall*, Allen and Keaton (like Alvy and Annie) were former lovers who had become closest friends; like the couple auditioning for a play at the end of *Annie Hall*, they first met when Keaton auditioned for Allen's live theater version of *Play It Again, Sam*, in the late 1960s. In her own life, Keaton (whose given name was Diane Hall) was developing a photographic eye (her mother was a photographer); she sang for a brief spell with a rock 'n roll band and eventually was the lead on Broadway in *Hair*. And, much the same as Annie, she had a personality that was both quirky and iconoclastic. This was the fourth of eight films that the two have made together spanning a period from *Play It Again, Sam* in 1972 to *Manhattan Murder Mystery* in 1993. (*Annie Hall*. Peter Cowie. London: British Film Institute, 1996.)
- *Annie Hall* was originally titled *Anhedonia*, which means "the inability to enjoy anything"—a fair description of the misanthropic Alvy Singer. (*For Keeps*. Pauline Kael. New York: Dutton, 1994.)

- "*Annie Hall's* wardrobe came directly out of Diane Keaton's closet. Allen defended Keaton's Goodwill/St. Vincent de Paul–designer sensibility to the film's irate costume mistress. And Keaton's patchwork of oversized men's pants, ties, vests, and hat proved to be fortuitous: the look was licensed and a line of apparel bearing the *Annie Hall* label flourished. Keaton's predilection for used clothes is illustrated again when, near the end of the film, we see Annie in the same well-worn flannel plaid shirt that Alvy had worn in earlier scenes." (*Inside Oscar*. Mason Wiley and Damien Bona. New York: Ballantine Books, 1993.)

MOVIE HISTORY

Alvy's bantering with Annie alludes to those memorable exchanges between men and women in the 1930s and 1940s screwball comedies such, as Cary Grant and Katharine Hepburn in *The Philadelphia Story*, William Powell and Myrna Loy in the *Thin Man* series, Cary Grant and Irene Dunne in *The Awful Truth*, and, of course, Spencer Tracy and Katharine Hepburn in *Adam's Rib* (see July) and *Woman of the Year*.

DID YOU KNOW...?

Diane Keaton won her first Academy Award for *Annie Hall* in 1978. Her second nomination—25 years later—was for her role as a middle-aged, divorced, successful playwright, Erica Berry, in *Something's Gotta Give*. The self-actualized Berry could be seen as the grown-up counterpart to Annie Hall, the wacky, emerging artist struggling with love.

MORE CLASSIC MOTION PICTURE FAVORITES

The African Queen, Far From the Madding Crowd, It Happened One Night, A Place in the Sun, Women in Love

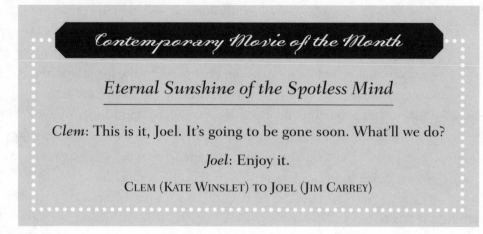

Contemporary Movie of the Month

Eternal Sunshine of the Spotless Mind

Clem: This is it, Joel. It's going to be gone soon. What'll we do?

Joel: Enjoy it.

CLEM (KATE WINSLET) TO JOEL (JIM CARREY)

THE DETAILS

2004, 108m/C; R; DVD. DIRECTOR: Michel Gondry. **SCREENPLAY:** Charlie Kaufman (*Being John Malkovich, Adaptation*). **CINEMATOGRAPHER:** Ellen Kuras. **AWARDS:** OSCARS: Best Original Screenplay. BAFTA (Britain): Best Editing, Best Original Screenplay. Writers Guild of America Award: Best Original Screenplay.

THE SETTING

Present-day Montauk, Long Island, and New York City.

THE STORY

Joel (Jim Carrey), a weary suburban single, wakes up one winter morning on Valentine's Day, calls in sick, and impulsively takes a commuter train out to a beach in Montauk, on Long Island. Some unexplainable metaphysical element draws him there. On the train home he meets Clementine (Kate Winslet), a free spirit (inclined toward manic depression) with dyed-blue hair. Like many ill-suited couples, they are polar opposites who feel a connection they don't understand. But, after two years in the relationship, Clem is bored with Joel's timidity and mundane approach to life. She avails herself of Lacuna, Inc., a brain-cleansing service, to erase all recollection of Joel. When he discovers what she's done, he responds in kind by showing up with all of his Clem memorabilia stuffed into two large shopping bags. "Does it cause brain damage?" he asks. "Technically speaking, the procedure *is* brain damage," the good doctor, Howard Mierzwiak (Tom Wilkinson), reassures him. And here is the crux of the story. *Which* causes more brain damage: remembering love or forgetting it? As Joel struggles to hold onto the memories of the woman he truly loves before they evaporate, the film grapples with the concept of memory itself and how it defines our lives. This twenty-first century screwball comedy raises plenty of questions about the nature of love.

READING THE MOVIE

1. A view of Joel and Clem flat on their backs on a frozen lake is a piece of visual romantic magic. What is the filmmaker's message?

2. The old adages "Opposites attract" and "Familiarity breeds contempt" are both examined in *Eternal Sunshine*. There are significant differences between the two, but what drew Clem and Joel together in the first place? And what ultimately drove them apart?

3. How would you describe the sets on the film? Do they detract from or contribute to the story, acting, and so on?

4. If you were the screenwriter or director of this film, would you change anything? The characters? The plot? The dialogue? The end? If so, how?

FINDING THE MEANING

5. Like its maze cinema predecessors *Memento* and *Mulholland Drive*, *Eternal Sunshine* obliges multiple viewings in order to unfold the mysteries and motives behind characters' actions. For example, there are frequent references to déjà vu, such as when Clem seductively solicits Joel to "meet me in Montauk." How does this somewhat metaphysical bent affect your enjoyment or understanding of the film?

6. How would you compare other screwball comedies, such classics as *The Awful Truth* (1937) and *The Lady Eve* (1941), or others with which you might be familiar, to the post-Freudian new-wave romantic comedy *Eternal Sunshine*?

7. The underlying theme of love longed for, love given and received, and love lost makes for a great film. Just before Joel and Clem meet, Joel thinks to himself, "Valentine's Day is a holiday invented by greeting card companies to make people feel like crap." And later, he ruminates to himself about his and Clem's relationship: "Are we like couples you see in restaurants? Are we the dining dead?" What statement is the filmmaker making about our culture? How might this relate to experiences in your own life?

8. After Mary (Kirsten Dunst) returns the personal files to all Lacuna clients, Joel and Clem listen to the tape of her listing everything she dislikes about Joel and the reasons she wishes to forget him. Just as we tend to blame our partner for our own unhappiness in life, her litany is an expression of her internal misery, which she projects onto Joel. How could this have been a moment of epiphany for Clem? (#19,1:37)

9. When Clem and Joel first meet on the train, he tells her that her name means "merciful," derived from *clemency*. She responds to him by saying, "Although it hardly fits. I'm a vindictive little bitch, if truth be told." Are there moments when she enacts this self-indictment? Do you find Clem to be a sympathetic character? (#1, :07)

10. As Joel's memories progressively disappear, he begins to rediscover his and Clem's earlier passion. From deep within the archives of his autobiography, Joel attempts to escape the procedure. As Dr. Mierzwiak and his crew chase him through the maze of his memory-library, Joel develops a resistance to the procedure. How does Joel's increasing awareness make him ever more in love with Clem? (#14, 1:10)

BONUS QUESTION

Conceptually, there is a link between *Eternal Sunshine* and the myth of Orpheus and Eurydice, in which Orpheus must descend into the depths of the Underworld in order to rescue his lover, Eurydice. How does the attempt to erase the innermost regions of memory seem like a version of hell?

HE SAID/SHE SAID

Clementine: Joely? What if you stay this time?

Joel: I walked out the door. There's no memory left.

Clementine: Come back and make up a goodbye at least, let's pretend we had one. . . . Goodbye, Joel.

Joel: . . . I love you. . .

Clementine: . . . Meet me in Montauk. . .

DID YOU KNOW. . .?

- Kaufman's title is based on an Alexander Pope poem illuminating a letter from "Eloisa to Abelard": "How happy is the blameless vestal's lot! The world forgetting, by the world forgot. Eternal sunshine of the spotless mind! Each pray'r accepted, and each wish resign'd." (DVD director and screenwriter's commentary)

- "The memory-erasing company, Lacuna Inc., takes its name from the Latin word meaning a cavity, hollow, or dip. Therefore, lacuna comes to mean a gap, deficiency, or loss. Additionally, in papyrology (the study of ancient manuscripts) a lacuna is a hole where part of the text is missing, and which can sometimes be re-constructed." (imdb.com)

- The Website www.lacunainc.com displayed in the film is an actual Website that announces, "Bringing you the revolutionary painless non-surgical memory erasing process." The entertaining pages offer "free evaluations," "testimonials," and "promotions." Check it out!

BEHIND THE SCENES

- According to Jim Carrey, he and Kate Winslet were allowed many chances to improvise. Much of their dialogue resulted from videotaped rehearsal sessions during which the two actors became close by sharing tales of their real-life relationships and heartbreaks. (DVD commentary with director and Jim Carrey)

CRITICALLY SPEAKING

In his review, Chris Norris equates the loss of memory with the actual loss of life: "Ruffalo's laptop ministrations often trigger that familiar Microsoft 'chirp' that indicates a completed function—a saved file, a deleted file, an obliterated person. You begin to understand that the procedure is akin to murder, much in the sense that [British author] Martin Amis described suicide as an act of global genocide: you're wiping out the whole world." (*Film Comment*, March/April 2004)

MORE CONTEMPORARY MOVIE FAVORITES

Breaking the Waves, Enemies: A Love Story, High Fidelity,
Leaving Las Vegas, Mississippi Masala

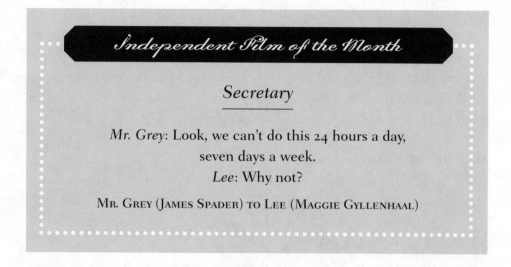

Independent Film of the Month

Secretary

Mr. Grey: Look, we can't do this 24 hours a day,
seven days a week.
Lee: Why not?

MR. GREY (JAMES SPADER) TO LEE (MAGGIE GYLLENHAAL)

THE DETAILS

2002, 111m/C; R; DVD. **DIRECTOR:** Steven Shainberg. **SCREENPLAY:** Erin Cressida Wilson, based on a story by Mary Gaitskill. **CINEMATOGRAPHER:** Steven Fierberg **AWARDS:** Independent Spirit Awards: Best First Screenplay. Sundance Film Festival: Special Jury Prize (for originality): Steven Shainberg. Paris Film Festival: Best Actress: Maggie Gyllenhaal.

THE SETTING

Present-day Los Angeles.

THE STORY

After a stint in a mental institution, Lee Holloway (Maggie Gyllenhaal) arrives at her parents' home in time for her sister's wedding. Within hours, Lee's surroundings unwittingly force her back into her habit of ritualized self-mutilation. She is unable to feel and, therefore, seeks a comfort of sorts in her sacred box of sharp instruments. Lee answers a newspaper ad for a secretarial position at a law office. In the scene where she responds to the ad for a secretary, Lee walks up a path bordered by trees. She is wearing a hooded purple cape when she enters the "wolf's" den on Ardmore Avenue. Although Lee appears to be innocent, we know that she has experienced deep trauma that led to her stay in a mental hospital. Mr. E. Edward Grey (James Spader, at his twisted best), a successful attorney, who just happens to be a sexual sadist, appears at first to be in control of himself and his surroundings, but we discover that he has his own self-doubts and inner demons. Lee and Mr. Grey's interactions are often discomfiting, but never boring. A fantastical love story, *Secretary* is an ardent advertisement for the romantic maxim, There is someone for everyone.

READING THE MOVIE

1. What is the symbolism in the characters' names? Mr. Grey lives on Ardmore Avenue. Lee's last name is Holloway. What do the characters' names say about them? How are the characters' attributes revealed through their actions?

2. Both characters are muted by their lack of emotional expression. Lee's doctor says, "Who's to say that love needs to be soft and gentle?" How does Lee express her affection and how does Mr. Grey express his desire?

3. As their feelings for each other develop, how does their relationship begin to change Lee and Mr. Grey as individuals?

4. At some point the scenes that anticipate Lee acting out through cutting convert into her willingness to follow Mr. Grey's orders. What does this say about Lee's character? How do you feel about her proclivities?

FINDING THE MEANING

5. Is Lee on an adventure of sexual emancipation (or something else?) as she dissolves the boundary between pleasure and pain? How does the issue of sadomasochism, as addressed in the film, make you feel?

6. Mr. Grey often seems at odds with his sadistic tendencies and, in fact, sometimes in despair over them. What are these moments? How does the actor, James Spader, convey his character's point of view?

7. How does the movie make you feel by the end? Is the ending consistent with your expectations?

8. There are several incidents that lead up to Lee's intentionally injuring herself. We could say that she embodies both sadist and masochist, and that Mr. Grey (a sort of cruel but tender Pygmalian) signifies her ability to surrender to an external source of control. When *Secretary* (which was written by a woman) was first released, there was a feminist uproar about Lee's treatment by a man in power. But, as Stephen Holden noted in his *New York Times* review of the film, "It could also be seen as a stylized critique of power and submission in the workplace and its inescapably erotic subtext." What did you feel while watching this scene? Do you think the film goes over the line of sexual politics in its depiction of Lee's treatment? (#13, :15)

9. Lee tells the newspaper reporter, "In one way or another I've always suffered . . . but I'm not as scared of suffering now. I feel more than I've ever felt and I've found someone to feel with, to play with, to love in a way that feels right for me. I hope he knows that I can see he suffers too, and that I want to love him." Just as Lee and Mr. Grey found each other in the movie, do you think that people find/create the love that fits their needs in life? (#23, 1:39:30)

10. Lee describes how she feels seen and accepted by Mr. Grey: "Each cut, each scar, each burn, a different mood or time. I told him what the first one was, told him where the second one came from. I remembered them all. And for the first time in my life, I felt beautiful. Finally, part of the earth. I touched the soil and he loved me back." And in the end, Mr. Grey finally surrenders to Lee's love for him and to his own for her. Are there any indications that theirs will be a lasting union? What might keep it fresh and alive for them? (#24, 1:44:44)

BONUS QUESTION

Lee walks into an environment that is alive with natural light, wood paneling, green plants, and thriving orchids, which seems to represent a Garden of Eden. How does this setting differ from her home environment? What is the connection between the film's story and the myth of Adam and Eve in the Garden of Eden?

HE SAID/SHE SAID

E. Edward Grey: Why do you cut yourself, Lee?

Lee: I don't know.

E. Edward Grey: Is it that sometimes the pain inside has to come to the surface, and when you see evidence of the pain inside you finally know you're really here? Then, when you watch the wound heal, it's comforting . . . isn't it?

Lee: I . . . That's a way to put it.

DID YOU KNOW...?

"The song that plays over Mr. Gray and Lee at the end of the movie is 'Chariots Rise' by Lizzie West. The original lyric is 'What a fool am I, to fall so in love,' but the director did not want to imply that Lee was being foolish, and asked if it could be altered. Because she wanted the song to be in the movie, Lizzie West re-recorded the line as 'What grace have I, to fall so in love.'" (imdb.com)

CRITICALLY SPEAKING

Stephen Holden, *New York Times*, 20 September 2002

Secretary, a small groundbreaking comedy, is a contemporary Cinderella story with a kink and a wink.

Mick LaSalle, *San Francisco Chronicle*, 27 September 2002

The movie, radiant with self-satisfaction, seems to have been intended as a provocation and as a daring exploration of sexuality. But it gets tripped up on two points: It provokes nothing but yawns, and the sex it explores is stuff everybody knows about and says, "So what?"

MORE INDEPENDENT FILM FAVORITES

Danny Deckchair, Don Juan DeMarco, Innocence, Punch-Drunk Love,
Brokeback Mountain

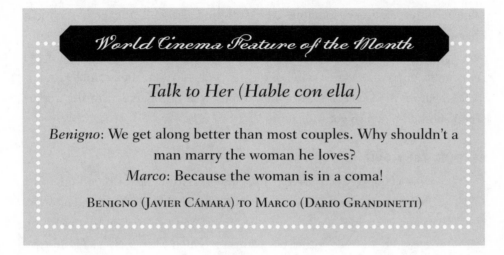

World Cinema Feature of the Month

Talk to Her (Hable con ella)

Benigno: We get along better than most couples. Why shouldn't a man marry the woman he loves?
Marco: Because the woman is in a coma!

BENIGNO (JAVIER CÁMARA) TO MARCO (DARIO GRANDINETTI)

THE DETAILS

2002, 112m/C and B&W; R; DVD (in Spanish with English subtitles). **DIRECTOR/ SCREENPLAY:** Pedro Almodóvar. **CINEMATOGRAPHER:** Javier Aguirresarobe. **AWARDS:** Oscars: Best Original Screenplay. BAFTA (Britain): Best Film Not in the English Language, Best Original Screenplay. Cesár (France): Best European Film. Los Angeles Film Critics Award: Best Director.

THE SETTING

Present-day Madrid and various locales in Spain

THE STORY

In *Talk to Her*, the two men, who develop the central and truest relationship in the film, are in conversation with themselves and each other. An emotional journalist recovering from a love affair that ended 10 years earlier, Marco Zuluaga (Dario Grandinetti) chastises Benigno Martín (Javier Cámara), a naïve nurse who has lived only with his mother, and now devotes his life to caring for Alicia, his sole patient (a young ballet student, tragically in a coma after being hit by a car four years earlier): "Your relationship with Alicia is a monologue!" However, he doesn't do much better himself. From the beginning, Marco and Benigno identify with each other's loneliness and suffering and, in fact, each of the main characters is suspended in his or her own separate world. Although the "conversations" between the men and women are, until the end, one-sided, it is the remarkably empathic Marco who, recognizing his love for Alicia, finally understands that it's not enough to just "talk to her." For one person to truly understand another, he's also got to listen.

READING THE MOVIE

1. The movie opens with Marco and Benigno sitting next to each other at a Pina Bausch dance production. Although they don't know each other, Benigno is curious about a man so intoxicated by emotion that he weeps. What are the other occasions on which Marco cries? Is there a pattern to what elicits this response from him?

2. The Bausch dances also provide a subtext to the story. What are the parallels between the characters and actions in *The Shrinking Lover* and *Talk to Her* and between the characters and the Bausch dancers? Does this add to your understanding of the film's characters and their actions?

3. The soundtrack offers a correspondence to the film's various actions. What are the emotional swings, and how are they countered by the music?

4. The obsessive Benigno says he wants to marry the comatose Alicia because he can talk to her. Marco, in frustration, humorously snaps, "People talk to plants, but they don't marry them." Similar to, but far less sinister than, the two women characters in Ingmar Bergman's film *Persona*, a relationship develops between Benigno and Marco. How does it change each of them?

FINDING THE MEANING

5. Why does Benigno go to the cinema to watch a silent movie? Does the foreshadowing in *The Shrinking Lover* add to or detract from your emotional resonance with the film?

6. What is the implied symbolism in Benigno's name? Does it accurately describe his character? When does Benigno's emotional unraveling begin and what is its progression? What clues do we see of how Benigno cannot distinguish between reality and fantasy?

7. Both Benigno and Marco live their emotional lives through two women who have no awareness of the men's sacrifices. They assume the female roles of taking care of comatose women who are never expected to recover. Although Almodóvar indicates that there is something a little creepy about their devotion, what else is he suggesting that is more humanistic and compassionate?

8. Before Marco's lover Lydia (a matador by profession and, like Marco, on the rebound) is gored by a bull in the ring, she subtly signals Marco that she wants to tell him something. What was it? Who eventually tells him and what effect does it have on his actions? (#6, :20:30)

9. Almodóvar has said, "Nature is amoral. These kinds of passions are part of our nature and go beyond our reason." What are your thoughts about Almodóvar's statement as it relates to Benigno's transgression against Alicia, and as a statement about life in general? What feeling does the complex and emotionally unnerving final third of the film evoke for you? (#21, 1:19:51)

10. *Talk to Her* is a film about being trapped in different kinds of prisons: physical, emotional, spiritual, and, finally, literal. How does the empathy that Marco offers Benigno free Benigno from his spiritual prison? How does it free Marco from his own emotional prison? (#22, 1:28 and #25, 1:35)

DID YOU KNOW...?

"When Marco asks Lydia her name, he says: 'It looks like you've been predestined to it.' That's because bullfighting is also known as 'the art of lidia.'"(imdb.com)

FROM THE DIRECTOR

In an interview with Lynn Hirschberg for *The New York Times Magazine*, Pedro Almodóvar explains his connection to his characters: "My goal as a writer is to have empathy for all my characters. In all my films, I have a tendency to redeem my characters. It is very Catholic—redemption is one of the most appealing parts of the religion. . . . I love characters who are crazy in love and will give their life to passion, even if they burn in hell." (5 September 2004)

CRITICALLY SPEAKING

David Edelstein, *Slate*, 22 November 2002
Almodóvar created [*The Shrinking Lover*], and its surreal Freudian landscape is one of the most wildly funny—and believable—portraits of desire ever put on film. The movie is the strangest experience: a matter-of-fact thing that swallows you whole.

Roger Ebert, *Chicago Sun-Times*, 25 December 2002
No director since Fassbinder has been able to evoke such complex emotions with such problematic material.

MORE WORLD CINEMA FAVORITES

Ali: Fear Eats the Soul, Girl on the Bridge, Under the Sun,
Warm Water Under a Red Bridge, Wings of Desire

March: Friends and Rivals

★ ★ ★ ★

Friend, the finest word in any language.

FLETCHER CHRISTIAN (MARLON BRANDO)
MUTINY ON THE BOUNTY, 1962
DIR. LEWIS MILESTONE

Maybe I wasn't his friend, but if I wasn't, he
never had one.

JEDEDIAH LELAND (JOSEPH COTTON)
CITIZEN KANE, 1941
DIR. ORSON WELLES

Featuring

CLASSIC MOTION PICTURE: *Julia*

CONTEMPORARY MOVIE: *25th Hour*

INDEPENDENT FILM: *The Station Agent*

WORLD CINEMA FEATURE: *Y tu mamá también*

PREVIEWS

☆ *Julia* is a powerful film about a lifelong friendship between two women, and the extent to which one friend will go to help another. Based on a story by Lillian Hellman, it stars Jane Fonda and Vanessa Redgrave, as Lillian and Julia.

☆ *25th Hour* is another controversial Spike Lee film. Edward Norton stars as Monty Brogan, a reforming drug dealer trying to reevaluate his life during his 24-hour countdown to incarceration. The film has garnered both rave reviews and criticism for its examination of an at-once sympathetic and loathsome character, who spends his last hours of freedom walking the streets of the city he loves, while examining the decisions that have led him to this predicament.

☆ *The Station Agent* is a thoughtful, often poignant look at loneliness and how we can find unanticipated friendships in the most unexpected places. Recluse Finbar and grieving artist Olivia find peaceful solitude together, but the hyperkinetic Joe insists on crashing their party. Genuine warmth pervades the film's humorous situations and quirky characters, and we come away feeling most fortunate to have met them.

☆ *Y tu mamá también* is set in the sociopolitical context of Mexico's socialist democracy. Best friends Tenoch and Julio become rivals for Luisa, a sexy older woman, in this award-winning, sexually explicit coming-of-age road film from Mexico. A comedy at heart, the film's underlying poignancy and hard life lessons about impermanency add depth and grace to the most popular film in Mexico's history. "You're so lucky to live in Mexico," Luisa explains. "Look at it—it breathes with life!" And the same can be said about this film.

Classic Motion Picture of the Month

Julia

You've been better than a good friend to me:
you've helped people.

JULIA (VANESSA REDGRAVE) TO (JANE FONDA)

THE DETAILS

1977, 118M/C; PG; DVD. **DIRECTOR:** Fred Zinnemann. **SCREENWRITER:** Alfred Sargent. **CINEMATOGRAPHER:** Douglas Slocombe. **AWARDS:** Academy Awards: Nominated for 11 Oscars. Won: Best Supporting Actress, Vanessa Redgrave; Best Supporting Actor, Jason Robards; Best Adapted Screenplay. BAFTA (Britain): Best Film; Screenplay; Best Actress, Jane Fonda; Cinematography. Directors Guild of America: Fred Zinnemann. Golden Globes: Best Actress: Fonda and Redgrave. New York Film Critics Award: Best Supporting Actor, Maximilian Schell.

THE SETTING

1920s–1970s, New York City, Long Island, Oxford, Paris, Berlin, Russia.

THE STORY

The film is based on Lillian Hellman's story "Julia" in her memoir *Pentimento*, and it focuses on two relationships: the friendship between Lillian and her dearest friend since childhood, Julia, and the 30-year-long love affair between Lillian and Dashiell Hammett, the famed author of detective stories (which were later turned into Hollywood movies, such as *The Thin Man* series). Fred Zinnemann's film adaptation stars Jane Fonda as playwright and author Lillian Hellman, and chronicles her deep and involving friendship with Julia (Vanessa Redgrave). The film increases in intensity when Julia persuades Lillian to transport $50,000 from America to Germany to fund an antifascist Resistance Movement during the 1930s—at great personal risk to Julia. At the same time, the film follows the romance of Lilly and her alternately tender and crusty Dash, who has great influence and impact on her progress as a writer. Fonda and Robards bring dimension to and breathe life into Lilly and Dash. This gripping film provides a portrait of female friendship, as well as a window into the romantic and working relationship of two important writers. But, perhaps most important, *Julia* also portrays what director Fred Zinnemann calls "conscience ... the ability to stand up to pressures infinitely greater than the individual."

READING THE MOVIE

1. What are the three primary lenses through which the story is told? How might the film have been different if it had been told from only one of these lenses?

2. *Julia* was noted for its effective cinematography. In addition to the lush scenery, what are some striking camera movements and angles? What is significant about the light and shading? Do you think the luxuriance of the set design is at odds with the content of the story?

3. The film was made in 1977. If the film were being made today, how might the focus of the story, characters, actors, costumes, set design, and location shots be different? Do you think the film could be made more effectively today, or do you think too much would be lost in an update?

4. While this film follows two different relationships, the title focuses on only one person: Julia. Why do you think this was the chosen title? In the end, does this film ultimately seem to be about Julia? Why or why not?

FINDING THE MEANING

5. Are there any indications in the childhood scenes of the paths that each of the girls will eventually follow?

6. Julia asks Lillian, "Are you as angry a woman as you were a child? I've always liked your anger, trusted it." In light of Lillian's behavior, what does she mean? And how was this supposed anger manifested in Lillian, both as a child and as an adult? (01:33:44)

7. What did you think about the portrayal of female friendship in this film? Did you find it believable? Desirable? Why or why not? Are there any films within the past three to five years based on the theme of friendship between women? If so, what are they and how do they compare with *Julia*?

8. The long-term relationship between Lillian Hellman and Dashiell Hammett was notoriously troubled. How is it portrayed in *Julia*? (:03:50; :36:15) Why do you think the filmmakers made this choice? How does their relationship work in the film as a whole? Does it seem necessary to our understanding of the relationship between the two women, or does it detract from this story?

9. *Julia* was adapted from Hellman's memoir "Julia" in *Pentimento*. Did you read the book? Which do you think was more successful?

10. The film opens with Jane Fonda's voice-over narration, which is the epigraph to *Pentimento*. (:01:30) It is a passage about old paint on canvas that, through age, reveals what was underneath, what was obscured "because the painter 'repented,' changed his mind.... I wanted to see what was there for me once, what is there for me now." This is a beautiful evocation of the mysteries of memory. How does this passage relate to the process in your own life of remembering and forgetting?

BONUS QUESTION

Jane Fonda fought hard to reverse the screen persona she had acquired from her roles as a ditzy newlywed in *Barefoot in the Park* in 1967 and as the bizarre nymph in *Barbarella* in 1968. During the 1970s, in addition to *Julia*, she starred in nine films, including two performances for which she won Oscars: her portrayal of a prostitute in *Klute*, with Donald Sutherland; the wife of a Marine officer, who befriends a paraplegic Vietnam vet (Jon Voight) in *Coming Home* and a socially conscious journalist in the prescient thriller *The China Syndrome*. How might Fonda's characters, including Lillian, be "in dialogue" with one another?

CULTURAL REFERENCES

- Lillian Hellman the playwright/author and her companion, Dashiell Hammett, both politically liberal and supportive of leftist causes, were hounded by Senator Joseph McCarthy during his anticommunist witch-hunt of the 1950s. Subsequently, they were blacklisted by Hollywood producers and prevented from working in the industry. (*Scoundrel Time*, Lillian Hellman. New York: Little, Brown, and Co., 1979.)

- Vanessa Redgrave supported the unpopular Palestinian–Arab cause. After she was nominated for an Academy Award as Best Supporting Actress, her life was threatened by Jewish Defense League members. During her live Oscar acceptance speech, she was at first roundly booed (undoubtedly by JDL members), but then received enormous applause when it became clear that she was antifascist, not anti-Semitic. Her speech in part read, "I salute you (all who stood firm and dealt a blow against . . . the Nixon and McCarthy witch hunt). . . . I pledge to you that I will continue to fight against anti-Semitism and fascism. Thank you." (*Vanessa Redgrave: An Autobiography*. Vanessa Redgrave. New York: Random House, 1994.)

BEHIND THE SCENES

During the early 1970s, both Jane Fonda and Vanessa Redgrave were political activists. However, even though they liked each other personally, their politics were divergent. Vanessa Redgrave had become an articulate spokeswoman for the Palestinian cause, even to the point of making a documentary about Palestine, while Fonda's interest in politics had waned. Thus, they agreed not to discuss politics during the shoot. (*Vanessa Redgrave: An Autobiography*. Vanessa Redgrave. New York: Random House, 1994.)

DID YOU KNOW...?

- A made-for-TV film about the relationship between Dashiell Hammett and Lillian Hellman—*Dash and Lilly*—was made in 1999. It starred Sam Shepard and Judy Davis, and was directed by the actress Kathy Bates.
- *Julia* was Meryl Streep's screen debut as the character Anne Marie, but she had originally tried out for the starring role of Julia.

CRITICALLY SPEAKING

Pauline Kael, *New Yorker*, 10 October 1977

[The film] is important-motion-picture land, where every shot is the most beautiful still of the month. *Julia* is romantic in such a studied way that it turns romanticism into a moral lesson.

Roger Ebert, *Chicago-Sun Times*, 1 January 1977

Many of the reviews of *Julia* went on and on about the relationship it portrays between two women, and have discovered in the movie all sorts of feminist lessons. That's wishful thinking. The only real relationship in the movie is the man–woman one, and, if anything, *Julia* documents how hard it was forty years ago for two women, even emancipated intellectual women, to meet each other on this level.

MORE CLASSIC MOTION PICTURE FAVORITES

All About Eve, The Deer Hunter, Fried Green Tomatoes, Jules and Jim, The Women, Wrestling Ernest Hemingway

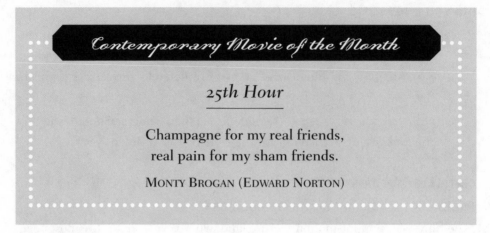

Contemporary Movie of the Month

25th Hour

Champagne for my real friends,
real pain for my sham friends.

MONTY BROGAN (EDWARD NORTON)

THE DETAILS

2003, 130M/C; R; DVD. **DIRECTOR:** Spike Lee. **SCREENWRITER:** David Benioff
(based on his novel of the same name). **CINEMATOGRAPHER:** Rodrigo Prieto.
AWARDS: Berlin International Film Festival: Nominated: Golden Berlin Bear,
Spike Lee.

THE SETTING

2002; New York City: Manhattan, Brooklyn; Texas: Austin, Elgin, El Paso.

THE STORY

25th Hour finds Monty Brogan (Edward Norton), a New York City player, examining the life choices that have led to his conviction as a drug supplier and a
seven-year jail sentence that begins the next day. Director Spike Lee doesn't
demand from us as viewers a specific response to Monty and his actions. On
the one hand, it's clear that he is a good son, a generous friend, and a loving
partner. Still, when his best friend Frank Slaughtery (an excellent Barry Pepper),
a driven Wall Street trader, says, "He profited from others' misery and he deserves
what he gets," we know he's right. Even though he has grown distant from Frank
and his other childhood friend, Jacob Elinsky (Philip Seymour Hoffman), a
socially inept English teacher, Monty chooses to spend his remaining hours with

them as he examines his life, says goodbye to his father (Brian Cox) and girl-friend Naturelle Riveria (Rosario Dawson), finds a home for Doyle the dog res-cued several years earlier, settles a score with his Russian Mafia drug suppliers, and comes up with a plan to buy himself some time from the fate that befalls a good-looking young man in prison. He's aware that his life, as he has known it up to this point, is over. And, indeed, at one point, Frank refers to his incarcer-ation, as ". . . going to hell and never coming back." The story revolves around his interactions with each of these people, all of whom somehow blame them-selves for what is happening to Monty. A subtext of the effect of September 11 on the city itself and its inhabitants brings both a relevance and gravitas to the story. And Norton brings a complexity to Monty's character. As described by A. O. Scott in his December 19, 2002, *New York Times* review, he can be "almost sociopathically controlled and terribly, childishly vulnerable. Monty is all of these things: an outlaw big shot and a messed-up kid; a dutiful son and a drug pusher who sweet-talks schoolgirls on the playground; a cocksure tough guy and a ter-rified pipsqueak." And Monty's controversial monologue in the mirror sequence alone is worth the price of admission.

READING THE MOVIE

1. What does the title mean in relationship to the story? What does this title emphasize or illuminate about the overall events of the film? Why does the film open up the way it does?

2. The film's color changes periodically to a garish intensity; what do the varying hues indicate?

3. Do you think this film was intended to seem realistic (as if the events were happening to real people) or more constructed (as if the events and characters were sociopolitical symbols)? Try to use specific events or scenes to support your opinion.

4. Did you read David Benioff's novel on which the film was based? How faithful is the film to the novel?

FINDING THE MEANING

5. Did you feel sympathy for Edward Norton's character Monty Brogan? If so, why; if not, why not? How was he similar to or different from common social or filmic portrayals of people who sell drugs?

6. How is friendship and loyalty different in Monty's relationships with Frank, Naturelle, and Doyle? How do these varying relationships affect Monty's fate in the film? Which character do you feel was his "truest" friend? What are the various kinds of loyalty that you experience in your own relationships?

7. The narrative makes clear that no character is blameless in terms of his or her life mistakes or in terms of Monty's situation. The characters continually ask themselves and each other the moral question of where they went wrong. How has each friend or family member (Jacob, Frank, Monty's father) played a part in Monty's circumstances? What responsibility do we owe our friends when we see them heading for a crisis?

8. One of the more painful scenes in the film is between Monty and his friend Frank, when Frank tries to assure Monty that he will "be there for you when you get out" of prison. (#12, 1:20) Is it believable, especially in light of Frank's earlier conversation with Jacob? (#7, :46) Is the film's dialogue convincing?

9. The sequence of Monty in the restroom of his dad's bar was controversial when the film was first released. What thoughts and emotions does this scene evoke for you, especially in light of the current fiery issues of illegal immigrants and immigration? (#6, :36)

10. People have had mixed reactions to the film's final montage. How did you respond to it? Did you find it believable or confusing or...? (#18, 1:58) How would you have ended the story?

CULTURAL REFERENCES

25th Hour was the first movie filmed in post-9/11 New York City.

MEMORABLE QUOTES

Jacob Elinsky: What do we say to him?
Frank Slaughtery: We say nothin'. The guy's going to hell for seven years. What are going to do, wish him luck?

BEHIND THE SCENES

According to director Spike Lee, after the fight between Monty and Frank, Monty stumbles over to the bench to pick up his coat. This was an intentional nod to Marlon Brando in *On the Waterfront*. (*Sight and Sound* magazine, Leslie Felperin, April 2003)

STRAIGHT FROM THE ACTOR

In an interview with Demetrios Matheou, Edward Norton describes his understanding of the Monty Brogan character: "You're grappling with a complicated humanity. In that sense Monty falls right in line with a lot of classical tragic heroes—you don't hate Othello, for instance, but he makes a terrible error and it destroys him. And the point is to see his destruction—you're supposed to derive a moral lesson from it. Spike and I talked about making sure the ending was an unequivocal statement: he's going down for what he did." (*Sight and Sound* magazine, April 2003)

STRAIGHT FROM THE DIRECTOR

In an interview with Leslie Felperin, Spike Lee discusses the inclusion of the September 11 subtext in the film: "When David Benioff wrote his original script 9/11 hadn't happened. But when it did I made a quick decision to put this stuff in. It took more deliberation to know how to incorporate it. We didn't want it to seem stuck on—it had to be seamless, but at the same time respectful of the people who got murdered, of the loved ones who got left behind. So we decided to use the music, locations, dialogue and visual references to recreate this mood of post 9/11 New York City and America." (*Sight and Sound* magazine, April 2003)

MORE CONTEMPORARY MOVIE FAVORITES

About a Boy, Donnie Brasco, GoodFellas, Master and Commander,
The Quiet American, Training Day

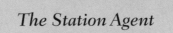

Independent Film of the Month

The Station Agent

Joe: Hey listen, if you guys do something
later, can I join you?
Finbar: We're not gonna do something.
Joe: No, I know, but if you do, can I join you?
Finbar: We're not gonna do something later.
Joe: Okay, but, if you do?
Finbar: Okay.
Joe: Cool.

JOE (BOBBY CANNAVALE) TO FINBAR (PETER DINKLAGE)

THE DETAILS

2003, 90M/C; R; DVD. **DIRECTOR/SCREENWRITER:** Thomas McCarthy.
CINEMATOGRAPHER: Oliver Bokelberg. **AWARDS:** BAFTA (British): Best Original
Screenplay. Independent Spirit Awards: Best Screenplay, John Cassavetes Award.
Sundance Film Festival: Audience Award; Special Jury Prize: Patricia Clarkson.
National Society of Film Critics Award: Patricia Clarkson, Best Supporting
Actress. San Sebastián International Film Festival: Special Jury Prize.

THE SETTING

Contemporary. Rural New Jersey.

THE STORY

Finbar McBride (Peter Dinklage), a four-foot, five-inch dwarf, works in Hoboken
at the Golden Spike model-train store, which is owned by his mentor and only
friend, a man named Henry, who is intensely protective of Fin. After Henry's

sudden death, Fin learns that he has inherited an out-of-use train depot in rural New Jersey. Upon his arrival in the picturesque town of Newfoundland, Fin hardly has time to settle into the ramshackle oasis before the aggressive but Joe Oramas (a hilarious Bobby Cannavale) shows up on Fin's doorstep with a "Hey, bro, you the man," and a café con leché. Cuban Joe has taken over his ailing father's food truck, "Gorgeous Frank's," which is parked a stone's throw away from Fin's new home. We soon understand that Joe's curiosity, rambling talkativeness, and eagerness to please are a result of his own isolation. Fin and Joe could hardly be more different, yet the endearing Joe opens up the world to Fin in the unexpected ways that only new liaisons can.

A short time later, another quirky resident, artist Olivia Harris, while driving to the market, runs into Fin (literally) as he walks to the Good to Go Deli on a country lane. At first, theirs is not a fortuitous meeting, but the repentant Olivia, too, shows up on Fin's doorstep, with a bottle of brandy as penance. Soon it appears that Fin and his depot assume the role of the old-time station agent: they become a surrogate community center for the nomadic souls of Newfoundland.

Similar to characters in another "stranger comes to town" movie such as Jim Jarmusch's *Stranger than Paradise*, the members of this unlikely trio, each lonely in his or her own way, learn that friends not only make life more interesting, they make our lives worth living. The wise saying "We inherit our family but we choose our friends" is no where more apparent than among the eccentric characters who populate Newfoundland, New Jersey, in this enchanting film.

READING THE MOVIE

1. What do you think of the casting of the three main characters? The director/screenwriter has said that he wrote the script specifically for Dinklage, Clarkson, and Cannavale. Can you imagine what other actors could have performed these roles?

2. What are some foreshadowings of events to come? In retrospect, were they noticeable enough or too subtle? For instance, in the train shop, while Fin is working at his desk on a model, he accidentally knocks

over a toy figure. What happens immediately after that? In another scene, when Olivia comes to Fin's station house to apologize, she drops her purse and the contents spill out. What does Fin notice that alerts him to something about Olivia?

3. Newfoundland, New Jersey, is an actual place. What is the significance/symbology of the setting to the film's story? How did the various sets of the film affect you emotionally? What are the social responsibilities of the historical station agent that Fin (unwittingly) inherits?

FINDING THE MEANING

4. In movie characters we often find qualities that resonate with us. What are qualities among Fin, Olivia, Joe, Emily, and Cleo that you experience in yourself? Who is the most like you? Who is the most unlike you? Which of them did you like the most and why?

5. We have the sense that Fin has lived in an angry, isolated state for most of his life. When he comes into contact with people in the real world, he begins to understand that each of them has their own cross to bear in life, such as when he learns about Olivia's loss (#6, :22). What are the similarities and differences among the types of losses each of the characters has sustained and how they've dealt with their losses? How do you tend to respond to loss in your own life?

6. Peter Dinklage, who portrays Finbar, really sets the dramatic and comedic pace of *The Station Agent*. Due to the character's solitude, much of the film is played in silence, almost as if quiet itself were another character. How did you respond to the stretches of silence in the film? Did you welcome them or did they make you uncomfortable? Why? How did this silence and slower pacing affect your understanding of the characters and their lives?

7. The relationship between Joe and Fin mellows, and they relax into what appears to be not only an acceptance but an appreciation of their differences. How are these changes indicated?

8. What is it about Cleo's character that allows Fin to fully open up to her?

9. Take a closer look at Olivia's paintings (#7, :25:18 and #17, 1:09:49). How might the images reflect Olivia's inner emotional state?

10. Fin has an explicit epiphany in this scene (#19, 1:19). The light on his face from the oncoming train seems almost beatific. How does this experience change him? What is each of the other characters' moment of insight about his or her own life? How did these insights affect you emotionally?

BONUS QUESTION

The Station Agent is beautifully and lovingly photographed by cinematographer Oliver Bokelberg. There are references to other contemplative artists' work, such as photographer Walker Evans's images of abandoned country buildings, Edward Hopper's paintings of a nude woman wistfully sitting on the edge of a bed, and Vermeer's glorious portraits. Can you identify those scenes? How do the images reflect various characters' inner lives?

HE SAID/SHE SAID

Finbar: Well, there are people called train chasers. They follow a train and they film it.
Olivia: Are you a train chaser?
Finbar: No.
Olivia: How come?
Finbar: I don't know how to drive a car. And I don't own a camera.
Olivia: That'd do it.

Emily: What do you do?
Finbar: I'm retired, actually.
Emily: Aren't you a little young to be retired?
Finbar: No, dwarves retire early. Common fact.
Emily: Yeah, lazy dwarves.

BEHIND THE SCENES

- According to the director's DVD commentary, the Newfoundland train depot that Finbar McBride inherits was completely renovated when the location scout found it. According to McCarthy, "It looked like a Starbucks inside." The set designer aged the building 100 years in three days.

- The book that Joe reads when he is sitting next to Fin on "the patio" is *All Quiet on the Western Front* by Erich Maria Remarque. This is a joke on Joe, as the last thing he is capable of, at that point, is being "quiet."

- Director McCarthy likens the diminutive actor Peter Dinklage (who plays Finbar) to "a John Wayne or a Gary Cooper. He's a classic archetypal Hollywood character who is better or worse, sometimes rude, sometimes enjoyable, but always true." (*Filmmaker* magazine, Nick Jarecki, Fall 2003, Vol. 12, #1)

- McCarthy worked closely on the script for three years with his three primary actors, especially Peter Dinklage, about whom the director says, "Peter's life experience as a dwarf was obviously very unique." But the two agreed that the story would not be "'a coming of height' story about a small person who deals with the challenges of being small," but rather about characters "who for different reasons choose to disconnect from their community." (*FLM* magazine, Thomas McCarthy, Fall 2003)

ABOUT THE DIRECTOR

Thomas McCarthy studied philosophy in college before he attended Yale Drama School and later acted in several Hollywood films as well as in a television series, *Boston Public*. He spent two years writing the script for *The Station Agent*, his first film, and one year gathering financial backing. Stumbling upon a train depot in a small New Jersey lakeside town got him to thinking about the story. During that time he began to notice how certain of his friends isolated themselves, one because of an illness and others because they were out-of-work actors. McCarthy became interested in "the themes of isolation and connection and disconnection. The train is such an obvious metaphor—how it connected everything," he says. "I think some of us forget the history, the impact of the train. It is already a technological fossil, but what it did for this country is amazing!" (*Filmmaker* magazine, Nick Jarecki, Fall 2003, Vol. 12, #1)

MORE INDEPENDENT FILM FAVORITES

The Adventures of Priscilla, Queen of the Desert; Me Without You; My Bodyguard; Spring Forward; Swimming with Sharks; Withnail and I

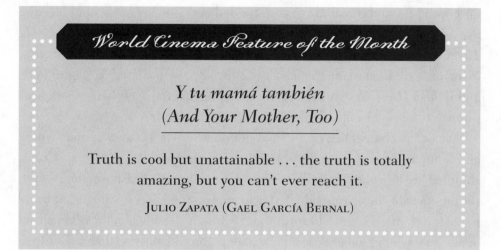

THE DETAILS

2001, Mexico, 105m/C; R; DVD, Spanish with English subtitles. **DIRECTOR:** Alfonso
Cuarón. **SCREENPLAY:** Alfonso Cuarón, Carlos Cuarón. **CINEMATOGRAPHER:**
Emmanuel Lubezki. **AWARDS:** Venice Film Festival: Best Screenplay. Independent
Spirit Awards: Best Foreign Film. Havana Film Festival: FIPRESCI Prize: Alfonso
Cuarón. National Society of Film Critics Award: Best Foreign Language Film. San
Francisco Film Critics Circle: Best Foreign-Language Film.

THE SETTING

Present-day Mexico City and Huatulco, Oaxaca, Mexico.

THE STORY

Y tu mamá también seems to leap back and forth between Francois Truffaut's
sophisticated *Jules et Jim* and the moronic *Beavis and Butt-Head Do America*.
Ostensibly, it is a coming-of-age journey about two sex-obsessed teenage males
in Mexico City and their road trip with a woman ten years their senior, to a distant (and imaginary) beach. But this multilayered movie is a masterwork of filmmaking, with depth and unspoken meaning. Cuarón's lucid storytelling skills
and his instinct for gaining access to unsettling emotional states carry his theme

far beyond its superficial likeness to the tedious *Summer of '42*, and give the movie the life-altering gravitas of other road movies. It is simular to *About Schmidt; The Adventures of Priscilla, Queen of the Desert; Going Places; Lost in America; Pieces of April; Rain Man; Thelma and Louise; Two for the Road; Voyage in Italy*; and *Wild at Heart*, in that each of the characters, because of their experiences through travel, is changed forever.

Tenoch Iturbide (Diego Luna) and Julio Zapata (Gael García Bernal), whose girlfriends are traveling in Italy for the summer, meet and flirt with Luisa Cortés (Maribel Verdú, who is married to Tenoch's cousin), at a lavish wedding—even the president of Mexico attends. Trying to impress the "older woman," they invite her to travel with them to a beautiful, secret beach. Later, when Luisa's husband admits to infidelity, in her despair, she eagerly joins the boys on their road trip to the fabricated destination. Along the way, explosively ripe sexual tensions, quarrels, and revelations arise among the trio. One of Luisa's teachings to the boys is that "the greatest pleasure is giving pleasure," and this movie is pure pleasure.

READING THE MOVIE

1. What is the symbolic significance of the name and the existence of the unspoiled, poignant paradise "Heaven's Mouth"?

2. Emmanuel Lubezki's camera is at the characters' level as all three of them feverishly, drunkenly give in to their sexual impulses. What effect does this camera angle have on you as the viewer? Do you feel like these sex scenes are gratuitous or an integral part of the story?

3. Cuarón is unafraid of sexuality, and the sex scenes in this film exude a titillating sensuality. How does the film use sex to reveal Julio and Tenoch's hidden and complex feelings toward each other, as well as reveal Luisa's unspoken devastating secret? What effect does the revelation of secrets have on each of the characters? Does the film evoke memories of a youthful romantic fling you have experienced?

4. Maribel Verdú creates the mysterious character of Luisa as a mercurial personality. On the one hand, she playfully seduces the boys for her own gratification, and then explosively turns on them when they disap-

point her—"Play with babies and you'll end up washing diapers!" she snaps at them. Nevertheless, there is another side to Luisa that is both world weary and untainted, as seen when she tells Tenoch and Julio, "Life is like the surf, so give yourself away, like the sea." How did you feel about her character throughout the film? In retrospect, how does the film's final revelation explain much of Luisa's behavior and her melancholy awareness? Do you feel differently about her in hindsight?

FINDING THE MEANING

5. In an early scene, a poster for the cult American film *Harold and Maude* (starring Ruth Gordon as a fun-loving, eccentric octogenerian, who, in a brief romantic fling, transforms the life of Harold, a morbid 20-year-old) is in the background. (#1, 01:07) What is this film's (clearly tongue-in-cheek) connection to it? What is the director telling us by referencing it?

6. Through the voice-over narrator's subversive sociopolitical comments, and the magic of his cinematic language, Cuarón introduces us to three Mexicos. Rich boy Tenoch's Mexico represents a ruling class of privilege, corruption, and social insensitivity and cruelty (#7, :19:45); Julio's Mexico represents a socially conscious but struggling middle class (#10, :25:35); and the Mexico of Tenoch's nanny/housekeeper and, later, the fisherman and his family represents the economically exploited, uneducated, impoverished caste. (#26, :1:20:30) There are many unspoken class differences between Tenoch and Julio. What are some examples of this disparate class system depicted in the film? Does director Cuarón make his political leanings apparent? What are they?

7. Cuarón skillfully uses the French New Wave technique of a third-person voice-over narrative. The director and his screenwriter-brother Carlos watched Godard's *Masculine/Feminine* together. But, rather than describing the inner life of one character, as Godard does, Cuarón uses the voice-over technique to "trace the interaction between characters and history and how the two continually intersect." (#16, :40:25;

#22, 1:03:10) (*Filmmaker*, Winter 2002) Does this technique work for you? Does it bring you deeper into the story or take you out of it?

8. Inherent in the film's title, and in the "older woman/younger man" theme, this film touches on the notion of Freud's theory of the Oedipal complex. It also, somewhat more subtly, demonstrates a theme of latent homosexuality. Do you see how these themes might be interconnected? If so, how; if not, why not?

9. One way or another, a road trip, like a spiral, always leads its protagonists back to the beginning, but on a deeper, wiser level. The adage "Wherever you go, there you are," is especially true in this film. How are Tenoch and Julio altered by what they think will merely be a free-spirited adventure? What self-knowledge do they gain? (#31, 1:36:00) Have you ever been transformed personally by a road trip or other journey? How, and why do you think it is that travel causes people so much internal change?

10. Compare *Y tu mamá también* with other road movies you have seen, such as *About Schmidt; The Adventures of Priscilla, Queen of the Desert; Going Places; Lost in America; Pieces of April; Rain Man; Thelma and Louise; Two for the Road; Voyage in Italy;* and *Wild at Heart.* How were the characters altered? What were the transformative factors? Who did they become? What might be the similarities and differences?

HE SAID/SHE SAID

Luisa: You have to make the clitoris your best friend.
Tenoch: What kind of friend is always hiding?

MOVIE HISTORY

- In 2001, *Y tu mamá también* broke all Mexican box-office records, when it had the highest-grossing theatre opening. (imdb.com)
- Gael García Bernal (Julio Zapata) also starred in *Amores Perros*, 2000, and *The Motorcycle Diaries*, 2004 (a road film about Ché Guevara).

ABOUT THE DIRECTOR

Mexican director Alfonso Cuarón has also directed the Hollywood features *A Little Princess* (1995), *Great Expectations* (1998), and *Harry Potter and the Prisoner of Azkaban* (2004).

STRAIGHT FROM THE DIRECTOR

In an interview, Alfonso Cuarón explains that a major theme of his film is "identity": "Here are two teenagers trying to figure out their identities as they grow up; a woman trying to find her identity as a liberated woman and a country that, in our opinion, is a teenage country trying to find its identity as a grown-up one." (*Filmmaker* magazine, Peter Bowen, Fall 2003)

CRITICALLY SPEAKING

Peter Travers, *Rolling Stone*, 11 April 2002

Cuarón's return to his roots adds to the resurgence in Mexican cinema marked last year by Alejandro González Iñarritu's *Amores Perros*. Cuarón's hot-blooded, haunting and wildly erotic film revels in the pleasures of the flesh without losing touch with thought and feeling. Its emotions are as naked as its bodies. The result shames Hollywood claptrap such as *40 Days and 40 Nights* that passes off crudity as the latest in cool. *Y tu mamá también* is in Spanish with English subtitles. Don't worry. Very little gets lost in the translation.

Desson Howe, *Washington Post*, 3 May 2002

The movie's about flesh *and* spirit. *Y tu mamá también*, punctuated with smart, touching narrative about the political situation in Mexico and the fatalistic connections between everyone, is compellingly intelligent. The boys' transparent, juvenile agenda leads to an ever-deepening saga about so many things: love, self-deception, fidelity and the ultimate affirmation of life.

MORE WORLD CINEMA FAVORITES

Autumn Tale, Dreamlife of Angels, Elling, Monsieur Ibrahim, Shower, Under the Sun

April: Heroes and Mavericks

★ ★ ★ ★

You think I'm licked. You all think I'm licked. Well,
I'm not licked. And I'm going to stay right here and fight
for this lost cause.

JEFFERSON SMITH (JAMES STEWART)
MR. SMITH GOES TO WASHINGTON, 1939
DIR. FRANK CAPRA

Woman in bar: Hey, Johnny, what are you rebelling against?
Johnny: What've you got?

JOHNNY (MARLON BRANDO)
THE WILD ONE, 1953
DIR. LASLO BENEDEK

Featuring

CLASSIC MOTION PICTURE: *To Kill a Mockingbird*
CONTEMPORARY MOVIE: *Hotel Rwanda*
INDEPENDENT FILM: *Whale Rider*
WORLD CINEMA FEATURE: *The Sea Inside*

PREVIEWS:

☆ *To Kill a Mockingbird* is the faithful adaptation of Harper Lee's Pulitzer
Prize–winning novel. We see life in a small Southern town in the 1930s

through the innocent eyes of two children, whose father is the defending attorney of a black man falsely accused of attacking a white woman. This masterful film is as powerful today as when it was first released in 1962.

☆ *Hotel Rwanda* is set during one of the worst atrocities in African history: the attempted genocide of the Rwandan people in 1994 by the Hutu militia. The refined and resourceful manager of an elegant Belgian-owned four-star hotel (portrayed by an utterly convincing and memorable Don Cheadle), Paul Rusesabagina uses the hotel as a sanctuary for over 1200 threatened refugees. We agonize with Paul as he and his guests are failed by the international community. But in the end, this story reminds us that the dignity and goodness of one person can make a difference.

☆ In the Australian film *Whale Rider*, we are introduced to Pai, a young girl whose spiritual awareness is matched by her perseverance to achieve her rightful place in her tribal lineage. But first she must convince the tribal elder, who happens to be her patriarchal grandfather, that, yes, a girl is destined to lead their people. The awe-inspiring New Zealand land and seascapes and the convincing performances (especially by new comer Keisha Castle-Hughes) make this film a delightful viewing and discussion experience. The ending is not only inspiring and uplifting, it's transcendent. It offers a mystical hope, even in the face of a harsh reality.

☆ *The Sea Inside* is based on the true story of quadriplegic Ramón Sampedro (Javier Bardem in a sensitive and compassionate performance) and his efforts to convince the courts in Spain of his right to die. After more than two decades of being bedridden, Javier is determined to end his life, but first, he must convince his family, his friends, and the legal system. This film delicately deals with issues that are currently in the political forefront.

Classic Motion Picture of the Month

To Kill a Mockingbird

If you just learn a single trick, Scout, you'll get
along a lot better with all kinds of folks. You
never really understand a person until you consider things
from his point of view... Until you climb inside of
his skin and walk around in it.

ATTICUS FINCH (GREGORY PECK)

THE DETAILS

1962, 129M/B&W; R; DVD. **DIRECTOR:** Robert Mulligan. **SCREENWRITER**:
Horton Foote. **CINEMATOGRAPHER:** Russell Harlan. **AWARDS:** Academy Awards:
Best Actor, Gregory Peck. Best Adapted Screenplay. Best Art Direction–Set
Decoration, Black-and-White. Cannes Film Festival: Gary Cooper Award, Robert
Mulligan. Golden Globes: Best Film Promoting International Understanding.
Best Actor, Drama, Gregory Peck. Best Motion Picture Score, Elmer Bernstein.
Writers Guild of America: Best American Drama.

THE SETTING

1932–1933. Macomb County, Alabama.

THE STORY

The film *To Kill a Mockingbird* is based on Harper Lee's semiautobiographical
novel about her childhood in Monroeville, Alabama in the 1930s. Scout, the child
protagonist, is six years old, her brother, Jem, is ten. Their widower father Atticus,
portrayed flawlessly by Gregory Peck in an Academy Award-winning performance), embodies fairness, compassion, and decency, qualities especially notable

in an environment of bigotry and prejudice. An adult Scout remembers, Macomb, her hometown, as "a tired old town," even in 1932, when she first knew it. "Men's stiff collars wilted by nine in the morning; ladies bathed before noon, after their 3 o'clock naps, and by nightfall were like soft teacakes with frosting from sweating and sweet talcum." Although it is a faithful adaptation of a major American work of literature, the film stands on its own merit.

READING THE MOVIE

1. Why does the film open up with the title sequence? Is it a foreshadowing?

2. In addition to the title, the mockingbird motif is carried throughout the film. Atticus tells his children that when his own father gave him his first gun, he warned him that he "could shoot all the blue jays I wanted—if I could hit 'em; but to remember it was a sin to kill a mockingbird." What do mockingbirds symbolize in the film?

3. Who narrates the film? What is the point of view (POV)? Is it consistent throughout the film? How does it (or doesn't it) serve the story?

4. Does the black-and-white cinematography add to or detract from your involvement with and pleasure in the film? (#2, :03) Would it have been more effective in color? Why or why not? What effect does the soundtrack have on you? Does it enhance the action in subtle ways or is it distracting?

FINDING THE MEANING

5. The film provides many indications of Atticus's devotion to his children and to his principles. In one scene he tells his son, Jem, "There's a lot of ugly things in this world, Son. I wish I could keep 'em all away from you. That's never possible." (#16, :46) What are other ways in which Atticus demonstrates how his parental skills are informed by his ethics? The movie has been inspiring people for well over 40 years. Does it inspire you? If so, in what ways?

6. Although *To Kill a Mockingbird* takes place in the Depression era, it was released in 1962, during the early years of the civil rights movement. If you experienced the era of civil rights in the 1960s, what was that period like for you? Did you see the film upon its theatrical release? What was your response to it? If you are too young to have personally experienced this period, what do you know about it? Do you think that the depiction of racism in the film is accurate to the period? Why or why not?

7. Is each character—Atticus, Scout, Jem, Robert, Mayella, Boo, the judge—fully developed and portrayed as a real person or one-dimensional? What are the qualities that make them believable or flat?

8. The film's producer and director have said that they encountered much resistance from the studios during the planning stages of *Mockingbird*. Why do you think that might have been? Would it be easier or more difficult to get a film like this made today? Why?

9. *To Kill a Mockingbird* has many emotional moments, but we never feel that the director is manipulating us. A testament to Mulligan's subtle style is the aftermath of the court scene. Although Atticus has lost his case, he has fought valiantly. As he prepares to leave the courtroom, the black observers in the balcony acknowledge this honorable man by standing and saluting him as he exits. (#30, 1:42) What makes this scene so powerful? How might it have been done in a more typical Hollywood style? And how would that have affected the outcome?

10. Alan J. Pakula, *Mockingbird*'s producer, said in an interview that the film depicts a "childhood we all wanted to have and most of us didn't. We are rooted in a street in which we know everyone. We are free to live our own mystery under the protection of the father. It's one of the great American myths, right up there with *Huckleberry Finn*." Do you agree with this statement? Does it apply to you? Why or why not?

BONUS QUESTION

About this film, Gregory Peck once said that the role was "something [I] had to do." Judging from what you know about Peck's biography, was he similar to the character of Atticus Finch? Why or why not? How does this role compare with others that he played throughout his career, such as *Spellbound, Duel in the Sun, Gentleman's Agreement, David and Bathsheba, The Snows of Kilimanjaro, Roman Holiday, Moby Dick, The Man in the Gray Flannel Suit, On the Beach, Cape Fear, Captain Newman, M.D., The Omen, MacArthur, The Boys from Brazil,* or any others with which you are familiar? Is there a consistent quality in the characters he elected to portray?

CULTURAL CONTEXT

1932–1933, the time during which the story takes place: Franklin Delano Roosevelt is elected president; Aldous Huxley's grimly prophetic *Brave New World* is published; Charles and Anne Morrow Lindbergh's baby is kidnapped; the first years of the Dust Bowl in Texas, Kansas, and Oklahoma; Adolph Hitler assumes power in Germany; Albert Einstein leaves Germany; Gertrude Stein publishes *The Autobiography of Alice B. Toklas*; Prohibition ends. Births: Edward Kennedy, Jacques Chirac, Mario Cuomo, Elizabeth Taylor, François Truffaut, Peter O'Toole, Sylvia Plath, John Updike, Johnny Cash, Michael Caine, Brigitte Bardot, Philip Roth, Susan Sontag, Ruth Bader Ginsburg, Willie Nelson.

1962, the year the film was released: The Cuban missile crisis; Rachel Carson publishes *The Silent Spring*; John Glenn is the first man to orbit around the Earth; African American James Meredith enrolls in the University of Mississippi under the order of the Supreme Court; Sean Connery creates Agent 007 in the first James Bond film, *Dr. No*; the Rolling Stones is formed; Doris Lessing publishes *The Golden Notebook*; Marilyn Monroe, William Faulkner, Herman Hesse, Eleanor Roosevelt, Isak Dinesen, Robinson Jeffers, and e.e. cummings die. Births: Jodie Foster, Tom Cruise.

MEMORABLE QUOTES

Scout as an adult recalling her friend, Boo: "Neighbors bring food with death, and flowers with sickness, and little things in between. Boo was our neighbor. He gave us two soap dolls, a broken watch and chain, a knife, and our lives."

BEHIND THE SCENES

- Brock Peters, who played Tom, started to cry while shooting the testifying scene, without rehearsing it this way, and Gregory Peck said that he had to look past him, instead of looking him in the eye, without choking up himself.

- In an interview on the DVD, the composer Elmer Bernstein explains how the idea for the film's score came to him: "I couldn't figure out what the film was about in a way that was an open door to walk through. Certain things were obvious—it was about racism, the Depression, the South. But the minute you say it's about the South, you get tied up with geography. Do you want banjos and the blues? I didn't want to get involved in geography. The question becomes what to get involved in, how to get into these issues. But then I realized that the film was about these issues, but seen through the eyes of children. That was the clue. Once I got that, that led to the tentative one-finger piano thing that children do when they are trying to pick out a tune. It gave me the bells and musical box effects and harps".

DID YOU KNOW...?

- According to Gregory Peck, the famed defense attorney F. Lee Bailey once confided to him that he became a lawyer "because of Atticus Finch."

- Although the watch Atticus uses is a prop, the sentimental value of the original watch, which belonged to Harper Lee's father, was significant enough that Lee gave the original to Gregory Peck because he reminded her so much of him.

STRAIGHT FROM THE ACTOR

About playing the role of Atticus Finch, Gregory Peck declared, "It was like climbing into a favorite suit of clothes. . . . I knew all about that man, those children, and that small-town background." (*Film Quarterly*, Mark Holcomb.)

CRITICALLY SPEAKING

An original review at the time of the film's release.
James Powers, *Hollywood Reporter*, 11 December 1962
One of the finest pictures of this or any year, *To Kill a Mockingbird* is certain also to be one of the best-loved. [It] is a genuine experience, so penetrating and pervasive it lingers long after the last image has faded. There is no question it will be one of the year's most honored films. Funny, sad, exalting in its theme . . . [it] could be a solid commercial hit as well. It certainly deserves to be.

A contemporary review.
Mark Holcomb, *Film Quarterly*, Volume 55., Number 4, Summer 2002
It is possible to enjoy and even champion *To Kill a Mockingbird* without turning a blind eye to its thematic flaws or overestimating its relevance. It daringly rejects the bland conformity of the not-so-recently-past (at the time of the film's original release) Eisenhower era by casting Atticus's futile challenge to the status quo in a heroic light. At the very least, it tells its story in the context of race and class, which precious few films have attempted to do even in the intervening four decades.

MORE CLASSIC MOTION PICTURE FAVORITES

Christopher Strong, On the Waterfront, Rebel Without a Cause,
Spartacus, The Wild One

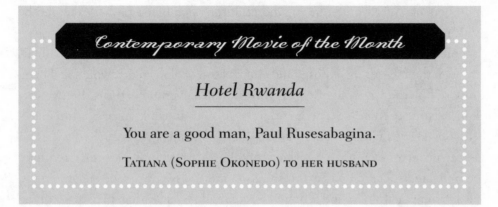

Contemporary Movie of the Month

Hotel Rwanda

You are a good man, Paul Rusesabagina.

TATIANA (SOPHIE OKONEDO) TO HER HUSBAND

THE DETAILS

2004, 121M/C; PG-13; DVD. **DIRECTOR:** Terry George. **SCREENWRITERS:** Keir Pearson and Terry George. **CINEMATOGRAPHER:** Robert Fraisse. **AWARDS:** Toronto International Film Festival: People's Choice Award. Political Film Society: PFS Award: Human Rights. Humanitas Prize: Best Film. Black Reel Awards: Best Actress, Drama, Sophie Okonedo. AFI Fest: Audience Award: Best Feature Film. Academy Awards: Nominated: Best Actor, Don Cheadle; Best Supporting Actress, Sophie Okonedo; Best Original Screenplay.

THE SETTING

1994; Kigali, Rwanda.

THE STORY

In *Hotel Rwanda*, Terry George, the director, recounts the horrific massacre of 1 million Rwandan people during a three-month period in 1994 in a country smaller than Massachusetts. Don Cheadle gives a phenomenal performance depicting a hero: Paul Rusesabagina, a quiet, meticulous, dignified Rwandan hotel manager in the capital city of Kigali, who, in the face of chaos and butchery, becomes an unlikely liberator. Cheadle's Rusesabagina embodies grace under pressure, and his efforts earned him a well-deserved Academy Award nomination for Best Actor. Paul Rusesabagina valiantly risked his life and the lives of his wife, children, and extended family, to provide sanctuary for increasing

numbers of Tutsi women, men, and children, as a blood bath—executed by
warring Hutus—waged on the streets and in the homes of innocent Tutsi tribespeople. The Tutsi and Hutu (an artificial differentiation between individuals
through the measuring of noses and comparison of skin colors, which had been
imposed by the governing Belgian government), eventually turns the two fac-
tions against each other. The fact that Paul is Hutu, while his wife, Tatiana, is
Tutsi makes his circumstances all the more alarming. We first see Paul as an
astute observer of human behavior, who has learned to work the system of a
complicated social order. As the situation around him worsens exponentially,
his inherent tactfulness and acquired resourcefulness allow him to barter for time
and human lives. Although watching *Hotel Rwanda* is an emotionally wearying
experience, we find solace in the lifesaving actions of one good man.

READING THE MOVIE

1. What is your overall response to the film? Did it change as you were
   watching it?

2. What techniques of filmmaking (lighting, music, sets, cinematography,
   editing, and so on) were used to convey the film's message? Were they
   effective? Why or why not?

3. What makes Don Cheadle's portrayal of Paul Rusesabagina so
   effective?

FINDING THE MEANING

4. Toward the beginning of the film, at Paul and Tatiana's home, they
   watch as a neighbor is brutalized by the militia. Tatiana beseeches Paul
   to "do something." Later, in bed, he explains to her that there is nothing he can do because he has been "storing up favors" for the day that
   they might need them. (#3, :11) "Family is all that matters," he tells her.
   And yet we see that he is conflicted about his position. How do you
   deal with this dilemma of balancing family and social responsibilities?

5. After Paul thanks him for shooting footage of the genocide, a slightly
   drunk Jack Danglish (Joaquin Phoenix), the American journalist,

responds, "I think if people see this footage, they'll say, Oh, my God, that's horrible. And then they'll go on eating their dinners." (#10, :43) Beginning with the war in Vietnam, the West has become accustomed to watching many kinds of atrocities on television. What is your experience of this phenomenon?

6. Paul is the personification of graciousness. And his work as a manager for a four-star hotel has taught him a lot. But he's also had to pay a steep price. What does he mean by the statement that a Cuban cigar is more valuable than money?

7. Do you feel that the film effectively shows the horror of the genocide? Some critics (see "Critically Speaking") have complained that it is a sanitized version of the massacre. Do you agree or disagree with this? Why?

8. In this scene Paul finally cracks. Aside from the horror around him and the helplessness he feels, what, on a deeper level, so severely affects him? (#16, 1:16:40)

9. The film alerts us to important past, present, and future global events. Perhaps even more dismaying and distressing than the story about the Rwandan genocide is the fact that similar circumstances exist in other parts of Africa right now, especially in the Darfur region of Sudan and Niger. What might be a way to use the information that *Hotel Rwanda* has brought to our attention to work toward ending these or other crises? Is it possible that what we "learn" from movies can actually change us? Yet how can we deal with compassion fatigue?

10. During his conversation with Jack, we learn from Benedict (the Kigali journalist) the difference between the Hutus and Tutsis. (#4, :13) We also learn the origin of this cultural division. What part did European colonial powers, which ignored traditional tribal boundaries, play in the problems in Africa?

HISTORICAL CONTEXT

The definition of "Hutu" and "Tutsi" has changed over time. Primarily it has distinguished between one group in positions of power over the other. Although Tutsi are generally considered taller than Hutu, the vice president of the National Assembly, Laurent Nkongoli, says that is erroneous, because even they cannot distinguish between themselves. Since the withdrawal of German and Belgian colonialism, the Tutsi have been considered the elite of the country. But the Hutu and Tutsi labels are designations of class or caste rather than tribe or ethnicity, as is usually portrayed by the media and militants.

MEMORABLE QUOTES

Tatiana: Why are people so cruel?
Paul: Hatred. Insanity. I don't know.

BEHIND THE SCENES

While writing the screenplay, Keir Pearson contacted the Rwandan embassy in Washington, D.C., to verify some information. He coincidentally spoke with a woman who had survived the Rwandan massacre by being sheltered in the Mille Collines Hotel by Paul Rusesabagina.

STRAIGHT FROM THE ACTOR

Don Cheadle admits that he knew little about the heroic man he would eventually portray in *Hotel Rwanda* before he read the script: "I had cursory knowledge about the massacre and I think like most people I became mostly aware of it when there were two million refugees in the camps with some of the militia sprinkled among them. . . . Look, we had OJ going on, we had apartheid abolished in 1994, so there were other events that sort of took [precedence] and I think there was no political upside for the western powers, because I think they found Africa was just black killing black and their attitude was: 'We will get to it when we can.'" Asked if the film will find an audience, he responds: "I don't know who the audience is but as an artist that is not my purview. What I do is go 'this is amazing, this is fascinating, I think there is a compelling story here, I hope it touches somebody and they will be moved by it' and then I go forward. What comes out afterwards, is a marketing issue." (filmmonthly.com, 23 December 2004)

CRITICALLY SPEAKING

David Edelstein, *Slate.msn.com*, 29 December 2004

Hotel Rwanda doesn't make the massacre of nearly a million people only 10 years ago even remotely credible: If it hadn't actually happened, it would be hard to believe that one portion of a country could be moved by the exhortations of generals and radio personalities to take machetes to the other. The movie, directed by Terry George, wastes no time trying to explain the attempted genocide of the Tutsis by the Hutus. Instead, it tells the true story of Paul Rusesabagina (Don Cheadle), the manager of a four-star, French-owned resort hotel who evolved into the Oskar Schindler of Rwanda.

Mick LaSalle, *San Francisco Chronicle*, 7 January 2005

What makes the film not just harrowing but transcendent is Cheadle. He does nothing traditionally heroic. He just presents a picture of basic decency, showing how, when combined with courage, decency can result in an awe-inspiring moral steadfastness. He depicts someone calling upon conventional strengths, such as resourcefulness, in a struggle to achieve nearly impossible ends. And he shows the emotional cost of the effort.... See "Hotel Rwanda" and you may feel as though you've been through a war. It takes a while to realize that most of the film's violence is suggested. The movie is not without gore, but the director somehow conveys a bloodbath without showing one. Most of the killing is off camera, and the film's terrors are psychological.

MORE CONTEMPORARY MOVIE FAVORITES

Ali, Braveheart, Copland, The Insider, Silkwood

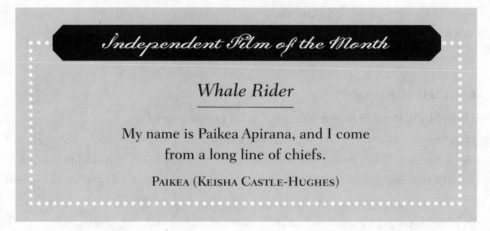

Independent Film of the Month

Whale Rider

My name is Paikea Apirana, and I come
from a long line of chiefs.

PAIKEA (KEISHA CASTLE-HUGHES)

THE DETAILS

2002, 101M/C; PG-13; DVD. **DIRECTOR/SCREENWRITER:** Niki Caro (based on
the novel by Witi Ihimaera). **CINEMATOGRAPHER:** Leon Narbey. **AWARDS:**
Academy Award nomination: Best Actress, Keisha Castle-Hughes. Independent
Spirit Awards: Best Foreign Film. Sundance Film Festival: Audience Award,
World Cinema. San Francisco International Film Festival: Audience Award, Best
Narrative Feature. Toronto International Film Festival: People's Choice Award.
São Paulo International Film Festival: International Jury Award, Best Film. Seattle
International Film Festival: Best Director.

THE SETTING

Contemporary New Zealand.

THE STORY

In *Whale Rider* we meet Paikea (Keisha Castle-Hughes), a quiet but charismatic
force. At her birth, both Pai's mother and twin brother die. The death of the
male child is devastating to Pai's paternal grandfather, Koro (Rawiri Paratene).
It is clear that Koro loves his granddaughter, but his pride and stubborn obser-
vance of tradition prevent him from seeing what Pai unswervingly demonstrates
to him: She is the latest in a long line of Whangara tribal chiefs that extends
back to her Maori namesake, Paikea, the Whale Rider of mythic legend. And it

is an inner spiritual knowing and sensitivity that connect Pai to her ancient ancestors as well as to her village tribespeople. When Koro takes the local boys to the sacred school of Maori warrior techniques to train and test them for courage, cleverness, and leadership, it's so obvious to us that none of them can hold a candle to Pai that we want to shake Koro out of his patriarchal stubbornness and force him to recognize the treasure he has in his granddaughter. Like a young Artemis warrior, Pai outfights, outswims, and outsings every male around her. It's rare to find a female character who balances the regal with the vulnerable. How Pai uses her unflagging spirit and determination to empower the other members of her tribe is as thrilling as how the whales help her do it. This is a refreshing modern-day fairy tale.

READING THE MOVIE

1. What does the title mean in relation to the story?
2. Why does the film conclude on this image? What is the message?
3. What emotions does this film elicit in you?
4. How do women and men differ in this film? What are the strengths of each?

FINDING THE MEANING

5. What happens between Pai and her grandfather, Koro, in this scene, without Koro understanding it? (#6, :17:20)
6. Have you seen another film that is similar to this one? What is it? What are the similarities? The differences? How does *Whale Rider* differ from other films about teenagers?
7. There are moments that our hearts break for Paikea. The unfairness of her grandfather's attitude toward her seems overly harsh, but he feels that it is his responsibility to find a leader for a tribe that is losing its people and power. Can you feel compassion for him, as does Paikea herself, or only anger? Might any sense of anger be better directed at something or someone else? Who or what might that be?

8. Koro says, "When she was born, that's when things went wrong for us." What does he mean? What is he referring to? (#9, :29) Is it possible for an ancient culture to adapt to the norms and standards of the modern world? Should it try? What are the losses and gains?

9. Do you think that the feminist perspective in the film is fresh or clichéd? Why? What are lessons about female empowerment that women can learn from Pai? How does Pai become aware of her calling? Is it gradual or swift?

10. The beached-whales scene is wrenching. (#20, 1:13) It is easy to substitute any number of environmental cataclysms in its place. And yet a miraculous outcome saves the day. What message is the director offering us here?

BONUS QUESTION

Another Maori film, *Once Were Warriors,* was a somber meditation about the dangers of assimilation and of a people losing touch with their traditions. *Whale Rider* also makes a statement about this subject. (#14, :49:34) What is the director saying about this? How does it differ from *Once Were Warriors*?

MEMORABLE QUOTES

Paikea: Why doesn't he want me?
Porourangi: He's just looking for something that doesn't exist anymore.
Paikea: A new leader? They exist.

BEHIND THE SCENES

According to director Caro, the book *Whale Rider,* upon which she based her screenplay, contains very little dialogue. Her main concern was "protecting the spirit of the book." The "great moments from the film [were] lifted verbatim from the book."

DID YOU KNOW...?

Whangara, the village where the film was shot, is an actual seaside community on New Zealand's East Coast. It is the home of a Maori tribe known as Ngati Kanohi, and they have lived on their land for a thousand years. Many members of the tribe were also extras in the film.

FROM THE SCREENWRITER

Whale Rider is adapted from the best-selling 1986 novel by Witi Ihimaera, the first Maori novelist to be published in New Zealand. About the source of his inspiration for the story, Ihimaera says, "A whale came up the Hudson River just when my daughters were visiting. They'd been complaining to me about the movies I'd been taking them to in which the boy is always the hero and the girl screams, 'Save me. . . .'" So I got to thinking about the ultimate journey that anybody could take, which to me is riding on a whale. Having the girl ride the whale, which is also a symbol of patriarchy, was my sneaky literary way of socking it to the guy thing." (*Script*, July/August 2003, Vol. 9, No. 4)

MORE INDEPENDENT FILM FAVORITES

Calendar Girls, George Washington, Ghost World, Jesus' Son

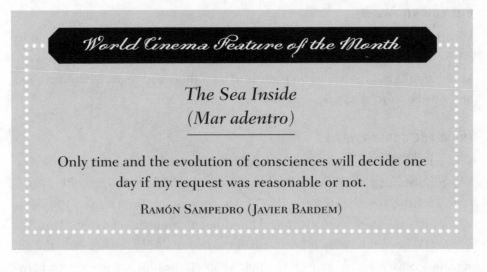

World Cinema Feature of the Month

The Sea Inside
(Mar adentro)

Only time and the evolution of consciences will decide one
day if my request was reasonable or not.

RAMÓN SAMPEDRO (JAVIER BARDEM)

THE DETAILS

2004, 125M/C; PG-13; DVD (in Spanish with English subtitles). **DIRECTOR:**
Alejandro Amenábar. **SCREENWRITERS:** Alejandro Amenábar and Mateo Gil.
CINEMATOGRAPHER: Javier Aguirresarobe. **AWARDS:** Academy Awards: Best
Foreign Film. European Film Awards: Best Actor, Javier Bardem; Best Director.
Golden Globes Award: Best Foreign Film. Goya Awards: Best Film, Director,
Actor, Actress (Lola Dueñas), Cinematography, Best Supporting Actor (Celso
Bugallo), Best Supporting Actress (Mabel Rivera). Independent Spirit Awards:
Best Foreign Film. Venice Film Festival: Best: International Film, Director, Actor.

THE SETTING

1996–1998; Galicia, Spain.

THE STORY

The subject matter of *The Sea Inside* is a stunningly complex one: Ramón
Sampedro, a quadriplegic fighting for his right to die in Spain, has been bedridden in his brother's house for nearly 30 years since he broke his neck in a diving
accident. The film follows his public battle with the courts and Church repre-
sentatives, as well as his private struggle with his family and friends. Ramón
takes refuge in writing poetry and behind a façade of irony, which serves him in

the face of potential despair. The philosophical and ethical concern of euthanasia is complicated and, naturally, the film must simplify it by providing characters as spokespeople for both sides of the issue. Ramón's family has steadfastly and selflessly cared for him throughout these many years. His angry older brother José (Celso Bugallo) has had to give up his life on the sea, his sister-in-law Manuela (Mabel Rivera) has tirelessly nursed him, and his father, Joaquín (Joan Dalmau), and nephew Javi (Tamar Novas) have built the many mechanical devices that he has designed as agents for his handicap. Apparently there were several women in love with Ramón, and we meet at least three of them: a right-to-die activist Gené (Clara Seguara); a beautiful attorney, Julia (Belén Rueda), who also is dealing with a debilitating illness; and Rosa (Lola Dueñas), a frazzled single mother of two, who visits Ramón after seeing him on television and falls in love. Javier Bardem, a powerful physical actor (on the order of Russell Crowe), is nothing short of astonishing in a role that demands complete physical immobility and aging 20 years. The humor, compassion, pleading, and anger that his character's eyes convey are palpable. Whatever side of the assisted right-to-die question you find yourself on, the sensitive and haunting *The Sea Inside* is worthy viewing.

READING THE MOVIE

1. What is the relation of the sound to the image in specific scenes or sequences?

2. What is the quality of acting among the cast? Are they believable in their roles?

3. Shooting a film about a bedridden character poses obvious problems for a film. How did the director handle this issue? Were the techniques used successful?

4. Is the change between Ramón's reality and his inner thoughts, flashbacks, and fantasies readily discernible? How?

FINDING THE MEANING

5. Julia, Ramón's attorney, is also suffering from a degenerative disease. According to the director, she was a composite character of several

women in Ramón's life. How does it serve the film to have this parallel story? Did the relationship between them, as portrayed in the film, feel authentic to you? Why or why not? What did you think about the way their relationship ended? (#13, 1:36:12) Did Rosa seem like a genuine portrayal of someone in love with Ramón? Why or why not?

6. The controversy over euthanasia is a central theme in the film. Do you think the director fairly offers both sides of the profoundly difficult "right to die with dignity" issue? How does or doesn't he do this? What is your opinion about Ramón Sampedro's fight for the right to assisted suicide?

7. In this tender scene between Ramón and his nephew Javi, we see the depth of Ramón's humanity and also of his patience. (#2, :11) Has there ever been a situation in your life that demanded such an acute act of patience toward a less experienced or aware person?

8. Ramón tells Rosa, "When you can't escape, and you constantly rely on everyone else, you learn to cry by smiling, you know?" He never loses his sense of humor (as in these scenes: #3, :16:45; #5, :33:30; #5, :37). What are other similar scenes you remember? Are we provided an explanation as to how he can maintain his generous spirit?

9. On a visit to the Sampedro home, the priest says to Ramón, "A freedom that ends life is no freedom at all." Ramón replies, "And a life that ends freedom is not a life either." How do you feel about the two scenes with Padre Francisco (José María Pou) and his attitude toward Ramón and his family? (#7, :58; #9, 1:05)

10. Do you think Ramón Sampedro was a heroic figure?

BONUS QUESTION

The Sea Inside opens up where Amenábar's earlier film *Open Your Eyes* (*Abre los ojos*; later made in the United States by Cameron Crowe as *Vanilla Sky*) ends. If you saw that film, do you remember the ending and how it relates to this film?

CULTURAL CONTEXT

On January 12, 1998, 55-year-old Ramón Sampedro ended his life by drinking cyanide in an elaborate plan that was videotaped and shown on Spanish television. His assisted suicide involved ten friends, each performing a single step without knowledge of one another's participation. After his death, hundreds of supporters of euthanasia wrote letters, confessing to allegedly assisting in his suicide. (DVD commentary)

BEHIND THE SCENES

The scene of Ramón's accident was shot in the same place, at the same time of day, and at the same time of year as when his catastrophe really happened.

DID YOU KNOW...?

- After his death, Ramón's derogatory open letter to the legal, political, and religious authorities in Spain was made public: "It is not that my conscience finds itself trapped in the deformity of my atrophied and numb body; but in the deformity, atrophy, and insensitivity of your consciences."

- Worried that moviegoers would pay more attention to Bardem's make-up—which aged him 30 years—than to his performance, the director decided to distribute a photo of him as the 55-year-old Ramón to Spanish newspapers before the film opened. The ploy worked: people forgot they were looking at a youthful man. (DVD commentary)

- Director Pedro Almodóvar, who directed Bardem in *Live Flesh*, has said about the actor, "Javier has become a specialist in doing roles which are very far from his own personality. It seems that he is interested in roles where the preparation takes almost as long as the shooting of the film. He really delves into a character very deeply." (*New York Times*, 4 March 2001)

FROM THE DIRECTOR

The Sea Inside is Alejandro Amenábar's fourth film. The 32-year-old had two pre-vious successes with *Open Your Eyes* in 1997 and *The Others*, 2001, starring Nicole Kidman. *The Sea Inside* won 14 of the 15 Goya Awards for which it was nomi-nated, the most for any Spanish film in history. Asked in an interview if *The Sea Inside* was similar to *The Others*, Amenábar responded, "I think there must be a connection at the back of my mind. I never thought that I'd make four films and they'd all be films about death. I don't think I'm the kind of guy who is obsessively talking about it. But in the last couple of years, I've found death around me, I've found myself in the cemetery consoling friends. In my films I don't think it's death so much as how we face it, how we deal with it, whether we want to search for something else, whether we want to find a way out and focus on our lives in the here and now." (*Indie London*, 2004)

FROM THE ACTOR

When Alejandro Amenábar first approached Javier Bardem to play the role of Ramón, Bardem needed a month to consider taking it. His primary concern was making the 30-year passage of time seem believable. "Then I started to read and talk to people who knew [Ramón], and then I saw the work of make-up artist, Jo Allen and I was completely amazed by that. I knew that would help me to be more confident. It was an amazing job. It helped me to see that this part of the job is done, she has done 50% of my job, which is to make people believe that I'm Ramón's age. So I didn't have to worry about that, I only needed to worry about the rest of it, filling that make-up with something truthful." (*Indie London*, 2004)

MORE WORLD CINEMA FAVORITES

Crouching Tiger, Hidden Dragon; The Full Monty; The Motorcycle Diaries; My Left Foot; The Story of Qiu Ju

May: Creative Forces

★ ★ ★ ★

An artist is never poor.

BABETTE (STEPHANE AUDRAN)
BABETTE'S FEAST, 1987
DIR. GABRIEL AXEL

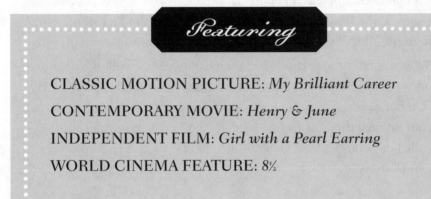

Featuring

CLASSIC MOTION PICTURE: *My Brilliant Career*

CONTEMPORARY MOVIE: *Henry & June*

INDEPENDENT FILM: *Girl with a Pearl Earring*

WORLD CINEMA FEATURE: *8½*

PREVIEWS

☆ In *My Brilliant Career* we meet Sybylla Melvyn, a turn-of-the-century heroine who lives in the Australian outback. The story chronicles the efforts of an independent-minded farm girl to fulfill her dream of becoming a writer. But family expectations of conformity to Victorian-era marriage and tradition might be a stumbling block. And then, there is the wealthy landowner-suitor to whom she is attracted. What's a girl to do?

☆ If you have ever wished that you'd lived in Paris during the height of the American expatriate years in the 1920s and 1930s, *Henry & June* is for you. This is an account of the love affair between writers Anaïs Nin and Henry Miller, which went beyond the sexual into a creative alliance that lasted for nearly 50 years. Philip Kaufman, the director, brings this erotic biography atmospherically alive. The visuals and the music of the period are delectable. Prepare yourself: This is a daringly sexy adult film about a woman's extraordinary sexual and creative awakening.

☆ *Girl with a Pearl Earring* is a sumptuous telling of a passionate yet unconsummated love that develops between the seventeenth-century Dutch painter Johannes Vermeer and a beautiful maid in the service of his household. Just as an appreciation for art and beauty brings them together, the film transports us with its magnificent look of the old masters, all the while sustaining a distinctly modern slant to the story.

☆ What a long, strange trip is Federico Fellini's 8½. If Fellini is already one of your favorite directors, if you've always wanted to watch a Fellini film but never got around to it, or if you've never heard of Fellini, put your rational thinking cap on hold and enjoy this carnivalesque, lyrically humorous look at a Fellini-like director's soul-searching and social commentary.

Classic Motion Picture of the Month

My Brilliant Career

Dear fellow countrymen, just a few words to
let you know that this story is going to be all
about me. So, in answer to many requests, here
is the story of my career . . . here is the story, of
my career . . . my brilliant career.

SYBYLLA (JUDY DAVIS)

THE DETAILS

1979, 100M/C; G; DVD. **DIRECTOR:** Gillian Armstrong. **SCREENWRITER:** Eleanor Witcombe (based on the novel by Miles Franklin). **CINEMATOGRAPHER:** Donald McAlpine. **AWARDS:** Australian Film Institute: Best Film; Best Director; Best Screenplay; Adapted; Best Cinematograph; Best Costume Design; Best Production Design. BAFTA Awards: Best Actress, Judy Davis. London Critics Circle Film Awards: Special Achievement Award, Gillian Armstrong. Cannes Film Festival: Nominated: Golden Palm, Gillian Armstrong. Golden Globes: Nominated: Best Foreign Film.

THE SETTING

1897; New South Wales, Australia.

THE STORY

"I make no apologies for sounding egotistical . . . because I am!" says Sybylla Melvyn (Judy Davis), a headstrong young woman, in *My Brilliant Career*. The film was adapted from an autobiographical novel by Australian writer Miles Franklin, and takes place in 1897 in the Australian outback. It is clear that Sybylla has grander plans for her life than those that her family and class would bestow. No, she belongs to the world of art and literature and music, and longs to broaden her intellect and develop her as-yet undeveloped artistic capacity. However, her dreams seem incongruous with her lot in life as the eldest of five or six siblings on a small, impoverished farm. Even when a nearly irresistible, wealthy, aristocrat bachelor, Harry Beecham (Sam Neill), enters her life and proposes marriage, this feisty could-be Cinderella cleaves ever more vigorously to her literary aspirations.

In her first starring role, a fresh Judy Davis is the epitome of a headstrong young woman who spurns the social expectations of turn-of-the-century Australia. Her broad, freckled face and unruly Gibson Girl–styled orange hair are a perfect metaphor for unconventionality and irreverence. Sybylla is a giant sunflower, loudly exclaiming her presence. And Davis's elemental energy and charisma ensure a remarkable performance.

READING THE MOVIE

1. What is striking about the *mise-en-scène* (setting, set decorations, and costumes)? Are some elements more successful than others? Why or why not? How does the dialogue work with the story?

2. How is this film similar to or different from other films with comparable themes?

3. The haunting melody Sybylla practices on the piano is from Schumann's "Scenes from Childhood" ("Kinderszenen"). What does this add to the story?

4. "Your family always had illusions of grandeur," Sybylla's father says rather accusingly to her mother. And once we see the refined environment in which she was brought up, we realize that, long ago, her mother, too, must have had a few exalted dreams of her own. Do you think there is a bit of resentment toward Sybylla from the women in her family for daring to dream of living a different kind of life?

FINDING THE MEANING

5. "Give me a chance to find out what's wrong with the world . . . and me," Sybylla tells a disappointed but patient Harry. "Find out who I am. Then I'll marry you." (#22, 1:15) What does Sybylla actually "find out about the world" and herself? How does this affect her?

6. After two years pass, Harry once again pursues this intelligent, independent, outspoken young woman. But, as before, Sybylla declares passionately, "I want to be a writer. And I've got to do it now. And I've got to do it alone." Does this seem like an overlay of 1970s feminism on nineteenth-century circumstances? How about the issue of women's self-esteem? Has the dependence a woman might have on her looks diminished during a century or has it increased? In what ways?

7. What is the quality of life, and what are the opportunities available, for a young Australian outback woman in the 1890s? For all of Sybylla's artistic ambitions, is her eventual progression from housemaid to housewife inevitable, given both the cultural repression of her gender as well as her parents' poverty? What are the subtle ways in which *My Brilliant Career* contends with these issues? What is the statement the film is making about the culture during the period it takes place? Does it seem realistic? Why or why not?

8. In the October 6, 1997, *New York Times Review,* critic Janet Maslin writes, "Miss Armstrong suddenly insists on Sybylla's independence, and tosses Harry to the vultures, and more or less knocks the audience on its ear. Is the viewer being hopelessly old-hat in feeling that Harry—who is handsome and nice, and says he would be delighted to see Sybylla pursue her career—isn't such a bad bet? Apparently so." (#26, 1:29:40) How did you feel about Sybylla's decision? What would you do?

9. Sybylla's Aunt Helen tells her that she has "a streak of wildness" that will get Sybylla into trouble all her life, so she must learn to control it and "cultivate a little more feminine vanity." (#7, :18) What is Sybylla's response to this admonition? And Aunt Gussie reminds Sybylla that

other women, too, have had their own doubts about love and marriage. (#20, 1:10) Is she one of the more sympathetic characters? Why?

10. Each character seems to have their own agenda for Sybylla: her parents, Grandma Bossier, Aunt Helen, Uncle Julius, Frank Hawdon, Mr. and Mrs. McSwatt, Aunt Gussie, and Harry Beechum. What have we learned about each of these characters that might make their opinions suspect?

BONUS QUESTION

Director Gillian Armstrong's career is filled with strong female characters. Which movies among the following have you seen? *Mrs. Soffel* (Diane Keaton), *High Tide* (Judy Davis), *The Last Days of Chez Nous*, *Little Women*, *Oscar and Lucinda* (Cate Blanchett), *Charlotte Gray* (Cate Blanchett). Are there any similarities among the female characters?

CULTURAL CONTEXT

According to the DVD commentary, during the late 1890s, there was a renewed sense of nationalism in Australia as it came of age. The writers and poets during that time, including Miles Franklin, began a movement of acceptance of and appreciation for Australia for what it was, with its bush, outback, and other natural splendors. According to Armstrong, there was also a social commentary in Miles Franklin's book, which reflected the fact that Australia had experienced an economic depression and a severe drought. This, in turn, instilled a public love of working people.

MEMORABLE QUOTES

Aunt Gussie: Loneliness is a terrible price to pay for independence. Don't throw away reality for an impossible dream.

Sybylla: I can't lose myself in someone else's life if I haven't lived my own yet.

BEHIND THE SCENES

Judy Davis plays her own piano solos in *My Brilliant Career*.

DID YOU KNOW...?

This was the directorial debut of Gillian Armstrong and the acting debut of Judy Davis.

ABOUT THE DIRECTOR

"Although Armstrong has often spoken in interviews about her discomfort at being confined to a category of woman filmmaker of women's films, and has articulated her desire to reach an audience of both genders and all nationalities, her work continually addresses sexual politics and family tensions. Escape from and struggle with traditional sex roles and the pitfalls and triumphs therein are themes frequently addressed in her films." (*The St. James Film Directors Encyclopedia*)

CRITICALLY SPEAKING

Janet Maslin, *New York Times*, 6 October 1979

Sybylla Melvyn (played by Judy Davis) is supposed to be plain. And she's sufficiently strange-looking, by movie-star standards, to strike the viewer as being something less than a ravishing beauty. But that effect lasts only a short while— only for as long as it takes to realize that Miss Davis brings an unconventional vigor to every scene she's in, even in a film that's as consistently animated as this one. Her Sybylla is a coltish creature, creating a merry chaos wherever she goes.

MORE CLASSIC MOVIE FAVORITES

Celeste, Chaplin, Isadora, Lenny, Testament of Orpheus

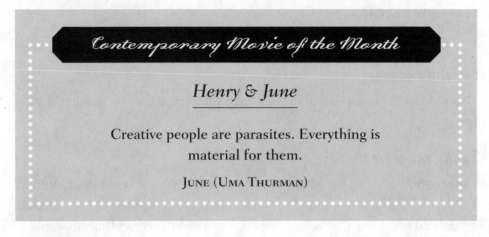

Contemporary Movie of the Month

Henry & June

Creative people are parasites. Everything is
material for them.

JUNE (UMA THURMAN)

THE DETAILS

1990, 136M/C; NC-17; DVD. **DIRECTOR:** Philip Kaufman. **SCREENWRITERS:**
Philip and Rose Kaufman. **CINEMATOGRAPHER:** Philippe Rousselot. **AWARDS:**
Academy Awards: Nominated: Best Cinematography, Philippe Rousselot.

THE SETTING

Early 1930s; Paris, France.

THE STORY

Henry & June is based on a portion of the "unexpurgated" diary of Anaïs Nin
written between 1931 and 1934. But it is also seasoned with Henry Miller's autobiographical novel *Tropic of Cancer*—a titillating account of an American writer's
adventures in Paris during the same years. Anaïs (Maria de Medeiros) and Henry
(Fred Ward) meet at a crucial point in their personal and professional lives, and
the film underscores the attraction of two hungry minds in search of artistic,
intellectual, and sexual liberation. Although they are each married to another,
the characters recognize in each other a kindred spirit. Essentially, *Henry & June*
provides a visually lush and intellectually stimulating account of two writers who
lived through a revolutionary creative period that spawned a variety of cultural
-isms, especially surrealism. Henry's financial struggles are accurately depicted,
as are his and Anaïs's internal creative wrestlings and uncertainties about the

quality of their written work. We see Henry writing in his cockroach-infested garret on the left bank which he shares with a hodgepodge of other artists and hangers-on. The wall he faces as he sits at his typewriter is covered with notes about his novel-in-progress. An ashtray overflows with cigarette butts as clouds of smoke circle around him like ethereal muses. Kaufman's atmospheric film brings the life and times of two great twentieth-century artists palpably alive.

READING THE MOVIE

1. What is the POV of the film? Is it consistent? Which scenes did you find the most interesting or compelling? The most arresting? Why?

2. Are the characters defined by their clothes, their conversation, or something else?

3. How effective was the soundtrack? Did it evoke the Paris of the 1930s?

4. June carries around "Count Bruga," a puppet that is modeled on Henry. (#5, :34:10; #16, 1:44:20) What is the symbolic meaning of the puppet?

FINDING THE MEANING

5. We see the life Henry lived in Paris cafés, in cinemas, and on city streets. His picaresque friends—pickpockets, magicians, circus performers, contortionists, prostitutes, a lawyer, writers, painters, and Gypsies—flit around him like the characters that will celebrate and memorialize them in *Tropic of Cancer*. The happy-go-lucky photographer, Brassai, sets up some of his most recognizable tableaux of the Parisian demimonde. Can you recognize which scenes are based on Brassai's photographs?

6. The film shows two distinct social strata: the upper class of Anaïs and Hugo's world and that of Henry's, as already mentioned. What are the differences and similarities between these two worlds and between the Parisians and the American expatriates?

7. Have you read any of Miller's or Nin's works? Did the film accurately convey your images of their material?

8. Who, of the three main characters, seems the most well developed and the most fully realized? How do you respond to the acts of infidelity portrayed? Is the film saying that artists are free to do whatever they wish in the service of their art? What is your feeling about this ethical question?

9. What did you think about June? Are Henry and Anaïs's literary depictions of her accurate or are they unfair? (#6, :38:28; #16, 1:46:15) Do you find her to be as compelling a character as do Henry and Anaïs? What about her do you respond to or discount?

10. The point is made a number of times throughout the film by several characters that artists view everything in life as merely material for their art. Do you think that is true of Anaïs and Henry? Do you think it is true in general? Why or why not?

BONUS QUESTION

The film garnered an NC-17 rating because of its highly sexual content. Do you think the sex scenes were handled tastefully? If so, why? Do you feel that certain scenes were gratuitous? If so, how would you have preferred them to be different? What is the director saying about the connection between eroticism and the creative process? Do you agree with him?

BEHIND THE SCENES

In the scene where Henry is first introduced to Anaïs and Hugo, Juan Luis Buñuel, the son of legendary Spanish director Luis Buñuel, plays the publisher.

DID YOU KNOW...?

If you enjoyed *Henry & June*, check out the documentary (and book) *Paris Was a Woman*. This film is about independent women artists and writers, both gay and straight (Gertrude Stein, Djuna Barnes, Sylvia Beach, Marie Laurencin, and Gisèle Freund, among them), who lived in Paris during the 1930s and were known as the "women of the Left Bank."

ABOUT THE ACTRESS: UMA THURMAN

In the following *New York Times* excerpt, Uma Thurman discusses women's roles in the postmodern world: "'While women today have many more options,' Ms. Thurman said, 'they still have hard choices to make. In the end, somebody has to bend,' she said with the hard-won wisdom of a Jamesian heroine. Hollywood has not provided her with many role models of female independence, personal or artistic, and Ms. Thurman said she was just trying to feel her own way. 'The challenge is to find the masculine that can bend without being emasculated and the feminine that can be strong without becoming unfeminine,' she said, 'and then somehow maintain that flexibility together.'"(*New York Times*, 22 April 2001)

ABOUT THE DIRECTOR

- Philip Kaufman also directed *The Right Stuff, The Unbearable Lightness of Being,* and *Quills*, among other films.

- Kaufman first came into contact with Miller's work in the 1950s while at the University of Chicago. He recalls that *Tropic of Cancer* (mentioned in the film as the book Henry is in the process of writing) "was the ultimate secret book everybody was reading."

CRITICALLY SPEAKING

Hal Hinson, *Washington Post*, 5 October 1990

Kaufman pulls enthralling performances from his main trio of actors. . . . De Medeiros's eyes are the soulful heart of *Henry & June*. A newcomer to film from the French theater, she brings a tremulous urgency to Nin's explorations, and we sense in her the danger she feels in unburdening herself of her bourgeois conventionality. As Miller, Ward gives a hilarious rendition of burly American bravado, but he keeps the character's vulgarities in balance with his artistic drives. This is a star performance with a character actor's authenticity. It's a driving, impassioned piece of comic acting. . . .

Watching *Henry & June*, what you see is a conception of the cinema so rare that it seems almost to have vanished from the scene. Imagine a movie that is sincere in its themes and its provocations, that is strikingly personal and concerns itself unabashedly with ideas and their expression.

MOVIE HISTORY

The films that Henry and Anaïs go to see:

La passion de Jeanne d'Arc by Carl Dreyer (1928)

Un chien andalou by Luis Buñuel and Salvadore Dali (1929)

Mädchen in Uniform by Leontine Sagan (1931)

MORE CONTEMPORARY MOVIE FAVORITES

Almost Famous, Bird, Carrington, Frida, Shakespeare in Love, Sylvia

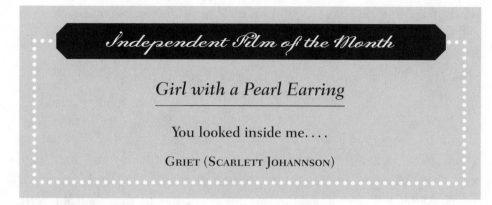

Independent Film of the Month

Girl with a Pearl Earring

You looked inside me. . . .

GRIET (SCARLETT JOHANNSON)

THE DETAILS

2003, 100M/C; PG-13; DVD. **DIRECTOR:** Peter Webber. **SCREENWRITER:** Olivia Hetreed (based on the novel by Tracy Chevalier). **CINEMATOGRAPHER:** Eduardo Serra. **AWARDS:** Polish Film Awards: Best European Film. San Diego Film Critics Society Awards: Best Cinematography, Eduardo Serra. San Sebastián International Film Festival: Best Cinematography, Eduardo Serra; Best Director. Academy Awards: Nominated: Best Art Direction–Set Decoration; Best Cinematography; Best Costume Design.

THE SETTING

1665; Delft, Holland

THE STORY

Griet (Scarlett Johannson), a young girl living in Delft, must leave home in order to work as a maid because her parents cannot afford to feed her. In the home of artist Johannes Vermeer (Colin Firth) she enters a world that is both restrictive and liberating. Her household duties are demeaning and the female members of the residence—including Vermeer's mother-in-law, wife and daughter, and the cook—all seem to have something against her. Perhaps it's Griet's beauty and apparent natural affinity for art which, she shares with the brooding master of the house. It's not long before Griet, who received training from her father, a tile painter until a kiln explosion rendered him blind, begins to see the complexity of colors in clouds and subtly offers compositional advice to Jan. When he recognizes her inherent gifts, he feels a kinship with the young girl and sets about to mentor her by teaching her to grind elements for mixing paints. It's a short distance from a shared passion for art to love. Everyone in the household senses it, but when Jan's menacing patron van Ruijven (Tom Wilkinson) commissions a painting of Griet by Vermeer, their fate seems sealed. She sits for the portrait that would come to be known as *Girl with a Pearl Earring* or "the Mona Lisa of the North." As the two enjoy a titillating but chaste personal exchange, they teach each other what it means to look closely and to see deeply. Although Vermeer and the painting are historical, the ethereal beauty remains anonymous. The authenticity of the period is ensured by Eduardo Serra's chiaroscuro-enhanced cinematography. And Scarlett Johansson as Griet displays an authority and presence previously reserved for European actresses. The secret that surrounds the painting lies in the "girl's" eyes, but this film miraculously brings to life a plausible account.

READING THE MOVIE

1. There is tremendous attention paid to the accuracy in set and costume design. What in particular do you notice? How are the different social orders—the peasants and the upper class—depicted through color and light?

2. *Girl with a Pearl Earring* won several awards for Art Direction and Cinematography. Beginning with the opening scene in which Griet is slicing and arranging root vegetables on a platter, which subsequent scenes could be described as painterly?

3. What do you think the pearl earrings initially symbolized for Vermeer? Vermeer's wife? Griet? How did this change? What do you think Griet eventually did with the earrings?

4. How do you feel about the actors chosen to portray the various roles? Did you find any of them especially compelling? Why?

FINDING THE MEANING

5. In two scenes, one early in the film and a second toward the end, Griet is seen standing in the middle of what looks like an eight-pointed star. What does its presence underscore about Griet's position in society, whether as a young woman, as the daughter of a recently impoverished family, or as the Protestant maid to a Catholic family?

6. What sort of man is Vermeer? He hides his feelings from everyone, including his wife, his patron, van Ruijven, and Griet. (#6, :23) How do we, as viewers, know how he feels toward each of these people? What are subtle clues to his ambivalent emotions and longings?

7. The camera obscura is a tangible representation of a different way of looking. (#9, :32) Griet has the capacity to see in a unique way, but she needs Vermeer to show her how. It also reminds us that in order to see clearly, you have to focus and block out the rest of the world. Why is this a significant symbol for the film? For Griet?

8. Although the film tells the story of one girl's transition into womanhood more than three centuries ago, her fears and longings are, in many ways, universal. Are there ways in which you identify personally with Griet? Considering the social structures of her time, what do you think the future held for Griet once she left Vermeer's household? What are her options? What might she have done if she lived during our time?

9. The Dutch Catholics were tolerated but expected to remain on the margins of society. In the opening scene, because Griet is going to a Catholic household, her mother says to close her ears, so she won't have to hear their Catholic prayers. (#1, :03) Vermeer actually converted to Catharina's Catholicism. What does this say about him?

10. What did you think about Vermeer's relationship with his wife? How do you think he felt about her? How did he treat her? Was she portrayed as a sympathetic character? What about her mother? Cornelia, Vermeer's daughter, plays a significant role in Griet's life while she lives in the Vermeer household. (#9, :35; #9, :36) What did you think of her?

BONUS QUESTION

Did you read Tracy Chevalier's novel of the same name? If so, what are the similarities between the film and the book? Do the differences bother you? Why or why not? Which do you prefer? Why?

CULTURAL CONTEXT

- Johannes Vermeer (1632–1675), a native of Delft who never left the small city, relied on the bourgeoisie for his living. A converted Catholic, Vermeer struggled to support a large family, including 11 children. Many of his paintings depict the wives or daughters of his Protestant patrons caught in the middle of common household actions—pouring a pitcher of water, writing a letter, or playing an instrument. Only 35 Vermeer paintings are known to exist today, and none of the models have ever been positively identified.

- Religious change in the Netherlands during the time the film takes place was an important issue. The Dutch had discarded the rule of the Catholic Spanish and were intent on distancing themselves from Catholicism.

HE SAID/SHE SAID

Catharina: Why don't you paint *me*?
Vermeer: Because you don't understand.

BEHIND THE SCENES

- On the set, members of the cast—especially Johansson—gave Colin Firth a hard time about his wig of long locks which give him a brooding seventeenth-century look for the film. She kept calling him "Fabio." "If your leading lady bursts into fits of laughter at the sight of you, it's a challenge," says Firth. (*People*, 1 December 2003)

- Johansson made a conscious choice to trust her instincts regarding her portrayal of Griet. "I did not read the book before or during filmmaking," she says. "It's written in a first-person narrative from my character's point of view. I just didn't want to be told what I should be feeling at a particular time." (*USA Today*, 1 December 2003, Claudia Puig)

DID YOU KNOW...?

- During the period she wrote the novel, Tracy Chevalier bought linseed oil (which is mixed with pigment to make paint) and left the bottle open, so that she could smell what Vermeer and Griet would have smelled.

- On her Website, Tracy Chevalier recounts the experience of first reading Olivia Hetreed's screenplay: "It was a strange experience reading someone else's version of my story. I felt a little sick as I read it, as if from the dizziness of someone else climbing inside my head and looking out through my eyes. Sometimes I was sorry when some scene or character was gone, but mostly I was impressed by how well Olivia had managed to translate a first-person book into a film. I was even envious of some of the visual details Olivia had invented, especially a scene in which Griet plays with the reflection of the bowl she's polishing and the Vermeer girls chase the spot of light around the courtyard. 'Why didn't I think of that?' I kept thinking as I read."

STRAIGHT FROM THE ACTOR: COLIN FIRTH

I'm interested in emotion, its complications, I'm not necessarily an optimist in terms of romantic love. I'm not the type of romantic who enjoys the weepy movie and then sighs sweetly about it. I'm more interested in the obstacles and the impossible than I am in resolution and happiness. (www.firth.com)

ABOUT THE DIRECTOR

Girl with a Pearl Earring is Peter Webber's debut feature film. The director worked in television for a decade, where he compiled an impressive list of documentary and drama credits. Webber's degree in art history provided insights into stylistically recreating the period in a way that recalls the work of Vermeer and his contemporaries.

STRAIGHT FROM THE DIRECTOR

Speaking about his excitement in beginning the direction of his first feature film, British filmmaker Peter Webber recalls his first visit, when he was 16 years old, to a soon-to-be-defunct repertory cinema—the Electric Cinema—in the Portobello section of West London. Many years later, his casting director suggested that he meet with the actors of *Pearl Earring* at the newly opened and refurbished Electric Cinema. "As I prepared to make the film I found my head flooded with images of the movies I had seen in those formative years. I remembered the intensity of Dreyer's *The Passion of Joan of Arc*. The dramatic sweep of Ophul's *Madame de*.... The creepiness of Hitchcock's *Rebecca*. And I realized that I had been gifted with a script full of rich cinematic possibilities, a script that would become a film about love and longing, about desire and repression, about art and inspiration. It is also a film that contrasts innocence and experience, the issue I had been contemplating as I went to my first casting session. The circle was completed as the adult filmmaker remembered the teenager cinephile and that first night at the Electric Cinema." (*FLM* magazine, Fall 2003)

MORE INDEPENDENT FILM FAVORITES

Basquiat, Before Night Falls, Love Is the Devil,
Pollack, Vincent and Theo

World Cinema Feature of the Month

8½

(Otto e mezzo)

I thought my ideas were so clear. I wanted to make an honest film. No lies whatsoever. I thought I had something so simple to say. Something useful to everybody. A film that could help bury forever all those dead things we carry within ourselves. Instead, I'm the one without the courage to bury anything at all. When did I go wrong? I really have nothing to say, but I want to say it all the same.

GUIDO (MARCELLO MASTROIANNI)

THE DETAILS

1963, 148M/B&W; NR; DVD (in Italian with subtitles). **DIRECTOR:** Federico Fellini. **SCREENWRITERS:** Federico Fellini, Ennio Flaiano, Tullio Pinelli, and Brunello Rondi. **CINEMATOGRAPHER:** Gianni Di Venanzo. **AWARDS:** Academy Awards: Best Foreign Language Film, Best Costume Design. Moscow International Film Festival: Grand Prix, Federico Fellini. National Board of Review: Best Foreign Language Film. New York Film Critics Circle Awards: Best Foreign Language Film

THE SETTING

Early 1960s; Rome, Italy.

THE STORY

This satire on filmmaking is one of the best films by one of the best world cinema directors. Federico Fellini crowds the picture with oddball characters and a biting humor that touches on practically everything: childhood memories, sex, marriage, infidelity, identity, spiritual quests, and, of course, making movies. While you're watching the film, remember that you are in the presence of a masterful filmmaker. Actually, more than his presence: you are in his mind. This truly stream-of-consciousness approach to movie-making is both energizing and bewildering. In interviews, Fellini was often asked, "What does the film mean?" His response: "What do you mean 'mean'? Like going to the circus, don't look for logic: watch for amusement."

READING THE MOVIE

1. The opening sequence of 8½ is one of the most recognized in the history of cinema. Why does the movie start the way it does? What do the tunnel, cars, odd people, and flight represent?

2. In terms of the cinematography, is there a pattern of striking camera movements and angles? What is their purpose? Do they serve to draw you into the film or keep you at a distance?

3. The Italian composer Nino Rota worked on many of Fellini's films. How is his delirious musical score a perfect counterpoint to Fellini's images in 8½?

4. Marcello Mastroianni, who plays Fellini's hero in a beautifully bored and baffled fashion, starred in many of Fellini's films. It has often been said that Mastroianni was Fellini's alter-ego. What do you think of his performance in 8½? What other films have you seen him in? (Check out the exceptional documentary on Mastroianni available on DVD: *Marcello Mastroianni: I Remember, Yes, I Remember*, 1997.)

FINDING THE MEANING

5. 8½ operates on several levels: It is a film-within-a-film-within-a-film. It's not only about the making of a film, it's about making *this* film. It also depicts images from Guido's memories, which collide with the present,

and his fantasies or wishful thinking. How did you respond to the stream-of-consciousness quality of the movie?

6. The working title for 8½ was *The Beautiful Confusion*. The fact that characters speak in a variety of languages—Italian, French, and English—and Italian dialects, is one indication of the fictional director's confused state of mind. Another is that the main actors portray more than one character. What are some other indications of this "beautiful confusion"?

7. Why do you think the film was so popular in its day? Why has it achieved—and maintained—the status of a world cinema classic? About 8½, the film critic Pauline Kael asked, "When a satire on a big, expensive movie is itself a big expensive movie, how can we distinguish it from its target? When a man makes himself the butt of his own joke, we may feel too uncomfortable to laugh. Exhibitionism is its own reward." Do you agree or disagree with Kael's assessment of this film? Why? Do you view 8½ as a masterpiece, as many do, or as an expensive demonstration of self-indulgence, as others have?

8. By the end of the film, Guido's wife has left him, his mistress has left him, and the young actress is unbearable. He fantasizes committing suicide. In this scene, why is everyone dressed in white? Is this paradise, a form of enlightenment, or a fantasy? (#25, 2:09:30)

9. One could make a case for at least two literary references in the film: the River Styx, which, in Greek mythology, souls on their way to the underworld must cross; and the three levels of Dante's *Divine Comedy*: hell, purgatory, and heaven. Where do these references occur in the film? In addition, Guido's wife tells him, "Lying is like breathing to you." And later: "It's a movie. Another invention. Another lie." (#20, 1:29:15) When he is caught in his lies, Guido often nervously touches his nose. What fairy tale figure might Fellini be referencing in this gesture?

10. In the car with the starlet, who was also the object of fantasy earlier at the spa, Guido seems to be deep in self-analysis, even revelation. (#24,

1:57) What does the scene represent? Why is his face in shadow? Guido seems to have a moment of clarity when he says, "All the confusion of my life . . . has been a reflection of myself! Myself as I am, not as I'd like to be." What does this imply?

BONUS QUESTION

Other films by Fellini include *I Vitelloni*, 1953; *La Strada*, 1954; *Nights of Cabiria*, 1957; *La Dolce Vita*, 1960; *Juliet of the Spirits*, 1968; *Fellini's Roma*, 1972; *Amarcord*, 1974; and *Intervista*, 1987. If you have seen any or all of them, how do they compare? 8½ inspired Bob Fosse's *All That Jazz*, 1979, and Woody Allen's *Stardust Memories*, 1980. If you have seen those films, what are the similarities to and differences from this one?

CULTURAL CONTEXT

Cleopatra, the Hollywood extravaganza starring Elizabeth Taylor and Richard Burton, was released the same year as 8½.

MEMORABLE QUOTES

Luisa: It's a movie. Another invention, another lie.

BEHIND THE SCENES

- Perhaps like a character out of his own movie, Fellini attached a note to himself, which he placed on the camera. The note read, "Remember, this is a comedy."
- Fellini never showed the script to the actors. Instead, he would individually tell them their lines each day. And, in fact, the actors never knew even how long their roles were to be.

ABOUT THE DIRECTOR

- As a young man, Fellini drew comics. The exaggerated, abstract quality of his drawing transferred to his filmmaking through his choice of people to portray his characters and the use of camera angles and depth-of-field.

- During the 1950s, Fellini was in therapy with a Jungian analyst. "ASI NISI MASE," the seemingly nonsensical magical children's rhyme in the film that has the power to move pictures, is an anagram for anima, which in Jungian psychology is the feminine aspect of a man's psyche.
- Fellini once said, "If film didn't exist, I would have been a circus director."

CRITICALLY SPEAKING

Pauline Kael, KPFA broadcast, Berkeley, California, 1963

8½ is an incredibly externalized version of an artist's "inner" life—a gorgeous, multiringed circus that has very little connection with what, even for a movie director, is most likely to be solitary, concentrated hard work. It's more like the fantasy life of someone who wishes he were a movie director, someone who has soaked up those movie versions of an artist's life, in which in the midst of a carnival or ball the hero receives inspiration and dashes away to transmute life into art.

Bosley Crowther, *New York Times*, 26 June 1963

Here is a piece of entertainment that will really make you sit up straight and think, a movie endowed with the challenge of a fascinating intellectual game. It has no more plot than a horse race, no more order than a pinball machine, and it bounces around on several levels of consciousness, dreams and memories as it details a man's rather casual psychoanalysis of himself. But it sets up a labyrinthine ego for the daring and thoughtful to explore, and it harbors some elegant treasures of wit and satire along the way.

MOVIE HISTORY

8½ is referenced in

A Hard Day's Night (1964)

The Godfather (1972)

Lenny (1974)

Eraserhead (1977)

All That Jazz (1979)

Stardust Memories (1980)

Brazil (1985)

The Adventures of Baron Munchausen (1988)

Santa sangre (1989)

Falling Down (1993)

Pulp Fiction (1994)

Romeo + Juliet (1996)

Wild Man Blues (1997)

8½ Women (1999)

Ghost World (2000)

Mulholland Drive (2001)

Cinemania (2002)

Adaptation (2002)

Big Fish (2003)

Wicker Park (2004)

MORE WORLD CINEMA FAVORITES

Andrei Rublev, Camille Claudel, Goya in Bordeaux, Topsy-Turvy, Wilde

June: Traveling Tales

★ ★ ★ ★

While armchair travelers dream of going places, traveling
armchairs dream of staying put.

JULIAN (BILL PULLMAN)
THE ACCIDENTAL TOURIST, 1988
DIR. LAWRENCE KASDAN

I've had my trip and that's more than enough to keep
me happy for the rest of my life.

CARY WATTS (GERALDINE PAGE)
THE TRIP TO BOUNTIFUL, 1985
DIR. PETER MASTERSON

Featuring

CLASSIC MOTION PICTURE: *It Happened One Night*
CONTEMPORARY MOVIE: *Catch Me If You Can*
INDEPENDENT FILM: *Hideous Kinky*
WORLD CINEMA FEATURE: *Ten*

PREVIEWS

☆ In *It Happened One Night* we meet Ellie (Claudette Colbert) and
Peter (Clark Gable) as they undertake a road trip by bus, car, and
hitchhiking. Ellie has just jumped ship, literally, to escape from her

interfering wealthy father. Traveling incognito by bus, she runs into newspaperman Peter and the sparks begin to fly in this screwball comedy, winner of multiple awards.

☆ *Catch Me If You Can* is based on the true story of Frank W. Abagnale, Jr. (Leonardo DiCaprio), an enfant terrible, who (by the time he was 19 years old) became one of the world's greatest con men and scam artists, and the youngest individual ever placed on the FBI's Most Wanted List. This supremely entertaining Spielberg film is a real charmer.

☆ *Hideous Kinky* imparts an intoxicating sense of place to the setting of Marrakech. Julia (Kate Winslet) is the 25-year-old mother of two young girls, Bea, 8, and Lucy, 6. Disenchanted with her life in London and her straying lover, and looking for enlightenment, in 1972, Julia carts off her daughters to exotic locales and adventures. But this self-absorbed mother has to lose nearly everything before she can appreciate what she's already got.

☆ *Ten* is a true road movie. In fact, we never leave the interior of a car. In this Iranian film, we eavesdrop on ten different conversations, as a woman driving through the streets of Tehran picks up her son, her sister, and various other travelers. It may seem slow to American viewers, used to 15-second sound bites, but the rewards of taking the entire journey are plentiful and satisfying.

Classic Motion Picture of the Month

It Happened One Night

You've given me a very good idea of the
hiking. When does the hitch come in?

ELLIE ANDREWS (CLAUDETTE COLBERT)

THE DETAILS

1934, 105M/B&W; NR; DVD. **DIRECTOR:** Frank Capra. **SCREENWRITER:** Robert
Riskin, based on the story "Night Bus" by Samuel Hopkins Adams.
CINEMATOGRAPHER: Joseph Walker. **AWARDS:** Academy Awards: Best Picture;
Director; Screenpla; Actor; Clark Gable, Actress; Claudette Colbert.

THE SETTING

1933; on route from Florida to New York.

THE STORY

This 1930s screwball comedy is perhaps the original road movie (a genre that
would become popular with the 1969 release of the Fonda/Hopper production
Easy Rider). An heiress, Ellie Andrews (Claudette Colbert), runs away from her
wealthy father in order to live with the gold-digging aviator King Westley (Jameson
Thomas), whom, against her father's wishes, she has already married (although
"in name only," he euphemistically reminds her). Traveling from Florida to New
York, the independent Ellie meets wisecracking newspaperman Peter Warne
(Clark Gable, in a role that prefigures James Stewart in *The Philadelphia Story*,
1939, and Cary Grant in *His Girl Friday*, 1940). They share the discomforts of a
long-distance bus ride, hitchhike, sleep under the stars in a hayfield and in motor
camps, while the pampered Ellie learns basic values from a working man, and

the cynical Peter is liberated by a free-spirited woman. During their adventures, this couple learns how to spend time together, a requisite for any romantic relationship. Will Ellie reach her husband? Will Peter get his story?

READING THE MOVIE

1. To accommodate a very short film schedule and a low budget ($350,000), most of the scenes are filmed on location. Can you pick out the few scenes that were filmed on a set?

2. Describe the quality of the acting.

3. Why does the movie start the way it does? What is the director trying to tell us?

4. What are other comedies from the 1930s that you have seen? How do they compare to *It Happened One Night*? How does it compare to other contemporary romantic comedies?

FINDING THE MEANING

5. *One Night* opens with Ellie refusing food from her father. (#2, :02:25) Midway, she welcomes a fried egg, donut, and coffee from the nurturing Peter. (#13, :36:10) How else does she gradually form an intimate alliance with him? How does Peter, in a sense, reparent Ellie?

6. In-between her intermittent flurries of diving off boats and back-talking, Ellie appears to be a modern, liberated, self-defining woman; yet there are moments when (for example, at the haystack she loses sight of Peter, or when she awakens at the second motor camp to find that apparently he has abandoned her) she seems utterly dependent on whichever man she is beholden to at the moment: Peter, her father, King. Nevertheless, it is Ellie who trumps the detectives at the bus station and, later, secures her and Peter's hitchhiking ride. How did you relate to Ellie?

7. Peter initially appears to be gruff and even conniving (as he bargains with Ellie to escort her to King, if she provides him with an exclusive story), but we see that he is also a protective and nurturing parental

figure as well. In what other instances does he break form with his conventional stereotypical character?

8. There is a bitter exchange between Ellie and Peter at her and Westley's reception. (#25, 1:38:20) How is this clash indicative of earlier disagreements? Or is it? If Ellie had proceeded with her marriage to King Westley, what kind of life do you think she would have had? (#24, 1:33:50) Which man would you have chosen? Why? What kind of life do you imagine Ellie and Peter have in 5 years? In 20 years? Do they stay together? What kind of life do they create?

9. The film reflects the economic and social realities of the era, and the Depression-weary American public undoubtedly found comfort in the fact that Ellie and Peter enjoyed their many adventures with little or no money. Often a movie subtext asks, Who needs money when you have love? In fact, one of the few musical numbers here, the tongue-in-cheek "Young People in Love Are Very Seldom Hungry," is a subtle reference to the period. What are other passages that comment on economic and social conditions during the Depression era?

10. *It Happened One Night* heralds, in a less lethal form of, our current "cult of celebrity," exemplified by the paparazzi. Ellie, the socialite, would have had little occasion to cross paths with Peter, the journalist. Yet when they meet, a new world of experiences and opportunities is made available to her. What are some of these experiences and opportunities?

BONUS QUESTION

The 1930s screwball comedies gave the American woman, as actress and heroine, a chance to speak her mind. By extension, the notion that good talk leads to good sex was an indispensable theme of this sophisticated genre. (Quite the reverse, in one of the most successful contemporary romantic comedies, *Pretty Woman*, Richard Gere gives Julia Roberts all that money can buy and she teaches him to feel, but does either of them say anything you can remember?) It's impossible to imagine King and Ellie enjoying the same kind of conversations that occur between her and Peter. Will their banter help the sassy Ellie decipher what, or whom, she really wants? How? What are other indications that the new couple might be destined for a generous and happy union?

HE SAID/SHE SAID

[*After hitching a ride by lifting her skirt*]

Ellie: Well, I proved once and for all that the limb is mightier than the thumb.

Peter: Why didn't you take off all your clothes? You could have stopped 40 cars.

Ellie: I'll remember that when I need 40 cars.

MEMORABLE QUOTES

Alexander: Do you mind if I ask you a question, frankly? Do you love my daughter?

Peter: Any guy that'd fall in love with your daughter ought to have his head examined.

Alexander: Now, that's an evasion! . . . Do you love her?

Peter: A normal human being couldn't live under the same roof with her without going nutty. She's my idea of nothing!

Alexander: I asked you a simple question. Do you love her?

Peter: Yes! But don't hold that against me. I'm a little screwy myself!

DID YOU KNOW...?

- When Clark Gable strips off his wet shirt at the motel, he is barechested. Subsequently, the undershirt industry nearly went bankrupt from the drop in sales.
- Twelve years later Frank Capra would direct the Christmas holiday classic, *It's a Wonderful Life* (1946).

ABOUT THE DIRECTOR

In his autobiography, *The Name Above the Title*, Capra explains how his personal success, as a result of *It Happened One Night*, at first frightened him, and he felt the pressure of making another blockbuster. To avoid work, he pretended to be sick, but then discovered that he really did have an undiagnosed illness and seemed to be dying. Capra received a visitor ("a faceless little man") who had been sent to try to remotivate the great director. The man ranted that Capra was wasting his God-given talent and influence. He compared Capra, whose message could reach hundreds of millions of people for a period of two hours, to Hitler, whose radio broadcasts could reach only 20 million for 20 minutes. It was an epiphany to Capra who, from that moment forward, committed himself as a filmmaker "to the service of man . . . down to my dying day, down to my last feeble talent. . . . Beginning with *Mr. Deeds Goes to Town*, my films had to *say* something."

CRITICALLY SPEAKING

Mordaunt Hall, *New York Times*, 23 February 1934

It Happened One Night is a good piece of fiction, which, with all its feverish stunts, is blessed with bright dialogue and a good quota of relatively restrained scenes. . . . And if there is a welter of improbable incidents these hectic doings serve to generate plenty of laughter. The pseudo suspense is kept on the wing until a few seconds before the picture ends, but it is a foregone conclusion that the producers would never dare to have the characters acted by Clark Gable and Claudette Colbert separated when the curtain falls.

MORE CLASSIC MOTION PICTURE FAVORITES

The Adventures of Priscilla, Queen of the Desert;
Alice Doesn't Live Here Anymore; Five Easy Pieces; The Scarecrow;
Sullivan's Travels; The Trip to Bountiful; The Wild One

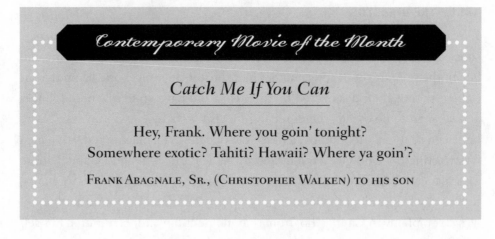

Contemporary Movie of the Month

Catch Me If You Can

Hey, Frank. Where you goin' tonight?
Somewhere exotic? Tahiti? Hawaii? Where ya goin'?

FRANK ABAGNALE, SR., (CHRISTOPHER WALKEN) TO HIS SON

THE DETAILS

2002, 141/C; PG-13; DVD. **DIRECTOR:** Steven Spielberg. **SCREENWRITERS:** Jeff Nathanson, based on the book by Frank Abagnale, Jr., and Stan Redding *Catch Me If You Can: The Amazing True Story of the Youngest and Most Daring Con Man in the History of Fun and Profit.* **CINEMATOGRAPHER:** Janusz Kaminski. **AWARDS:** BAFTA: Best Supporting Actor, Christopher Walken. National Society of Film Critics Award: Best Supporting Actor, Christopher Walken. Screen Actors Guild Awards: Best Supporting Actor, Christopher Walken. Academy Award: Nominated: Best Supporting Actor, Christopher Walken; Best Music, Original Score, John Williams.

THE SETTING

1960s. New York: New Rochelle, New York City; Hollywood; Atlanta; New Orleans; Miami; Tampa; Montrichard, France.

THE STORY

Sixteen-year-old Frank W. Abagnale, Jr. (Leonardo DiCaprio), is happy with his family and home life, until his adored father (Christopher Walken) runs into trouble with the IRS., which is investigating his financial affairs. The family loses both their home and livelihood. But Frank is loyal to his father and has learned his charming, if devious, ways of dealing with the world. After his parents' inevitable divorce, Frank runs away from his old life and into serial nonviolent crime. Like a chameleon, Frank easily assumes the profession of whomever he encounters if they happen to intrigue him: an airline executive, a doctor, an attorney, or even "Bond, James Bond" after he sees *Goldfinger*. This savvy trickster utilizes his gifts of impersonation and forgery as he hightails it around the world on phony identities and fake checks. It isn't long before the FBI is hot on his trail in the person of Carl Hanratty (Tom Hanks). But over the next few years, his nemesis develops into something that lies somewhere between law enforcer and friend, perhaps even father surrogate. This saga of invention is at once a madcap adventure and a poignant exploration of the importance of family and friends and how these roles are sometimes blurred. The question, Who says crime doesn't pay? must surely have been invented for Frank Abagnale, Jr., a cool cat who always lands on his feet. And one can't help but root for him.

READING THE MOVIE

1. What era of movie history does the title sequence evoke? Can you think of any films from that period that this film resembles?

2. Describe the editing/montage.

3. Does the film accurately portray the manner, atmosphere, and setting of the 1960s?

4. Is the film believable as a "true" story? Does the fact that it's true affect your perception of it?

FINDING THE MEANING

5. What were the funniest or most enjoyable scenes in the movie? Why?

6. What are the factors in both Frank's and Carl's biographies that contribute to a deeper connection between them?

7. Why is this scene important? How does it shape your feeling about each character? (#15, 1:32:20) Why does Frank's father ignore his son's plea for help?

8. Carl Hanratty says, "Sometimes it's easier livin' the lie." (#20, 2:10:40) What does he mean by this? Could that ever be true in your own life?

9. Does Frank seem to feel any compunction about his actions? If so, how is this displayed in the film? How does this make you feel about him?

10. It is often said, "Life is stranger than fiction." Does that apply to this story? (#13, 1:16:43; #14, 1:29:40) Which specific aspects of this story does this adage apply to?

11. Would you say that a life of crime pays off for Frank?

BONUS QUESTION

The reasons Frank follows his life of crime are complicated. It's most obvious to blame Frank's father's influence on him, but how did his mother also contribute to his development? How does the film explain the motive of his actions? How would you explain his behavior?

MEMORABLE QUOTES

Brenda: Frank? Frank? You're not a Lutheran?

Frank: [pretending to be an ER doctor]: Do you concur?
Intern: Why didn't I concur?!

BEHIND THE SCENES

- One of DiCaprio's favorite sequences in the movie is when Frank, Jr., sees the airline pilot coming out of the limousine like royalty, and he decides that's the life he wants to have. He wants that respect, even though he's only 16 years old. He wants to live that life. (www.bbc.co.uk/films)

- In an interview, Tom Hanks says that even though his character, FBI Agent Hanratty treats Frank, Jr., as a criminal and is determined to put him in jail, he's also worried about Frank's soul. "He sees him perhaps as the son he never had—a sort of fragile human being who's worth trying to redeem somehow."

DID YOU KNOW...?

- When Leo DiCaprio was cast in the role, the real Frank Abagnale, Jr., didn't think DiCaprio was "suave" enough to play him. But after he saw the film, he thought the actor had been perfect. (www.spielbergfilms.com)

- When asked if he had any regrets about his life of crime, Frank Abagnale, Jr., replied, "Yes, I have a lot of regrets. Though some people are fascinated with what I did as a teenager and find it very exciting, I lost my entire youth, 16–21 running from the police and 21–26 sitting in prison. Being on the run was a very lonely life. I never got to go to a senior prom, a high school football game or share a relationship with someone my own age. Even though I know where it brought me today, I wouldn't want to have to live it over again." (spielbergfilms.com)

ABOUT THE DIRECTOR

When asked during an interview what drew him to the Frank Abagnale, Jr., story, Spielberg responded, "His chutzpah and his imagination in the scams and stings he pulled off were so imaginative and so courageous. Amazing. In a way, he's sort of the anti-hero that you root for, even though you know he's going to have to pay a price and go to jail." (bbc.co.uk/films)

MOVIE AND TELEVISION REFERENCES

Perry Mason (1957)
Sing Along with Mitch (1961)
Dr. Kildare (1961)
Goldfinger (1964)

MORE CONTEMPORARY MOVIE FAVORITES

Almost Famous; Meet the Fockers; Oh Brother, Where Art Thou?;
The Straight Story

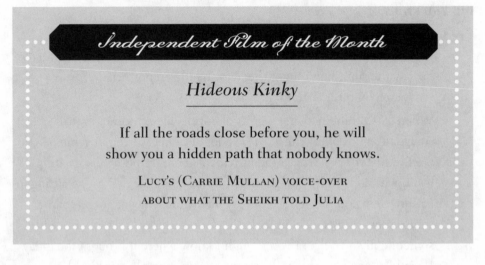

Independent Film of the Month

Hideous Kinky

If all the roads close before you, he will
show you a hidden path that nobody knows.

LUCY'S (CARRIE MULLAN) VOICE-OVER
ABOUT WHAT THE SHEIKH TOLD JULIA

THE DETAILS

1998, 99M/C; R; DVD. **DIRECTOR:** Gillies MacKinnon. **SCREENWRITER:** Billy MacKinnon (based on the novel by Esther Freud). **CINEMATOGRAPHER:** John de Borman. **AWARDS:** Evening Standard British Film Awards: Best Technical/Artistic Achievemen, John de Borman (Cinematography).

THE SETTING

1972; Marrakech, Morocco.

THE STORY

The spiritually lost Julia (Kate Winslet) has brought her two young daughters to Marrakech from London in search of a few lessons in enlightenment from a Sufi master. But, only 25 herself, the self-absorbed Julia didn't count on the difficulties she would encounter in this exotic and not-always-friendly country. Bea (Bella Riza), 8, and Lucy (Carrie Mullan), 6, often turn out to be more sensible than their mother—the children becoming the parent. For one thing, aside from an infrequent check from the girls' father, Julia has no idea how she will support them. She does some translation work and makes and sells cloth dolls, but things get desperate. When they meet Bilal, a street entertainer, they throw their lot in together, and a new dimension to the adventure begins. The charismatic Bilal (Said Taghmaoui) is enormously likable, and the movie is more amusing when he's entertaining the girls and enticing Julia. But, alas, he's as ineffectual at supporting a family as is Julia. Their trip to his village is an authentic piece of tribal life, but a discovery there about Bilal's past has them packing within a few days. It's evident that Julia loves her daughters, but has she the maturity and the maternal instinct for self-sacrifice? The film occasionally has trouble holding its focus, and feels almost like a travelogue, but, as always, Winslet is open, nuanced, and solidly grounded in her character. And the girls (both first-time actors) offer natural, unaffected performances. The vivid North African colors and flamboyant characters make the film a mesmerizing odyssey.

READING THE MOVIE

1. What does the title mean in relation to the story?
2. Do the soundtrack, hairstyles, and costumes do the job of transporting you back to the 1960s and 1970s?
3. How is the city of Marrakech and the Moroccan landscape a character in the film?
4. Do you feel there is a coherence and narrative momentum to the film or is it merely a series of vignettes? Could you easily follow the action? Are the actors given sufficient time to develop scenes?

FINDING THE MEANING

5. Is Julia a believable character? Does Winslet's performance capture the character of an early-1970s hippie mama with dreams of enlightenment? Why or why not? How are the two children's performances authentic? What did you learn from Kate Winslet's character, Julia?
6. At six years old, is it realistic to believe that a child, such as Lucy, could somehow possibly apprehend her mother's shortcomings? How do you suspect that Julia's cavalier attitude about parenting would be looked upon in the politically correct twenty-first century? (#6, 16":20)

7. From her audience with the new sheikh, Julia finds that "no matter where you go, there you are." Have you ever had this experience during your own travels? If so, what was it?

8. Critic Ruthe Stein of the *San Francisco Chronicle* wrote, "The problem for any filmmaker trying to evoke the period known as the '60s is that it's aged so badly. Not even Winslet could look good in purple harem pants." Do you agree with this statement? Why or why not?

9. A road movie is one in which characters embark on a journey of self-discovery through travel. How does this movie do that for the characters in *Hideous Kinky*? (#21, 1:09:15)

10. How does this film portray cultural differences between the English and the North Africans? (#12, :28:20; #13, :30:25)

SHE SAID/SHE SAID

Lucy: Bea, when you grow up, would you like to be a shepherd?
Bea: I don't think so.
Lucy: What, then?
Bea: I want to be normal.

MEMORABLE QUOTES

Bilal: Learn and work. That is the only secret.

BEHIND THE SCENES

Hideous Kinky is based on an autobiographical novel by Esther Freud, the great-granddaughter of the legendary Sigmund, and the daughter of the painter, Lucian. Her own mother had taken Esther and her sister to live among a Sufi Islamic sect in Morroco.

DID YOU KNOW...?

This was Kate Winslet's first film after *Titanic*, although that movie was not released until shooting wrapped on *Hideous Kinky*.

ABOUT THE ACTRESS

Winslet has done several nude or seminude scenes in films including *Hideous Kinky, Holy Smoke*, and *Iris*. She says, "I like exposing myself. There's not an awful lot that embarrasses me. I'm the kind of actress that absolutely believes in exposing myself." (8 April 2002, World Entertainment News Network)

CRITICALLY SPEAKING

Janet Maslin, *New York Times*, 16 April 1999
The colors and music of the Moroccan setting are so enveloping (and so appealingly photographed by John de Borman) that the film creates a sensual identity that reaches beyond its storytelling. . . . The atmosphere is an overwhelmingly strong aspect of the audience's experience, and the characters' way of penetrating that atmosphere creates its own momentum.

MORE INDEPENDENT FILM FAVORITES

Japanese Story, Morvern Callar, Rabbit-Proof Fence, Sideways, Smoke Signals, World Traveler

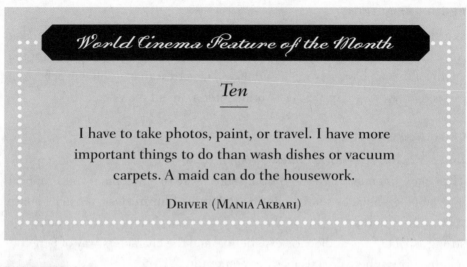

World Cinema Feature of the Month

Ten

I have to take photos, paint, or travel. I have more
important things to do than wash dishes or vacuum
carpets. A maid can do the housework.

DRIVER (MANIA AKBARI)

THE DETAILS

2002, 94M/C; NR; DVD (Farsi with English subtitles). **DIRECTOR/SCREENWRITER:**
Abbas Kiarostami. **CINEMATOGRAPHER:** Abbas Kiarostami. **AWARDS:** Cannes
Film Festival: Nominated: Golden Palm, Abbas Kiarostami.

THE SETTING

Contemporary Tehran, Iran.

THE STORY

As she maneuvers throughout the streets of Tehran on her daily errands, the
Driver (Mania Akbari)—she is never named—chauffeurs her seven-year-old
son, Amin (Amin Maher) around town and stops to offer a lift to six different
women: her sister, a friend, a prostitute, and other strangers. At some point, we
understand that this is a pilgrimage of sorts, during which the women and child
ostensibly are just going about living their lives, while underneath, the churnings
of internal conflicts that they share with each other give meaning to their existence and the story. The entire action of the film takes place in the interior of an
automobile and is recorded on two small digital cameras mounted on the dash-
board. About the use of a digital camera, the director has said, "What dramati-
cally distinguished the performance of a digital camera from that of a 35mm

camera, was the reaction of simple people, who responded so naturally and spontaneously in front of it." And, indeed, as viewers, we feel that we are privy to some serious, even intimate conversations among real people about motherhood, marriage, heartbreak, religion, and so on. Although directed by a man, the film is utterly sympathetic to women's treatment in Iran and confident in its depiction of their predicament and concerns.

READING THE MOVIE

1. Although it is a series of vignettes or chapters, do you feel that *Ten* is a cohesive or complete film? Why or why not? Is there a plot?

2. How does the director make Tehran, Iran, into a character in the movie?

3. What is the timeframe of the story?

4. How did you feel about virtually sitting in a car for 90 minutes while watching the film? Was it claustrophobic? Or did you feel a sense of intimacy? Is the setting appropriate for dealing with the characters' psychological states? Why or why not?

FINDING THE MEANING

5. How is the concept of voyeurism used as a theme and a concept in *Ten*? Did you have the sense that you were truly eavesdropping on actual conversations?

6. In Chapter 10, what is the director's purpose in not showing the mother's face? What does the film show that is universal about motherhood? What are the similarities and differences between this Iranian mother and son and an American mother and child? What about the similarities and differences in relationship and marriage? (#7, 1:08:09)

7. What aspects of Iranian culture are portrayed in the film? Were you surprised at the directness of the subject matter, especially in the scene with the prostitute? (#4, :36:40) What do you think the director is saying about Iranian society? Is he sympathetic to women's causes? If so, how does he display this opinion?

8. In what ways might the topics addressed in *Ten* be relevant to your own life? (#8, 1:16:60)

9. How do the characters evolve, especially the Driver and her son? Does the resolution seem authentic?

10. The Driver tells her son, "A woman has to die so as to be able to live." (#1, :15:32) What do you think she means? Do you agree with her? Why?

BONUS QUESTION

What are some techniques and approaches to filmmaking that World Cinema director Abbas Kiarostami uses that you do not see in American films? Do you feel that you have entered a different culture and learned something about it? What is that?

MEMORABLE QUOTES

Prostitute: [to the driver, who is a married woman]: You are wholesalers. We are retailers.

Driver: You can't live without losing. We come into the world for that.

BEHIND THE SCENES

All but one of the characters in *Ten* are nonactors, real people entangled in their everyday lives. The Driver and her son are, in fact, related. The only professional actor is the prostitute (whose face we never see). No nonprofessional actor would play this role, because they did not wish to be identified with prostitution.

ABOUT THE DIRECTOR

- Iranian director Abbas Kiarostami is considered one of the most visionary figures in international cinema. His films both challenge viewers' expectations of modern filmmaking and convey a deeply humanist philosophy. He explores complex issues with deceptive simplicity. He finds story ideas in the lives and people around him.

- Kiarostami has said that he finds nonactors no less interesting than professional actors, and he prefers to work with nonprofessional actors. In fact, he generally invites those in his film to portray aspects of their actual lives.

- In terms of costumes and makeup, Kiarostami allows his actors to wear their own clothes and wear whatever makeup they would normally use. "There is a sense of unity between someone's character and how they dress," he says in the DVD commentary. "No one knows better than the person what best represents them. People dress to match their inner feelings, more than their purple blouse."

CRITICALLY SPEAKING

A. O. Scott, *New York Times*, 28 September 2002

Ten . . . is a work of inspired simplicity. . . . These diffuse, inconclusive exchanges feel true to the random texture of daily life, and they allow the film's theme to develop slowly and organically within the boundaries of its formal artifice, so that by the end you feel that the lives of the characters, and the complicated society they inhabit, have been illuminated.

Frederic Brussat, spiritualityhealth.com

Kiarostami has created a parable about living in the present moment and taking what we can from each new situation. Amin's mother starts out in deep unhappiness, allowing her son's criticism of her to rock her self-esteem. In her encounters with others, she acquires a sense of inner peace, which enables her to allow things naturally to unfold. *Ten* is a marvel not only as a pioneering use of digital video but also as a winning parable about inner peace.

MORE WORLD CINEMA FAVORITES

Bread and Tulips, Central Station, In This World, Kikujiro, Learning Italian, Monsieur Hulot's Holiday, Taste of Cherry

July: Independent Spirits

★ ★ ★ ★

I dressed my maids as Amazons and rode
bare-breasted halfway to Damascus. Louis
had a seizure and I damn near died of
windburn ... but the troops were dazzled.

ELEANOR OF AFQUITAINE (KATHARINE HEPBURN)
THE LION IN WINTER, 1968
DIR. ANTHONY HARVEY

Featuring

CLASSIC MOTION PICTURE: *Adam's Rib*

CONTEMPORARY MOVIE: *Big Fish*

INDEPENDENT FILM: *Real Women Have Curves*

WORLD CINEMA FEATURE: *Respiro*

PREVIEWS

☆ It doesn't get much better than the verbal jousting between Kate
Hepburn and real-life love Spencer Tracy in *Adam's Rib*. The two play
happily married attorneys who suddenly find themselves on opposite
sides of the old cultural double standard: It's okay for guys, but not for
gals. To paraphrase Bette Davis in *All About Eve*, it's going to be a very
bumpy court case. So hang onto your popcorn.

☆ *Big Fish* is a whimsical narrative about Edward Bloom, who finds more merit in the fantastical than in the quotidian. But on his deathbed, Will, his son—soon to be a father himself—pleads with this larger-than-life figure to at last reveal the facts about his tall tales. In the process, he discovers that there may not be much difference between myths and truth. This enchanting movie is a bit of storytelling sorcery.

☆ *Real Women Have Curves* is a charming female-empowerment account of Ana, an 18-year-old recent high school graduate who has a full scholarship to Columbia University. But first she must convince her family. This full-figured first-generation Mexican-American refuses to succumb to popular-culture's body image ideal. During the course of a summer, while working in her sister's dressmaking shop, she learns a few important lessons about herself, her culture, and love.

☆ *Respiro* is the captivating tale of Grazia, a beautiful mother of three, who is much too spirited for the other members of her remote island community in Sicily. They are ready to pack her off to Milan for "treatment," but her devoted fisherman husband will not allow it, until . . . The elements of the land and sea are palpable, as is the passion Grazia feels for her husband, her children, and Nature. Based on an Italian legend, the haunting *Respiro* evokes the magic of fables and the transforming power of love.

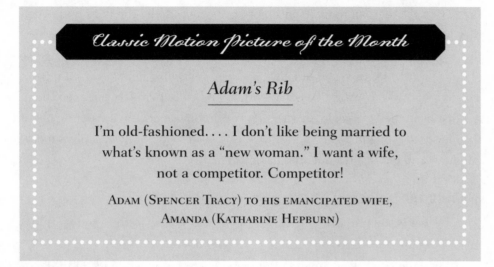

Classic Motion Picture of the Month

Adam's Rib

I'm old-fashioned. . . . I don't like being married to what's known as a "new woman." I want a wife, not a competitor. Competitor!

ADAM (SPENCER TRACY) TO HIS EMANCIPATED WIFE, AMANDA (KATHARINE HEPBURN)

THE DETAILS

1949, 101M/B&W; NR; DVD. **DIRECTOR:** George Cukor. **SCREENWRITER:** Ruth Gordon and Garson Kanin. **CINEMATOGRAPHER:** George J. Folsey. **AWARDS:** ACADEMY AWARDS: Nominated: Best Screenplay. Golden Globes: Nominated: Best Supporting Actress, Judy Holliday. Writers Guild of America: Nominated: Best Written American Comedy.

THE SETTING

Late 1940s; New York City.

THE STORY

"Do you believe in equal rights for women?" the fiery defending attorney, Amanda Bonner (Katharine Hepburn) asks a prospective juror. No, this isn't 1979, it's 1949! That's right, the feminist leaning of *Adam's Rib* affords this classic romantic comedy a delightfully endearing anachronism. Amanda, a trial attorney, is married to Adam Bonner (an assistant district attorney, played by Spencer Tracy). One morning the contented couple wake up, unaware that the front-page news is about to change their lives (at least for a while). A woman, Doris Attinger (Judy Holliday), has shot her philandering, husband Warren (Tom Ewell). Amanda says, "Brava!" Adam hollers, "Contempt of the law!" So by the day's end, when they find themselves on opposite sides of the court case . . . well, you see where this is going. Tracy and Hepburn have a ball with each other through the guise of their alter-egos, Adam and Amanda, and we are giggling right along with them. This is what movies were like when costars had *real* chemistry between them, not just headlines in *People* magazine. As critic Bowsley Crowther wrote about the movie, "We might say, in short, that it isn't solid food but it certainly is meaty and juicy and comically nourishing." *Bon appétit!*

READING THE MOVIE

1. What is the purpose of the theatrical stage setting in the opening title sequence?

2. In what ways does Amanda Bonner show her independence in the film?

3. What significance does the hat that Adam buys for Amanda play in the story?

4. Will Adam ever be able to "tame" Amanda's independent spirit? Should he try?

FINDING THE MEANING

5. What is the biblical reference to the film's title? How is it a motif throughout the film?

6. Is there a parallel between the two couples—Amanda and Adam, and Doris and Warren? What are the similarities and differences the film suggests? What must Amanda and Adam each concede to the other for the sake of their marriage? What do you think of the ending of the film? Is it as strong as the rest of the story? Why or why not?

7. What did you think when Amanda encouraged the circus "strong lady" to lift Adam in front of the court? Was she playing fair? (#20, 1:06:45) When Adam entered Kip's apartment with a licorice gun, was he justi-fied in making his argument? (#27, 1:29) Why or why not?

8. At one point, Amanda tells Adam, "Deep down I know you agree with everything I want and hope and believe in. We couldn't be as close if you didn't . . . at least if I didn't think you did." (#13, 41:55) Do you think she sees Adam clearly or is she projecting her mindset onto him? What makes you think so? Is it necessary for couples to hold all the same political, ethical, and spiritual positions in order to get along? Why or why not? Who are some well-known public couples that belong to different political parties?

9. What is the deeper message of the hilarious sequence that transposes Doris and Beryl into men and Warren into a woman? (#9, 1:14:06) How does it counterpoint Adam and Amanda's struggle?

10. *Adam's Rib* was released 13 years before Betty Friedan published *The Feminine Mystique*. Do you think *Adam's Rib*—as a commercial "feminist" film—was ahead of its time in 1949? Have the "times" caught up with it?

BONUS QUESTION

What other roles have you seen Katharine Hepburn and Spencer Tracy play? (See feature: "Did You Know. . .?") How does *Adam's Rib* compare? Which other of their individual films have you seen?

CULTURAL REFERENCES

Since the end of World War II, and the return home of the soldiers, there had been a concerted effort to remove women from the workplace and return them to the role of homemaker. But women weren't so eager to surrender their hard-won independence. In fact, in the final years of the war, a poll announced that 80 percent of working women wanted to keep their jobs.

MEMORABLE QUOTES

Kip Lurie: Lawyers should never marry other lawyers. This is called in-breeding; from this comes idiot children . . . and other lawyers.

BEHIND THE SCENES

- Katharine Hepburn and Spencer Tracy were a famous off-screen duo from the time they met in 1941 to his death in 1967, although the Catholic Tracy remained married to his wife.
- Ruth Gordon and Garson Kanin, the screenwriters, were a married team.

DID YOU KNOW...?

- When they first starred together, both of their careers were foundering. Hepburn was 42 years old and Tracy, who had never been a Hollywood romantic lead, had aged beyond the adventurer/hero roles that made him famous. But her sharp intelligence and his bemused masculinity made for an extraordinary on-screen pairing. Decades beyond their final role together, in the American Film Institute's poll of 100 Biggest Stars, Tracy was voted number nine, while Hepburn crowned the actress list at number one.
- Tracy and Hepburn made six additional films together: *Woman of the Year* (1942), *Keeper of the Flame* (1942), *State of the Union* (1948), *Pat and Mike* (1952), *The Desk Set* (1957), and *Guess Who's Coming to Dinner* (1967).

ABOUT THE DIRECTOR

George Cukor (1899–1983) was considered the "actress's director," because of his many successful films about women. He is said to have discovered Katharine Hepburn when he hired her in 1932 to play the role of the daughter of a shell-shocked WWI vet (John Barrymore), for whom she must care, in *Bill of Divorcement*. They went on to complete nine films in all, including some of Hepburn's most famous roles: *Little Women* (1933), *Sylvia Scarlett* (1935), *Holiday* (1938), *The Philadelphia Story* (1940), and *Pat and Mike* (1952), for which she reteamed with Spencer Tracy. (*Katharine Hepburn*. Barbara Leaming.)

CRITICALLY SPEAKING

Bosley Crowther, *New York Times*, 26 December 1949

Mr. Tracy and Miss Hepburn are the stellar performers in this show and their perfect compatibility in comic capers is delightful to see. A line thrown away, a lifted eyebrow, a smile, or a sharp, resounding slap on a tender part of the anatomy is as natural as breathing to them. Plainly, they took great pleasure in playing this rambunctious spoof.

Molly Haskell, *From Reverence to Rape: The Treatment of Women in the Movies*, 1987

Adam's Rib, that *rara avis*, a commercial "feminist" film, was many years ahead of its time when it appeared in 1949, and still, alas, is. Even the slightly coy happy ending testifies to the fact that the film strikes deeper into the question of sexual roles than its comic surface would indicate and raises more questions than it can possibly answer.

MORE CLASSIC MOTION PICTURE FAVORITES

Harold and Maude, Isadora, The Lion in Winter,
The Madwoman of Chaillot, One Flew Over the Cuckoo's Nest,
Tucker: The Man and His Dream, Zorba the Greek

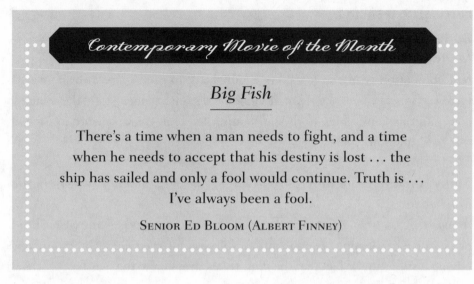

Contemporary Movie of the Month

Big Fish

There's a time when a man needs to fight, and a time
when he needs to accept that his destiny is lost ... the
ship has sailed and only a fool would continue. Truth is ...
I've always been a fool.

SENIOR ED BLOOM (ALBERT FINNEY)

THE DETAILS

2003, 122M/C; PG-13; DVD. **DIRECTOR:** Tim Burton. **SCREENWRITER:** John
August (based on the novel by Daniel Wallace). **CINEMATOGRAPHER:** Philippe
Rousselot. **AWARDS:** Academy Awards: Nominated: Best Original Score, Danny
Elfman. BAFTA (British) Nominated: Best Adapted Screenplay, Best Supporting
Actor, Albert Finney; Best Foreign Film; Achievement in Special Visual Effects.
Golden Globes: Nominated: Best Motion Picture—Musical or Comedy; Best
Supporting Actor, Albert Finney. Best Original Score—Motion Picture.

THE SETTING

1950–2000; Ashton, Alabama.

THE STORY

The eccentric Edward Bloom (Albert Finney) is more comfortable hiding behind
his preposterous stories than he is revealing himself. This independent spirit
has spent a lifetime embellishing every event of his early life. But now, on his
deathbed, his estranged son, Will (who has gone the opposite extreme of his
fabulist father to become a "just the facts, Ma'am" journalist), has returned
home from Paris, where he lives with his pregnant wife, to finally come to terms

with his father. "Dad, you're like Santa Claus and the Easter Bunny combined
. . . You're just as charming, and just as fake," Will (Billy Crudup) tells Edward.
During much of *Big Fish*, Edward's recounting of his improbable stories is spell-
binding: heroic, athletic, and lifesaving feats; discovery of a secret town; a spell
at a circus; and 10,000 daffodils. And the characters he's met along the way: a
witch; a werewolf; Siamese twins; a mermaid; a lonely, misunderstood giant;
and more. There's not a little resemblance between Wallace/Burton's Edward
Bloom and James Joyce's Leopold Bloom, from his masterpiece *Ulysses*. Both
are humane and generous wanderers on a quest for love, and each finds fulfillment only in his fantasies. As the young Ed Bloom (Ewan McGregor) says,
"There are some fish that cannot be caught. It's not that they're faster or stronger
than the other fish. They're just touched by something extra." The same can be
said of Ed himself and of *Big Fish*.

READING THE MOVIE

1. Who, among all the fantastical characters, did you find the most engag-
    ing? To whom, among the main characters, did you most easily relate?
    Which among Edward Bloom's fabricated stories was most entertaining
    to you?

2. There are a number of references to other movies and to mythical sto-
    ries. How many can you spot?

3. Do you think there was a balance between the male and female char-
    acters and their characterizations? If not, should there be?

4. The film covers a number of time frames (the father's childhood, ado-
    lescence, young adulthood, and old age; the son's childhood and adult-
    hood). Are the transitions easy to follow?

FINDING THE MEANING

5. Will Bloom says, "Man tells so many stories that he becomes the sto-
    ries. They live on after him, and in that way he becomes immortal." Is
    this part of the purpose of memory, in that, as long as we remember
    someone, they are immortal? *Big Fish* is an oasis of storytelling among

the many special-effects-driven Hollywood movies. Why are stories so important to us, especially stories about our families? Is the purpose of telling stories to hide or to reveal? Both? Is the "truth" just a series of selected facts? Can it ever be anything else?

6. What do you think the big fish represents? What does it represent for Ed? Why does he connect the big fish to Will's birth? Why does he repeat this story at Will's wedding? (#1, :03)

7. One of the roles of the artist is to stir our imaginations. *Big Fish* is about nothing if not the importance of the imagination to alleviate our often mundane lives. Do you think Ed tells stories in order to make his life seem more interesting and exciting than it really is?

8. We see Joseph Campbell's book *The Hero with a Thousand Faces* twice in *Big Fish*. First, on Edward Bloom's chest when he is dozing (Josephine [Marion Cotillard], Will's wife, enters the room and places it on the nightstand). Later, we see it still on the nightstand during a scene between Ed and Will. What do you think is the significance of this book to the film? Campbell described myth as something "that never was, but always is." What did he mean by this? What is the importance of mythology in our lives?

9. As charming as Edward, Sr., may seem to most people, did the thought ever cross your mind that Will may have a point? That his father is a narcissist and a compulsive liar? Does considering this possibility make you feel differently about the characters, or the story? Why or why not? Is Will justified in his anger toward his father? (#18, 1:35)

10. Ed Bloom, Sr., says, "Truth is, I've always been thirsty." What do you think he means by this statement? He makes many references to grow-ing out of things, moving on, to experiencing anything that is "more" (adventurous, dangerous, exotic, and so on). What can be the result of this kind of thinking? What resemblance might this ethos bear to "the American Dream"? On the other hand, do you think the town of Spectre might represent the dangers of contentment and compla-cency? (#8, :32)

BONUS QUESTION

One of the most important themes in *Big Fish* is that of death. The young Edward decides to look into the witch's eye and see his own death. (#1, 12:30) What does he see? Do you think this foreknowledge helps him to live life more on the edge, that it helps him to forgo some of life's inherent dangers and plunge headfirst into adventure? Would you choose to know your own death if you could? Why or why not?

HE SAID/SHE SAID

Josephine: I'd like to take your picture.
Senior Ed Bloom: Oh, you don't need a picture. Just look up *handsome* in the dictionary.

MEMORABLE QUOTES

Senior Ed Bloom: They say, when you meet the love of your life, time stops, and that's true. What they don't tell you is that when it starts again, it moves extra fast to catch up.

DID YOU KNOW...?

Director Tim Burton says he looked for "a pair" of actors to play the roles of Ed Bloom as a young man and as an older man. He couldn't consider one without the other. But when he saw photos of a young Albert Finney playing the rogue in *Tom Jones*, he noticed a striking similarity to Ewan McGregor. But, even more importantly, he says, he recognized the same spirit in both men. (DVD commentary)

ABOUT THE DIRECTOR

When Tim Burton took on the project of directing *Big Fish*, his father had recently died, and he had been thinking about the father–son issue that is prominent in the film. Burton also directed *Pee-wee's Big Adventure* (1985), *Beetlejuice* (1988), *Batman* (1989), *Edward Scissorhands* (1990), *Batman Returns* (1992), *Ed Wood* (1994), *Mars Attacks!* (1996), *Sleepy Hollow* (1999), *Planet of the Apes* (2001).

STRAIGHT FROM THE SCREENWRITER

In an article John August wrote for *Script* magazine, he describes his reaction to the—as yet unpublished—novel *Big Fish*: "The writing was simple, weird and imaginative. It clearly offered a lot of cinematic moments. But what attracted me most were the things that weren't even on the page. I knew that the son, Will, was a reporter in Paris and married to a pregnant French woman. That's nowhere in the story, but I was absolutely certain it was true. There wasn't a circus anywhere in the book, yet I immediately sensed where it would fit. In short, I knew so much about the story I wanted to tell that I had to write the script immediately." (*Script* magazine, January–February 2004)

MOVIE REFERENCES

The Wizard of Oz (1939)
8½ (1963)
Deliverance (1972)
Monty Python and the Holy Grail (1975)
Pee-wee's Big Adventure (1985)
Edward Scissorhands (1990)
Batman Returns (1992)
O Brother, Where Art Thou? (2000)
Identity (2003)

MORE CONTEMPORARY MOVIE FAVORITES

Blue Sky, Forrest Gump, Wilde

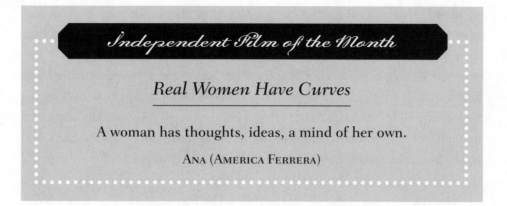

Independent Film of the Month

Real Women Have Curves

A woman has thoughts, ideas, a mind of her own.

ANA (AMERICA FERRERA)

THE DETAILS

2002, 90M/C; PG-13; DVD. **DIRECTOR:** Patricia Cardosa. **SCREENWRITER:** George LaVoo and Josefina Lopez (teleplay) (based on the play by Josefina Lopez). **CINEMATOGRAPHER:** Jim Denault. **AWARDS:** Independent Spirit Awards: Producers Award. Nominated: Best Debut Performance, America Ferrera. Sundance Film Festival: Audience Award; Special Jury Prize: Best Actors, America Ferrera and Lupe Ontiveros. San Sebastián International Film Festival: Youth Jury Award, Patricia Cardosa.

THE SETTING

2002; East Los Angeles, California.

THE STORY

Ana Garcia (America Ferrera), a first-generation Mexican-American teenager, is a vibrant young woman, comfortable with her mind, her body, and her sexuality: a true independent spirit. Although she lives in East L.A., Ana has just graduated from the prestigious Beverly Hills High School, where she was a star student. It often takes just one person who believes in us to get us started on the right track, or to set us straight when we've veered off. Mr. Guzman (George Lopez), her English teacher, is that person for Ana. Through personal connections he helps her achieve a full scholarship to Columbia University. The trouble is, according to cultural custom, her parents expect her to stick around East L.A. and help support the household, even if it's only on a measly salary. And then there is the issue of Ana's full figure, about which her mother—no size 10 herself—continually torments her. She also nags her to find a man, get married, and have children. For the summer, she is roped into working at the down town sewing factory owned by her sister Estela (Ingrid Oliu), where, unexpectedly, she learns to admire the hardworking team of women who teach her solidarity and teamwork. She teaches them a thing or two as well. "You're all cheap labor for Bloomingdale's!" she shrieks at them. But she also sets an example of a young woman who is comfortable in her own skin. The fun begins when they start discarding their clothes and comparing their cellulite. It's our good fortune that this was an HBO production, rather than that of a Hollywood studio, which surely would have cast Jennifer Lopez as Ana. In America's Ana, there are no pretensions to glamour or anything forced. What we have is the genuine article: smart, spunky, and always real.

READING THE MOVIE

1. Does the title of the film work? Why or why not? What other meanings could the word *curve* have? What is an alternative title?

2. Which scenes work the best? Which are the most humorous? Which are the most touching?

3. What do you think of Ana? Is she a strong person? Why or why not? Do you see her as lazy (as does Carmen), defiant, or resentful? Or is she just a teenager? Why did she quit her job at the burger joint?

4. This is a feminist movie in which men are not demonized. In fact, without exception, they are presented in a positive light. What roles do the male characters serve in *Real Women Have Curves*?

5. What are some cultural and institutional forms of prejudice in the movie? How would you compare and contrast Ana's sister, Estela, with the clothing distributor, Mrs. Green? (#8, :40). Ana refers to her sister's business as a "sweatshop." (#6, :34) Is Estela's little factory really a sweatshop? Do you agree that selling a dress for $18, which later sells

at Bloomingdale's for $600, is "just not right"? (#3, :17) What does Ana learn while working there about herself, her sister, her mother, and other Chicanas?

FINDING THE MEANING

6. *Real Women* explores the timeless battle between mother and daughter, both strong women in this case. What did you think about Ana's mother, Carmen? Did you sympathize with her manipulative ways or find them objectionable? Do you think she was portrayed as a three-dimensional character? What is Estela's relationship with her mother like? What do you think of the film's ending? (#16, 1:17:15) Carmen is adamantly opposed to Ana's going to college. (#12, :59:13) Why? Do you think there is some sublimated jealousy there? That, perhaps, Carmen is envious of Ana's youth and opportunities—opportunities she never had? Is she projecting a dislike of her own body onto Ana? What do you think Ana wrote about in her college-entrance essay?

7. Ana must somehow resolve her loyalty to her culture, even as she struggles to move forward in her life. Have you had difficult experiences trying to balance the values of your culture or belief system with those of your country, peers, or family?

8. In Los Angeles, the biggest subculture is Mexican or, more generally, Latin American. What are the biggest ethnic minorities where you live? Do you think there are similar issues between the older and younger generations in those subcultures?

9. This film is a positive portrayal of large women and addresses some of the sexual, personal, and cultural biases regarding weight. How does Ana struggle with the beauty myth, and cultural standards of beauty? Are Americans too obsessed with being thin? Or, in fact, are Americans actually too fat? What's behind this dichotomy? How does it affect women?

10. In the end, in order to achieve her independence, Ana has the difficult task of being forced to choose between her mother and her future. Why is this predicament one of the reasons the film resonates with so many people?

MEMORABLE QUOTES

Estela: *This* is cellulite.

Jimmy: You're not fat. You're beautiful.

DID YOU KNOW...?

- *Real Women Have Curves* was originally a stage play by Josefina Lopez that was produced for television by HBO.
- This was 18-year-old America Ferrera's first movie role.

ABOUT THE DIRECTOR

Patricia Cardosa, who is a Fulbright scholar, has a master's degree in archaeology, and was raised in Bogotá, Columbia. She spent ten years trying to get financing for *Real Women*. In an interview with *DGA* magazine, Cardosa explains what attracted her to Josefina Lopez's play: "Although I grew up in a different country, in a different financial class, the issues were the same. My mother, even though she was an architect from MIT, was just as controlling as Ana's mother [in the film]. I grew up having curves too. I visited dress factories in East Los Angeles and talked to dress designers. They told me that manufacturers complained that the factories should only use a size 4 model and that there would be a curve police to ensure the patterns were cut without curves! It's an issue that is a big part of women's lives, including my own." (*DGA* magazine, March 2002)

CRITICALLY SPEAKING

Desson Howe, *Washington Post*, 15 November 2002

Real Women Have Curves may be one of the oldest stories ever told: American immigrants trying to keep their children steeped in old-country tradition. But it

feels like one of the freshest, thanks to America Ferrera, who makes one cheeky, tough and adorable daughter.

Claudia Puig, *USA TODAY*, 24 October 2002

What will undoubtedly resound powerfully with audiences of *Real Women Have Curves*, particularly women, is the film's message that there is beauty in all shapes and sizes. . . . *Real Women* feels like an authentic portrayal of a segment of American life that we seldom see on film. Looking as if it were plucked from real life, the largely unknown cast is neither glossy nor glamorous. But the movie avoids a stereotypical portrayal of life in East L.A.; it's not seen as grimy or violence-ridden. Ana's family members are hard workers who own their own home, and the film shows the simple beauty of their neighborhood.

MORE INDEPENDENT FILM FAVORITES

The Apostle, Napoleon Dynamite, The Piano, Rushmore

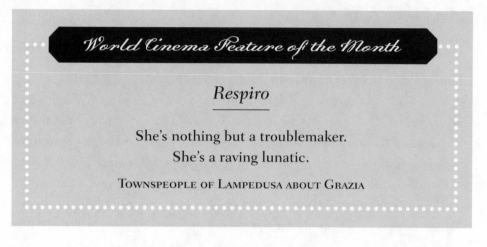

World Cinema Feature of the Month

Respiro

She's nothing but a troublemaker.
She's a raving lunatic.

TOWNSPEOPLE OF LAMPEDUSA ABOUT GRAZIA

THE DETAILS

2002, 90M/C; PG-13; DVD (Italian with English subtitles). **DIRECTOR/ SCREENWRITER:** Emenuele Crialese. **CINEMATOGRAPHER:** Fabio Zamarion. **AWARDS:** Cannes Film Festival: Critics Week Grand Prize. Young Critics Award: Best Feature. Italian National Syndicate of Film Journalists: Best Actress, Valeria Golino. David di Donatello Awards: Best Producer, Domenico Procacci.

THE SETTING

Contemporary Lampedusa, Sicily.

THE STORY

Lampedusa, a tiny fishing village off the west coast of Sicily, is so self-contained and insular that its inhabitants cannot tolerate the attractive, free-spirited Grazia (Valeria Golino). The townspeople confuse her unconventional behavior with madness and throw epithets at her: "raving lunatic ... public menace ... troublemaker." But there are also indications that Grazia may *be* either mentally unstable or perhaps epileptic. What's curious is that it's only acts of cruelty toward her children or animals that set her off. This often childlike, unselfconscious fertile beauty is a combination of animal vitality and Aphrodite–sea goddess. It is apparent, however, that Grazia, the youthful mother of three—

Marinella (Veronica D'Agostino); a teenage daughter, Pasquale (Francesco Casisa), perhaps 12; and 10-year-old Filippo (Filippo Pucillo)—and her virile, devoted fisherman-husband Pietro (Vincenzo Amato); are deeply and irresistibly in love with each other. The family does its best to keep a lid on this human Vesuvius, but Grazia's eruptions are as natural as lightning in a thunderstorm. The word *respiro* means "I breathe," and as the title suggests, links among the landscape, climate, and human behavior are as spiritual as they are biological. Indeed, we feel the unrelenting heat on the characters' skin, and the sharpness of the craggy terrain beneath their feet. We swim in the engulfing blueness of sea and sky reflected in Grazia's eyes. There is a mystical, lyrical quality to *Respiro*, especially its music and haunting ending, which are pure cinematic poetry.

READING THE MOVIE

1. What does the title mean in relation to the story? What is the significance of Grazia's name ("grace") to the story?

2. Why does the film start like it does? What is the director telling us?

3. Is the director trying to make a statement about the film? What is it? Is he trying to conjure a sense of place? How does he go about that?

4. In what ways might it be said that the lifestyle in the community of Lampedusa is a primitive existence?

FINDING THE MEANING

5. When Grazia frees the wild dogs from their confinement, what is she asserting? (#20, :54:58) How does it reflect her personality?

6. What kind of mother do you think Grazia is? Why? (#4, :12:25 ; #13, :36:07)

7. How would you describe the relationship between Grazia and Marinella?

8. About his character, the director says, "She's just going through a phase in her life where she's oppressed and feels the need to change. Every time she enters a scene I want everyone to feel unstable." What do you

think about Grazia's behavior? Do you sympathize with her? Do you think she is manic-depressive? Should she have gone to see the doctor in Milan? Do you know anyone who resembles Grazia?

9. It seems as if the town's inhabitants are a bit afraid of the spontaneous Grazia. Is there reason to be or not? Why? Or do they have other feelings about her? (#10, :28) What might those be?

10. How do you feel about the way the film ends? (#28, 1:27:20) What do you think happens after the family returns home? Will the townspeople have changed their attitude toward Grazia?

BONUS QUESTION

Respiro is similar to the 1950 Italian film *Stromboli*, directed by Roberto Rossellini and starring Ingrid Bergman, who plays a Czech refugee who marries an Italian fisherman and lives on his isolated home island of Stromboli. It also resembles the American film *Blue Sky* (1991), which stars Jessica Lange as an irrepressible military wife of Tommy Lee Jones. If you have seen one or both of these movies, how do they compare to *Respiro*? Are there other films of similar content that you can think of?

CULTURAL REFERENCES

Respiro was inspired by an Italian legend of a beautiful young woman who is scorned by her small town neighbors. When she disappears, leaving only her dress on the beach, they are guilt-ridden. Through the power of prayer and contrition, she is restored to life.

DID YOU KNOW...?

The Greek-Italian actress Valeria Golino has been in several American films, including *Rain Man*, *Leaving Las Vegas*, *Escape from L.A.*, and *Frida*.

ABOUT THE DIRECTOR

Emenuele Crialese graduated from the New York University Film School.

CRITICALLY SPEAKING

Stephen Holden, *New York Times*, 28 March 2003

Respiro . . . bursts with such pulsing vitality and sensual appreciation of nature that you can almost taste the salty air and feel the sun beating down on your shoulders. It's easy to envy its characters, who vent their feelings in fiery eruptions that quickly cool and whose minds remain uncluttered (uncorrupted, you might say) by the nagging temptations served up by modern mass media.

Kevin Thomas, *Los Angeles Times*, 23 May 2003

The film doubtless works better for those able to accept it unquestioningly as a charming fable of the redemptive, healing power of love that it means to be. Crialese certainly does capture the overwhelming sensuality of its many beautiful people and its sun-drenched locale. All that hot Sicilian blood is palpable, but to his credit Crialese resists caricature and is wonderful with actors.

MORE WORLD CINEMA FAVORITES

Chocolat, Juliet of the Spirits, Muriel's Wedding, Shirley Valentine

August: Life Transformations

★ ★ ★ ★

Something's like crossed over in me and I can't go back.

THELMA (GEENA DAVIS)
THELMA AND LOUISE, 1991
DIR. RIDLEY SCOTT

I'm just changing.

MERMAID MADISON (DARYL HANNAH)
SPLASH, 1984
DIR. RON HOWARD

Featuring

CLASSIC MOTION PICTURE: *Bagdad Café*

CONTEMPORARY MOVIE: *Pleasantville*

INDEPENDENT FILM: *Thirteen Conversations About One Thing*

WORLD CINEMA FEATURE: *Ma vie en rose*

PREVIEWS

☆ In the middle of the desert sits a forgotten truck-stop café and motel. The *Bagdad Café* is about making a home and connections wherever you find yourself. A plus-sized German woman, who has left her husband, shows that kindness and generosity of spirit are gifts that everyone needs; and that by extending them to others, they boomerang back to you. Meet a clan of eccentric characters who bring real magic to the screen.

☆ In *Pleasantville*, teenaged David and Jennifer, sparring siblings in late 1990s Anytown, USA, find themselves trapped in the 1958 sitcom of the title. Before being transported, David wanted only to retreat from life, while Jennifer recklessly ran into it—libido first. But in a new environment, they have an opportunity to colorize the town's gray inhabitants and, perhaps, refurbish their own lives. *Pleasantville* is a late-twentieth-century version of *It's a Wonderful Life* and *The Wizard of Oz*. And you can't go wrong with that.

☆ *Thirteen Conversations About One Thing* examines the concept of destiny, coincidence, bad luck, good fortune, serendipity, whatever you call it, with meticulous skill and perceptive insight into human nature. The stories of several characters who do not know one another (but who will meet, perhaps fleetingly or perhaps with life-changing consequences) nestle into one another like a mystical jigsaw puzzle. The brilliant use of clichéd phrases, such as, "Fortune smiles at some and laughs at others" proves just how true clichés often are. However, this intelligent film is anything but a cliché

☆ In *Ma vie en rose* (*My Life in Pink*), Ludovic is a good-natured seven-year-old boy who cross-dresses because he believes he is a girl. But his proclivity both confounds and causes problems for and between his parents, among his neighbors, and among his classmates at school. This infectious Belgian comedy-drama entertains, while it makes us think about gender confusion, intolerance, and the wisdom of innocence.

Classic Motion Picture of the Month

Bagdad Café

Rudi Cox: May I come in?
Jasmin: As a painter or as a gentleman?
Rudi Cox: As a man.

RUDI (JACK PALANCE)
JASMIN (MARIANNE SÄGEBRECHT)
BAGDAD CAFÉ, 1987

THE DETAILS

1987, 124M/C; PG; DVD. **DIRECTOR:** Percy Adlon. **SCREENWRITERS:** Percy and Eleonore Adlon. **CINEMATOGRAPHER:** Bernd Heinl. **AWARDS:** César Awards, France: Best Foreign Film. Independent Spirit Awards: Best Foreign Film. Berlin Film Critics' Ernst Lubitsch Award: Best Comedy. Bavarian Film Awards: Best Screenplay. German Film Awards: Outstanding Individual Achievement, Actress Marianne Sägebrecht. Seattle International Film Festival: Best Film. Academy Awards: Nominated: Best Music, Original Song, Bob Telson for the song "Calling You."

THE SETTING

Late 1980s; the California Mojave desert.

THE STORY

A German couple is way out of their element in the heat and barrenness of the California desert. This must surely be the vacation from hell. After a fight with her boorish husband in the middle of nowhere, Jasmin (Marianne Sägebrecht) stalks off to . . . she has no idea where. Sometime later, she spies a dilapidated roadside café and a bit apprehensively enters a new world. Inside the café the first thing Jasmin notices (good German hausfrau that she is) is the inch of dust that covers everything. As she looks into the dark eyes of Brenda (CCH Pounder), the black, furiously angry proprietor of the place, she fantasizes being held hostage among an African tribe of cannibals and being put in the cauldron for stewing. Even that, we think, would be better than where she has come from. As she walks into the café, her little purse looks just like a doctor's bag. The maternal Jasmin is here to heal, to repair broken hearts and damaged souls. This bizarre band of misfits includes the blocked painter, Rudi (Jack Palance); Brenda's husband, Sal (G. Smokey Campbell); her piano-playing son, Salomo (Darron Flagg); her daughter, Phyllis (Monica Calhoun); the tattoo artist, Debby (Christine Kaufmann); and the Native American cook, Cahuenga (George Aguilar). A café is a place people go to for nourishment—both physical and spiritual. They are there for transformation but don't know it yet. By the end, magic is on the move, and the once barren and desolate truck stop is a convivial cabaret.

READING THE MOVIE

1. What is the significance of the setting?

2. How are the costumes (especially of Jasmin and Rudy) significant?

3. There are several recurring motifs in the film. What do you think the yellow thermos signifies? What's the meaning of the boomerang?

4. The director lends a surreal quality to the film by using colored lens filters, fast editing, and silly scenarios or fantastic visions. What is the effect of these elements on the way you feel about the characters?

FINDING THE MEANING

5. In an early scene Jasmin is dressed in white. What does this represent? She seems more attractive than Debbie, the extremely cold, plastic tattoo artist–beauty with the perfect legs. What is a decided contrast between the two types of beauty or womanhood? (#6, :32:50; #8, :42:52)

6. When Jasmin opens her suitcase, she realizes that she took her husband's by mistake. Now, she will have to make an entirely new wardrobe for herself. (#5, :21:50) This is symbolic of an internal trans-

formation. What are other indications that she (as well as the other characters) is undergoing change?

7. The four men all seem emotionally and psychologically beaten. Life is colorless and monotonous, drab and sterile. Each, in his own way, senses the inertia and near-paralysis of the others and tries to be of some small comfort. They are a band of misfits. What is the central crisis at the root of this film? Which characters do you find most sympathetic and why? Do you identify with any of the characters?

8. Rita Kempley wrote, "There's something condescending about an Aryan Mary Poppins dropping by to save a black family from debt and despair. Nevertheless, it's a winning story of friendship, extended family and rediscovered femininity." (*Washington Post*, 6 May 1998) Do you agree with her assessment? Why or why not?

9. The opening scenes exemplify a desert of the heart. There is military-type music; everything is regimented. The husband and wife have grown to dislike each other intensely. Even the camera angles and frames are askew—everything is off-kilter here. How are the characters' feelings sublimated in their actions? (#1, :00:25)

10. Janet Maslin wrote, "*Bagdad Café* is too slow-paced to work as a comedy, and its screenplay manages simultaneously to be both shapeless and pat (Jasmin likes to clean, and Brenda doesn't; Brenda has too many children, and Jasmin has none)." (*New York Times*, 22 April 1988) Do you think the film works as a comedy? Why or why not?

BONUS QUESTION

Are there other Classic Motion Picture films you can think of that have similar themes?

MEMORABLE QUOTES

Sheriff Arnie: She's a tourist; what she wears is her business.

[After Jasmin has left]
Cahuenga: Magic? It's gone.

BEHIND THE SCENES

The cafe was the Sidewinder Café (now renamed the Bagdad Café) on the famed old Route 66, between the east and west off-ramps of I-40, near Newberry Springs, east of Barstow, on Highway 40, California.

ABOUT THE DIRECTOR

The script grew out of a 1984 trip that director Percy Adlon and his producer wife, Eleonore, took across the United States. Barstow, California, reminded them of purgatory.

CRITICALLY SPEAKING

Rita Kempley, *Washington Post*, 6 May 1988

Marianne Sägebrecht of Munich's avant-garde cinema is the unlikely heroine of Percy Adlon's first English-language film, *Bagdad Café*, a gingerly, happy little fable about a Mojave Desert oasis run dry. With its foibles and quirks, it's something like a Sam Shepard play by way of the Black Forest. . . . The movie does seem to have been pulled from a hat, a series of surprises tossed off by Adlon and his producer wife, Eleonore.

Janet Maslin, *New York Times*, 22 April 1988

Bagdad Café . . . takes much more delight in the zaniness and variety of its characters than many viewers will. Mr. Adlon . . . finds a tantalizing exoticism in all the wrong places, and seems most captivated by the fact that many of the film's characters are black (and a couple are American Indians, notably a local sheriff with long braids). That Jasmin can let her hair down, figuratively and literally, to become close to an irate black woman and her children is virtually the greatest miracle the film has to offer.

MORE CLASSIC MOTION PICTURE FAVORITES

Accidental Tourist, Altered States, Educating Rita

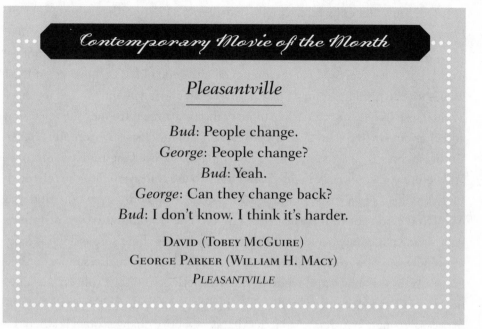

Contemporary Movie of the Month

Pleasantville

Bud: People change.
George: People change?
Bud: Yeah.
George: Can they change back?
Bud: I don't know. I think it's harder.

DAVID (TOBEY MCGUIRE)
GEORGE PARKER (WILLIAM H. MACY)
PLEASANTVILLE

THE DETAILS

1998, 124M/C; PG-13; DVD. **DIRECTOR/SCREENWRITER:** Gary Ross.
CINEMATOGRAPHER: John Lindley. **AWARDS:** Los Angeles Film Critics Association
Awards: Best Supporting Actress, Joan Allen; Best Production Design. Boston
Society of Film Critics Awards: Best Supporting Actor, William H. Macy; Best
Supporting Actress, Joan Allen. Academy Awards: Nominated: Best Art
Direction–Set Decoration; Best Costume Design; Best Music, Original Dramatic
Score, Randy Newman.

THE SETTING

1958; "Pleasantville," USA, and a contemporary USA town.

THE STORY

Once upon a time ... there were television sitcoms in the 1950s (*Father Knows
Best, The Donna Reed Show, My Three Sons*) that rendered family life as perfect. Father worked, Mom (or Uncle Charlie, in the latter's case) cooked and

cleaned, and kids enjoyed an idyllic existence. What could be better? Well, *Pleasantville* sets out to answer that question. As the film reveals (and of course as we already know), these shows instilled in the viewer a desire for a fantasy world that never was, and yet the dream of "the good old days" persists. At least it does for the nostalgia-hungry David (Tobey McGuire), an introverted teenager living in the late 1990s, who finds more comfort sitting in front of the television and channel-surfing than asking a girl out on a date. His sister, Jennifer (Reese Witherspoon), is just the opposite. During a tussle over the remote control—and before you can say *Twilight Zone*—the two are transported to the teletown, Pleasantville—circa 1958—and the fun begins. The siblings are now Bud and Mary Sue, and they find themselves trapped in surroundings where restrooms have no toilets, library books are blank, nobody knows about sex, and the myopic metropolis has one road that loops back on itself. To make matters more confusing, everything is black and white in this synthetic, circuitous suburb—a statement about the dangers of reductive thinking. At first, Pleasantville seems harmless enough in its repression, but that perspective changes quickly when the utopian, stereotypical family values the townspeople uphold begin to collapse. As the story progresses, color begins to peek through the monochromatic flatness—a rose here, a rouged cheek there—and soon this original and thought-provoking film has us reflecting on our own lives, the importance of individual freedom, and the dangers of absolutism. This play on the *Back to the Future* notion invites us to take a fresh look at our own authentic world as we comprehend that even a society inundated with a high divorce rate and unemployment, AIDS, and global warming still has more to offer than a one-way ticket to Pleasantville.

READING THE MOVIE

1. Why does the movie start the way it does? How did you respond to the opening title sequence of channel surfing?

2. In terms of the cinematography, is there a pattern of striking camera movements or angles? What is the director's purpose?

3. What experience or awareness precedes each character's becoming colorized? Does this enhance or detract from your involvement with the

story? What are various meanings implied by using the metaphor of color?

4. How do the paintings in the book that Bud brings to Mr. Johnson (Jeff Daniels) reflect various circumstances in the film?

FINDING THE MEANING

5. According to the director, Gary Ross, the film is a kind of merging of 1950s innocence with late-twentieth-century eroticism. When does Betty (Joan Allen) first get a glimpse of the possibility that another world exists? (#17, :43:40) While the other characters in Pleasantville are moving *toward* their sexual awakening, Jennifer/Mary Sue (Reese Witherspoon) is moving away from it. Why is this happening? What is the film saying about "values," their collapse, and what replaces them?

6. *Pleasantville* contains aspects of drama, satire, and a morality play. In what ways do these styles converge or conflict with one another? How might this resemble actual life?

7. One of the primary and deeper issues at play in the film is the question of free will. In what ways does it enhance the characters' lives? In what ways does it disturb or change their lives? Which two characters from Pleasantville are the first to experience an existential crisis? How does the film show that it takes only one event or one influence to change a person's life forever? When does Bud first realize that he cannot stop the characters from changing their routine lives?

8. In the case of Dave, his inability to engage with those around him leads to him completely removing himself from his actual world and entering a "fantasy" world. (#3, :02:15; #3, :05:10) Are there ways in your own life that you experience this disengagement with or avoidance of experience? How can you become more connected?

9. What are the differences and similarities between Dave/Bud's real mother (Jane Kaczmarek) and his Pleasantville mother, Betty, and how they interact with him? How do you think Bud's life will be different after he returns from Pleasantville?

10. When Bud's Pleasantville girlfriend offers him an apple, it is a direct "quote" from the myth of the Garden of Eden. (#27, 1:12:10) What are the many other references to this myth? Do they work? Why or why not? How does the progression from innocence to wisdom in the film reflect all human emotional evolution? (#14, :34:10) What does the film say might happen when life becomes too perfect, or habitual, and lacking in complexity?

BONUS QUESTION

From what you know (either what you experienced personally or what you have read, seen in movies or television series from the time, or been told) about the 1950s (the culture, music, art, literature, ethos, and so on), what about *Pleasantville's* depiction of that era is accurate? What is distorted? What are the ways the film depicts the change from a (perceived) utopian 1950s into the expanded consciousness of the 1960s? Have you seen films made during the 1950s? How do they compare to this one?

MEMORABLE QUOTES

Betty: What goes on up at Lover's Lane? . . .
Mary Sue: Well, sex.
Betty: Oh. What's sex?

[After the remote control has broken]
TV repairman: We'll fix you for good. You want something that will put you right in the show.

[Coming home to an empty house]
George: No wife, no lights, no dinner!

Jennifer: We're, like, stuck in Nerdville!

BEHIND THE SCENES

In the DVD commentary, director Gary Ross acknowledges these references to earlier films:

- The scene of J. T. Walsh (Big Bob), in front of the bowling alley score-card, summons up George C. Scott's speech in front of the American flag in *Patton* (1970).

- The division of a "segregated" courtroom ("black-and-white characters downstairs and "colored" characters upstairs") suggests *To Kill a Mockingbird* (1962). (See April: Heroes and Mavericks.)

- Notice the Native American in the upper-left-hand corner in the test pattern on the TV: the figure changes from smiling to angry and, finally, to crying, as the movie progresses and gets closer to "reality."

- Director Ross wanted the *Pleasantville* set design to "run rampant with false nostalgia to set up the need for colorized lives." He requested that set designer Jeannine Oppewall (*L.A. Confidential*) create the town from her personal memory of the late 1950s, rather than do extensive research.

DID YOU KNOW...?

- Bud (David) reads to his marveling Pleasantville classmates from the classics *The Adventures of Huckleberry Finn* and *Catcher in the Rye*. These books are numbers four and two, respectively, of the most widely banned in America.

- Director Ross is the son of screenwriter Arthur Ross, who penned *The Creature from the Black Lagoon* and *Brubaker* (starring Robert Redford), and was blacklisted in the aftermath of the House Un-American Activities Committee in the 1950s. He admits that much of his own life philosophy is colored by his father's experience that, even living in a seemingly progressive environment, political repression is always a possibility.

ABOUT THE DIRECTOR

Gary Ross also directed *Seabiscuit* (2003); and he wrote *Big* (1988), with Tom Hanks, and *Dave* (1993), with Kevin Kline. *Pleasantville* is his directorial debut. In an interview for CNN, Ross corroborates what his film suggests, that "pleasant" doesn't always equal "good." "You can drain the life and nuances and complexity out of things by homogenizing them to make everything harmoniously dull, flat, conflict-free, strife-free.... In a complex and troubling world, who wouldn't want to simplify? Everybody does. Everybody wants to simplify and put up a picket fence. The tougher thing is to give yourself that kick to be alive and to be fully engaged and stay alive.... I guess if the movie has a message, it's that it's worth that price, as difficult or strife-ridden as it may be." (cnn.com, 12 Oct. 1998, Jamie Allen)

MOVIE AND TV REFERENCES

Sherlock, Jr. (1924)
The Wizard of Oz (1939)
Citizen Kane (1941)
I Love Lucy (1951)
I Married Joan (1952)
The Honeymooners (1955)
Fahrenheit 451 (1966)
Back to the Future (1985)
The Truman Show (1998)

MORE CONTEMPORARY MOVIE FAVORITES

American Beauty, Being Julia, The Hours, Multiplicity

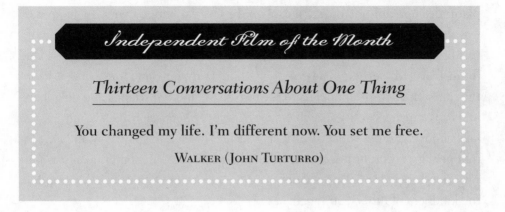

Independent Film of the Month

Thirteen Conversations About One Thing

You changed my life. I'm different now. You set me free.

WALKER (JOHN TURTURRO)

THE DETAILS

2001, 104M/C; R; DVD. **DIRECTOR:** Jill Sprecher. **SCREENWRITERS:** Karen Sprecher and Jill Sprecher. **CINEMATOGRAPHER:** Dick Pope. **AWARDS:** Boston Society of Film Critics Awards: Best Supporting Actor, Alan Arkin. San Diego Film Critics Society Awards: Best Director; Best Original Screenplay; Best Editing, Stephen Mirrione. Florida Film Critics Circle Awards: Best Ensemble Cast.

THE SETTING

Contemporary New York City.

THE STORY

Insurance claims adjuster Gene (Alan Arkin) can't stand to be around anyone who is too "smiley," like Wade (William Wise), the nicest, most generous guy in his office; while Dorrie (Tia Texada) can no longer bear the company of Bea (Clea DuVall), a sweet young housekeeper who has lost her sense of optimism. *Thirteen Conversations About One Thing* examines what effect we can have on others with whom we are either intimately involved or whom we barely know. In the cases of Troy (Matthew McConaughey), a brash, overconfident attorney, and Walker (John Turturro), an adulterous college physics professor, we see how life, as we are accustomed to it, can change in an instant, sometimes irrevocably, and how little control we actually have over our own actions. Accompanied by numerous platitudes and aphorisms, such as, "I once knew a happy man. His happiness was a curse," "Wisdom comes suddenly," and "Faith is the antithesis of proof," this brilliant series of 13 interrelated little moral fables is philosophy illustrated through everyday events. The questions about faith, fate, and free will that haunt the film's characters compel us to see ourselves, and our friends and neighbors, in these characters and realize that—even if only subconsciously—we too are anxious about the same concerns. Most of us feel broken in some way and long for that person, event, or belief that will make us whole. But sometimes just "putting on a happy face" isn't enough, and we must admit that we all depend on the kindness of others, strangers or not.

READING THE MOVIE

1. Many people have reacted to this film overwhelmingly positively, while some have called it slow and boring. What is your reaction? Why do you think the film elicits such forceful responses?

2. How does the nonlinear or nonchronological sequencing of the story affect your comprehension and enjoyment of the film? Why would the director use this technique?

3. There is an occasional flurry of white objects throughout the film. What do you think this motif of white matter represents?

4. Regarding the music, the director says, "The music is from the perspective of God. It knows what's going to happen before the characters do." What are some scenes that might support that statement?

FINDING THE MEANING

5. The "chapter intertitles" both reach forward to the next scene and back into the previous scene. Do you think this is an effective transitional technique? Why or why not?

6. The director used several Edward Hopper paintings to illustrate the internal states of mind of several characters. What was she trying to convey in these scenes? (#2, :10:08)

7. Why are characters often placed either in front of or behind glass? The film opens and ends with Patricia looking through a window (in her apartment and on the subway train). What do you suppose she is thinking about in these scenes?

8. What are the philosophical quandaries that the director addresses through her characters' situations and dialogue?

9. Beatrice says, "My eyes have been opened. I can never go back." Are people better off living under an illusion? (#9, 1:11:12)

10. Other characters in *Thirteen Conversations* question what their lives would look like "if things had happened differently." (#12, 1:35:45) What is your perspective on the simplistic explanation that "everything happens for a reason, or for the best?"

BONUS QUESTION

During the film all the characters' lives move forward in some way, yet there is no "Hollywood ending," in the sense of the customary resolution. What do you think might happen to the characters after the film ends? Will Troy be arrested? Will Gene's attitude ever change? Will Walker and Patricia reunite? As Troy's friend suggests, do we get a second chance in life?

MEMORABLE QUOTES

Beatrice: You're right. Life isn't fair.

Walker: It's perverse, isn't it? People spend years developing their minds and educating themselves, but in the end, they just want to shut them off.

Dick: In life, it only makes sense when you look at it backwards. Too bad we've got to live it forwards.

ABOUT THE DIRECTOR

Jill Sprecher studied literature and philosophy at the University of Wisconsin, Madison. After moving to New York City, she was mugged twice within the same year. The second time, she sustained a head injury and, like the housecleaning character played by Clea DuVall, underwent brain surgery. Despondent as she tried to make a living in the world of independent film, she was cheered one day when a stranger on the subway made simple human contact—by smiling. These events, along with Bertrand Russell's book *The Conquest of Happiness*, gave birth to this thoughtful and sensitive film. *Thirteen Conversations About One Thing* is Sprecher's second film. Her directorial debut was *Clockwatchers* (1997).

STRAIGHT FROM THE DIRECTOR

Speaking about her life as she progressed from being a struggling graduate student (at New York University's Cinema Studies Program), writer, and then independent filmmaker living in New York City, Jill Sprecher revealed during an interview in *Creative Screenwriting* magazine, "We lived above a bar, so it was like your neighbors were having a party every night. I slept on a couch until this past year that we've been living at our brother's house in LA. I can honestly say that I've slept on a couch my entire adult life. That goes along with writing, especially with independent films. It's a very expensive hobby." (*Creative Screenwriting*, May/June 2002)

MORE INDEPENDENT FILM FAVORITES

The Apostle, George Washington, Greenfingers, Personal Velocity, Raising Victor Vargas, Waking Life

World Cinema Feature of the Month

Ma vie en rose (My Life in Pink)

I'm a boy now, but one day I'll be a girl.

LUDOVIC (GEORGES DU FRESNE)

THE DETAILS

1997, 88M/C; R; DVD. Belgium (in French with English subtitles). **DIRECTOR:** Alain Berliner. **SCREENWRITERS:** Alain Berliner and Chris Vander Stappen. **CINEMATOGRAPHER:** Yves Cape. **AWARDS:** Golden Globes: Best Foreign Language Film. European Film Awards: Best Screenwriter. Seattle Lesbian & Gay Film Festival: Audience Award: Best Feature.

THE SETTING

A contemporary middle-class suburb of Paris, France.

THE STORY

In *Ma vie en rose*, the director visualizes a half-real, half-fantasy world as full of vibrant colors, living dolls, and synthetic landscapes. But there is a dark undertone as well. This charming story about a seven-year-old boy who believes that he is, in fact, a girl, contains themes and questions that deal with the universal and recognizable issues of conformity and individuality, the need for acceptance and the pain of exclusion, the importance of the support of our parents, and the prejudice and even violence bred by the fear of the "other" or anyone who is different. The boy, Ludovic (Georges Du Fresne) contentedly inhabits the "real" world with his family and a fantasy world occupied by Pam and Ben, French versions of Barbie and Ken. Everything is fine until Ludo decides that when he grows up he will be a woman and marry his next-door neighbor, Jérôme. His loving parents, Hanna Fabre (Michèle Laroque) and Pierre Fabre (Jean-Philippe Écoffey), become increasingly concerned, especially as Jérôme (Julian Rivière) is the son of Pierre's boss. Uncertain as to the difference between the sexes, Ludo asks his older sister, who has just started menstruating. She explains the biology lesson of X and Y chromosomes, and Ludo imagines the hand of God tossing down the requisite X and Y, with the X accidentally falling in the trash can outside his parents' window. It was all a simple mistake. As logical as this may sound to Ludo, the neighbors begin to turn against the household, and a series of unfortunate events disrupts the entire family's life. This film has a lot to teach us about gender and transgender issues, and it does so through the wondering eyes of an extraordinary child.

READING THE MOVIE

1. Does the opening of the film successfully bring you into the story?

2. How would you describe the director's cinematic style? How do the director and cameraman indicate exaggerated behavior and emotions?

3. What do you think of Ludovic? Did you find him sympathetic or maddening, or both? What does the actor, Georges Du Fresne, bring to the character?

4. What purpose do the dolls Pam and Ben serve in the film? What do you think of their song, "I long to be happy, / it's like a neurosis!"? What does it say about the film's "real" characters?

FINDING THE MEANING

5. Do you find Ludo's parents sympathetic characters? How does their relationship with Ludo change during the film?

6. The scene in which Ludo enters the garden party dressed in his mother's clothing establishes many of the central themes, as well as the tone of the film. (#4, :07:40) Why does Pierre call Ludo "the joker"? What's the significance of the Joker archetype? What does this say about Pierre?

7. What function does Ludo's grandmother play in his life? What role does she play in the film? (#6, :15:00)

8. Are gender differences in *Ma vie en rose* clearly delineated? If so, how? Ludo believes himself to be cross-gendered, a "girlboy," as he says. How does the film insightfully address the nature/nurture issue?

9. During Ludo's supposed "crisis of identity," he is the only one who doesn't really seem to be having a crisis, but his family gradually goes berserk. Yet, significantly, we rarely see Ludovic alone. What is the director conveying about Ludo's "problem"?

10. In this scene we see the children and adults of Ludo's neighborhood leaving, respectively, for school and work in the mornings. They seem in harmony with their perfect homes and their perfect families. (#4, :11:00) What is the undercurrent in this atmosphere? What is missing?

BONUS QUESTION

Was the ending satisfactory? In his October 3, 1997, review, *New York Times* critic Stephen Holden wrote, "For all its charm and daring, *Ma vie en rose* doesn't come fully to grips with its subject." Do you agree with him? Is that a failing of the film? Was a resolution necessary, or given one, would it have even been believable?

MEMORABLE QUOTES

Granny: We all have to face reality.

Ludovic: I'm a girlboy.

Principal: His tastes are too eccentric for this school.

Psychologist: There may be things that you'll have to wait to say until you get older.

ABOUT THE DIRECTOR

Ma vie en rose is the first film by Alain Berliner, a Belgian, who worked from the original screenplay by Chris Vander Stappen. Vander Stappen says she was hassled as a child for being a tomboy, and now identifies herself as a lesbian. (DVD Commentary)

CRITICALLY SPEAKING

Stephen Holden, *New York Times*, 3 October 1997

Childhood transvestism could hardly look more dignified than in the regally poised figure of Georges Du Fresne, the extraordinary young actor who plays Ludovic Fabre in *Ma vie en rose*. Although Ludovic is only seven, when dressed as a girl, this dark-eyed misfit who insists he belongs to the opposite sex contemplates the world with the serene hauteur of a natural-born diva. . . . For all its charm and daring, *Ma vie en rose* doesn't come fully to grips with its subject. Except for a scattered tear or two, Ludovic maintains a remarkable composure in the face of some vicious slings and arrows.

Roger Ebert, *Chicago-Sun Times*, 13 February 1998

The film is careful to keep its focus within childhood. It's not a story about homosexuality or transvestism, but about a little boy who thinks he's a little girl. Maybe Ludovic, played by a calmly self-possessed 11-year-old named Georges Du Fresne, will grow up to be gay. Maybe not. That's not what the movie is about. And the performance reflects Ludovic's innocence and naivete; there is no sexual awareness in his dressing-up, but simply a determination to set things right.

MORE WORLD CINEMA FAVORITES

*Little Voice; My Life as a Dog; Spring, Summer, Fall, Winter . . .
and Spring; The Taste of Cherry; Under the Sand; Wild Strawberries*

September: Working Stiffs

★ ★ ★ ★

It says, "Plenty of work in California.
Eight hundred pickers wanted."

UNCLE JOHN (FRANK DARIEN)
THE GRAPES OF WRATH, 1940
DIR. JOHN FORD

That was last year. This year I'm trying to earn a living.

JOE GILLES (WILLIAM HOLDEN)
SUNSET BOULEVARD, 1950
DIR. BILLY WILDER

Featuring

CLASSIC MOTION PICTURE: *Norma Rae*
CONTEMPORARY MOVIE: *Gosford Park*
INDEPENDENT FILM: *American Splendor*
WORLD CINEMA FEATURE: *Dirty Pretty Things*

PREVIEWS

☆ *Norma Rae* won numerous awards after its release in 1979, most
notably for actress Sally Field, who, in the best role of her career, portrayed widowed Norma Rae Webster, a mill worker in Alabama, whose
common sense makes up for a lack of formal education. Norma Rae's

admiration for Reuben, a union organizer from New York City, and her anger over low wages and inhumane working conditions at the local cotton mill, provoke her to unite forces in a collective effort to fight oppression. Moving and memorable.

☆ *Gosford Park* is a marvelous *Upstairs, Downstairs* for the twenty-first century. Sir William McCordle is the sort of *nouveau riche* everyone loves to hate, especially those who want something from him. He is murdered during a weekend of festivities, and the solving of that mystery exposes many others. With an impeccable cast, set design, and rendering, *Gosford Park* is a masterful whodunit.

☆ *American Splendor* is unlike any other film you have seen (or are apt to see). Based on the autobiographical comic books by Harvey Pekar, the film invites us into the small universe of Pekar's existence that includes his eccentric friends and coworkers at a VA Hospital in Cincinnati, his increasing success as a chronicler of the mundane, and his relationship with a woman who complements his own quirkiness. Offbeat and thoroughly entertaining.

☆ Although billed as a thriller, *Dirty Pretty Things* is more of a drama, with some dark comedy thrown in for leavening. Okwe, a cabbie and hotel night clerk, and his worker friends are all struggling immigrants, each from a different country and with a unique story. *Things* is more character- than plot-driven, but the plot (what part will Okwe, a doctor from Nigeria, play in the black market organ business he has uncovered?) brings us into the often harrowing world of victimized immigrants. A real eye-opener.

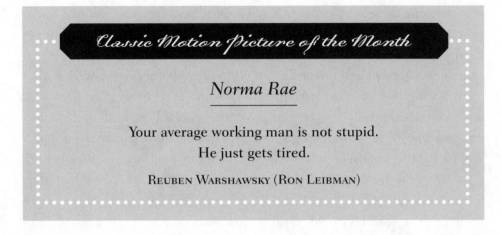

Classic Motion Picture of the Month

Norma Rae

Your average working man is not stupid.
He just gets tired.

REUBEN WARSHAWSKY (RON LEIBMAN)

THE DETAILS

1979, 114M/C; PG; DVD. **DIRECTOR:** Martin Ritt. **SCREENWRITERS:** Harriet Frank, Jr., and Irving Ravetch. **CINEMATOGRAPHER:** John A. Alonzo. **AWARDS:** Academy Awards: Best Actress, Sally Field; Best Music, Original Song; Nominated: Best Picture; Best Screenplay. Cannes Film Festival: Best Actress; Technical Grand Prize: Martin Ritt. Golden Globes: Best Actress. National Society of Film Critics Award: Best Actress. New York Film Critics Circle Awards: Best Actress.

THE SETTING

Summer, 1978; Henleyville (Opelika), Alabama.

THE STORY

When fast-talking New Yorker Reuben Warshawsky (Ron Leibman), an organizer for the Textile Workers Union of America, drives into the small town of Henleyville, his goal is to unionize the cotton mill, the town's only industry, and make a better life for its employees. But he'll need some help. Enter Norma Rae (Sally Field), whose entire family is employed by the mill. Her mother is going deaf from the ear-shattering noise of the machines and her father has his own factory-related health issues. When we are introduced to another family of seven whose dinner one night is comprised of "six turnips," we get a clear picture of just how destitute these people are. In an attempt to keep her quiet, Norma Rae is promoted to a spot-checking position, but she quickly discovers where her loyalty lies and what matters most to her. Sally Field's multidimensional performance is fervent and forceful as an entirely sympathetic widowed mother of two, who lives with her parents and kids and has experienced hard luck with men. Her honesty with herself and with, her children, husband, employers, and coworkers sometimes gets her into trouble, but Reuben, whose own zeal for fighting against oppression is contagious, inspires her to selflessly work for a better life for every mill worker. That this political film was directed by a man who himself had been blacklisted during the McCarthy era, adds an undercurrent of authority. *Norma Rae* remains an important film today, especially in light of the adjustments that union organizations are now making in their policies.

READING THE MOVIE

1. What kind of world does the film stage? Are we invited to identify with the characters and, thus, situate ourselves in that world?

2. Sally Field won many awards for her role as Norma Rae Webster. What are the qualities of her performance that so deeply affect viewers?

3. Regarding the look of the film, director Martin Ritt told the cinematographer John A. Alonzo, "I want a voyeuristic look. I want the camera to breathe; and I want the audience to breathe with it." Do you feel that the film achieves this objective? Why? Do you think the pace of the film is successful? Why or why not?

4. In his March 2, 1978, review, *New York Times* critic Vincent Canby writes, "In short, swift, effective scenes Norma Rae dramatizes the limits imposed on imaginations by both poverty and tradition." Can you identify the scenes to which he is referring?

FINDING THE MEANING

5. Why does Norma Rae get the spot-checking job? What is the statement she makes by giving it up? What views about the job do the writers and director advocate?

6. How does the church minister respond toward Norma Rae and the union organizing effort? Is this what you would expect from a religious leader? (#15, :57:10)

7. What did you think of Norma Rae's husband, Sonny (Beau Bridges)? Do you think it was reasonable for him to resent her work for the union? (#19, 1:08:30) Should she have dealt with him in a different way?

8. There is a lot of talk these days about men and women who have "emotional affairs" with individuals outside their marriage or committed relationship. Do you think Norma Rae's relationship with Reuben qualifies as such? Why or why not? (#18, 1:05:07)

9. In what ways is *Norma Rae* realistic? In what ways is it unrealistic? How does union politics, as depicted in the film, compare to what is currently happening among American labor unions? Have you had any direct contact with a union? What has been your experience?

10. Does the film, by emphasizing Norma and a single union organizer, downplay the many other workers, particularly blacks, who were involved in the organizing drive? If so, what might have been the filmmakers' motive for this?

BONUS QUESTION

Can you think of one or two other films that have strong female characters who are working for a social cause (for example, *Silkwood, Erin Brockovich, Rosa Luxemburg, North Country*, and others)? How might that film help us understand this one? How do they differ, and why?

CULTURAL REFERENCES

The DVD includes an excellent 20-minute documentary, *Backstory: Norma Rae*, which explains that the film is based on an actual union organizing campaign at the J.P. Stevens Mill in Opelika, Alabama. The character of Norma Rae is a composite of several people, including Crystal Lee Sutton, who became a spokesperson for the union. The producers of the film, Tamara Asseyev and Alex Rose, read an article in the *New York Times*, which inspired them to hire Irving Ravetch and Harriet Frank, Jr., to write a script and Martin Ritt to direct it.

MEMORABLE QUOTES

Norma Rae: Forget it! I'm stayin' right where I am. It's gonna take you and the police department and the fire department and the National Guard to get me outta here!

Reuben Warshowsky: It comes from the Bible—according to the tribes of your fathers, ye shall inherit. It comes from Reuben Warshowsky—not unless you make it happen.

DID YOU KNOW...?

- It took ten years to get a union contract at J.P. Stevens after the workers won the election.
- Jane Fonda, Marsha Mason, Jill Clayburgh, and Diane Keaton declined the role of Norma Rae. Fonda (*The China Syndrome*), Mason (*Chapter Two*), and Clayburgh (*Starting Over*) were all up for Best Actress Oscars the year Sally Field won it in 1980.
- Norma Rae Webster is listed as number 15 (out of 50) in the American Film Institute's poll of "100 Heroes and Villains."

ABOUT THE DIRECTOR

Martin Ritt (1914–1990) started out as both a director and actor in theatre and early television. During the 1950s he was targeted by the House Un-American Activities Committee, which inspired the crossover to film and his concentration on social issues. Several of his films are imbued with the voice of social conscience: *The Great White Hope* (1968), *Sounder* (1972), *Conrack* (1974), and *The Front* (1976). Others include *Hud* (1963), *Cross Creek* (1983), *Murphy's Romance* (1985), *Nuts* (1987), and *Stanley and Iris* (1990).

ABOUT THE ACTRESS

Prior to the Academy Award ceremony, Sally Field went on record with her feelings about the Oscar: "I think it's exploitative, over-commercialized, frequently offensive and shouldn't be televised." Asked whether she would show up or not, she responded, "Sure, I'll be there. If I said I wasn't coming, they'd still go on with the show."

After her win that evening, Field quipped, "I do feel like the Academy is slacking off in the class quotient—after all, I won. . . . It's like the Groucho Marx line about I wouldn't want to be in a club that would have me as a member." (*Inside Oscar*. Mason Wiley and Damien Bona. New York: Ballantine Books, 1993.)

CRITICALLY SPEAKING

Vincent Canby, *New York Times*, 2 March 1978

The film's principal appeal is not the manner in which this uphill struggle is fought and won, but in the way that Mr. Ritt, his writers and his cast reveal the natural resources of the characters—their grit, their emotional reserves and their complex feelings for one another. The politics of the film are worthy but they are never as surprising as the people, especially Norma Rae, whose personality is defined in her often comic, sometimes brutal, sometimes touching encounters with ex-husbands, lovers, children, parents, strangers.

Frederic and Mary Ann Brusatt, spiritualityhealth.com

This inspiring movie really connects with our emotions. Director Martin Ritt tackles the subject of unions with an earnestness that is rarely seen in films today. Screenplay writers Irving Ravetch and Harriet Frank, Jr., wisely focus on people rather than abstractions. The story's heroes are well developed and understandable; and there are no cardboard villains.

MORE CLASSIC MOTION PICTURE FAVORITES

The Dresser, The Fountainhead, Grapes of Wrath, Matewan,
Modern Times, Nine to Five, On the Waterfront

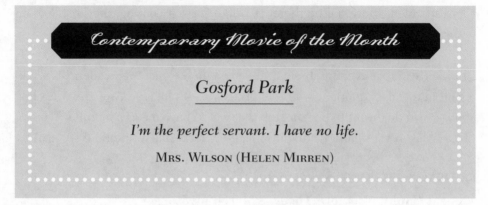

Contemporary Movie of the Month

Gosford Park

I'm the perfect servant. I have no life.

MRS. WILSON (HELEN MIRREN)

THE DETAILS

2001, 138M/C; R; DVD. **DIRECTOR:** Robert Altman. **SCREENWRITER:** Julian
Fellowes (based on an idea by Robert Altman and Bob Balaban).
CINEMATOGRAPHER: Andrew Dunn. **AWARDS:** Academy Awards: Best Original
Screenplay. Writers Guild of America: Best Screenplay Written Directly for the
Screen, Julian Fellowes. Screen Actors Guild Awards: Best Supporting Actress,
Helen Mirren; Outstanding Performance by an Ensemble. National Society of
Film Critics Awards: Best Director; Best Screenplay; Best Supporting Actress,
Helen Mirren. New York Film Critics Circle Awards: Best Director; Best
Screenplay; Best Supporting Actress, Helen Mirren. Golden Globes: Best Director;
Best Motion Picture. AFI Awards: Director of the Year, Robert Altman.

THE SETTING

November 1932; countryside estate, outside London, England.

THE STORY

Robert Altman's *Gosford Park* owes a large debt to Jean Renoir's 1939 classic *The
Rules of the Game,* in which a group of aristocrats gather in a French country
estate for a weekend of decadence and self-indulgence and end up having to
solve the murder of one of their own. Renoir himself played Octave, an obser-
vant character, who, like the director, was a benevolent humanist. His
line, "Everyone has his reasons," certainly applies as well to Altman's characters.

It seems that everyone at Gosford Park has a secret, except the ladies' maid, Mary (Kelly MacDonald), and by the end, after all the other character's personal mysteries have been revealed one by one, Mary has acquired the biggest secret of all and, consistent with her intrinsic decency, feels compelled to preserve it. It's hard to imagine this Upstairs, Downstairs confection–cum–murder mystery/social satire being any more enjoyable. Although in a first viewing it may be difficult to keep all the labyrinthine subplots and surplus of characters straight, it's worth the extra effort, and there will be lots to discuss. So here's a quick cast of characters to help keep you on track. The bulldog Sir William McCordle (Michael Gambon) and his glacial, much-younger wife, Lady Sylvia (Kristin Scott Thomas), welcome guests for a weekend shooting party at their lavish country estate. The guests include their daughter Isobel (Camilla Rutherford) and Lady Sylvia's aunt, the Countess of Trentham (a hilarious Maggie Smith). Other members of the local nobility are guests: Lord Stockbridge (Charles Dance); his wife, Louisa (Geraldine Somerville); and Freddie Nesbitt (James Wilby). There are a few celebrities for color: actors Ivor Novello (Jeremy Northam), Henry Denton (Ryan Phillippe), and Morris Weissman (Bob Balaban), a producer of Charlie Chan mysteries. The large service staff includes Mrs. Wilson (Helen Mirren), the head of the household staff; her sister Mrs. Croft (Eileen Atkins), the cook; Elsie (Emily Watson), the maid, who is having an affair with Sir William; Probert (Derek Jacobi), Sir William's valet; Jennings (Alan Bates), the butler; George (Richard E. Grant), a footman; Robert Parks (Clive Owen), Lord Stockbridge's valet; and the already mentioned Mary. This dazzling ensemble crew doesn't miss a beat, but with two cameras covering the action and the witty repartee, you may miss a line here and there. The intrigue begins the moment the guests arrive, and we become privy to the complications inherent in deceit, betrayal, revenge, love, and money. The intrigue increases after the murder of Sir William. And what good is a British murder mystery without the appearance of a police inspector (Stephen Fry) who bungles his way through an investigation à la Tati's Hulot and Sellers's Clouseau. We receive a number of false leads, so it takes some effort to stay up with (let alone ahead of) the clever unveiling of the murder plot. But what a sumptuous feast it is.

READING THE MOVIE

1. What is your response to *Gosford Park*? Is the complexity of the plot too off-putting? Are there too many subplots? Too many characters? Or do you relish the challenges this multifaceted film presents?

2. Mary (Kelly MacDonald), Lady Constance's maid, is the newest among a crew of highly experienced service staff. She is filled with questions about everything. What purpose might her inquisitiveness play in the film? According to Mrs. Wilson (Helen Mirren), what is "the gift of a good servant that separates them from the rest"?

3. What do you notice about the camera angles? Does it seem as if the camera is always moving about (if only slightly) and following the characters? During group scenes, two cameras were shooting at all times. What was the intention of the director in this process?

4. The director's attention to detail is astonishingly meticulous. Which details were you most struck by? Why?

FINDING THE MEANING

5. There is always a servant present in each scene with the aristocrats. What's the purpose of this? Is there something we should read into it or not? How did the interactions between servant and master or mistress alter when another aristocrat entered their midst? (#8, 1:03:24)

6. Are we meant to know everything about every character? What is the director's purpose in either disclosing or concealing information about the characters?

7. Did you solve the mystery about who the murderer was before it was revealed? If so, what were the tip-offs?

8. How do you feel about the characters in general? Which ones were the most sympathetic? Why? Which ones did you dislike? Why? Did you find any redeeming qualities in any of the characters, or were they all strictly one-dimensional? Do you think Mary and Robert Parks will see each other again? Are they destined to have a relationship? What do you think happened to Elsie, Sir William McCordle's lover? (#14, 2:03:36)

9. The film takes place between the two World Wars. What are the subtle indications that this lavish lifestyle may be coming to an end? Who are the most modern-leaning characters? (#14, 2:05:10)

10. Did you ever see the long-time British television series *Upstairs, Downstairs*? What are the similarities and differences between it and *Gosford Park*?

BONUS QUESTION

How do Altman's other ensemble-acted films (M*A*S*H, 1970; *Nashville*, 1975; *The Player*, 1992; *Short Cuts*, 1993; *Ready to Wear*, 1994; *Cookie's Fortune*, 1999; and *The Company*, 2003) compare to *Gosford Park*?

HE SAID/SHE SAID

Henry: You British really don't have a sense of humor, do you?
Elsie (head housemaid): We do if something's funny.

BEHIND THE SCENES

- None of the actors who played servants wore any makeup.
- Eileen Atkins (Mrs. Croft, the cook) co-created the classic British series *Upstairs, Downstairs* (1971), which was shown on (PBS) *Masterpiece Theatre*.
- The filmmakers brought onto the set two servants, who had worked during the 1930s as a butler and a cook. They were available to the actors at all times and informed them about the correct manner in which tasks should be performed.

MORE CONTEMPORARY MOVIE FAVORITES

Broadcast News, A Day Without a Mexican, Election, Good Will Hunting, Working Girl

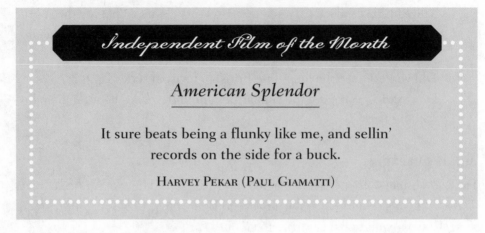

Independent Film of the Month

American Splendor

It sure beats being a flunky like me, and sellin'
records on the side for a buck.

HARVEY PEKAR (PAUL GIAMATTI)

THE DETAILS

2003, 105M/C; R; DVD. **DIRECTOR:** Shari Springer Berman, Robert Pulcini.
SCREENWRITERS: Shari Springer Berman, Robert Pulcini (based on the comic
book series *American Splendor* by Harvey Pekar and the graphic novel *Our Cancer
Year* by Pekar and Joyce Brabner). **CINEMATOGRAPHER:** Terry Stacey. **AWARDS:**
Sundance Film Festival: Grand Jury Prize. Toronto Film Critics Association
Awards: Best First Feature. National Society of Film Critics Award: Best Film;
Best Screenplay. National Board of Review: Best Breakthrough Performance by
an Actor, Paul Giamatti. New York Film Critics Circle Awards: Best Actress,
Hope Davis. Cannes Film Festival: FIPRESCI Prize. Edinburgh International
Film Festival: New Director's Award. Boston Society of Film Critics Awards:
Best Screenplay. Academy Awards: Nominated: Best Screenplay Based on Material
Previously Produced or Published.

THE SETTING

1950–2000; Cleveland, Ohio.

THE STORY

A self-taught intellectual, the unconventional Harvey Pekar is a file clerk at the
local VA hospital in Cincinnati. His humdrum life is getting him down until,
with the help of his now-successful friend, underground comix guru Robert

Crumb, Harvey discovers that the examined life is indeed worth living—especially through his *own* comic book series *American Splendor*. As do most writers, Harvey finds his material in the cast of characters who surround him. They include his unwittingly comical co-workers at the hospital, who are absolutely delighted to see themselves caricatured in classic comix style, and, eventually, the sardonic Joyce Brabner (who gives Harvey a run for his money in the oddball department), a fellow comic books aficionado who, within a few hours of meeting him, declares, "I think we should skip the courtship thing and just get married." There it is, right in front of us: soul mates in action. Sure, it's easy to laugh at a sad sack like the obsessive–compulsive Harvey, but as a working-class everyman, he speaks poignantly and truthfully to the issues that many of us face, such as trying to balance our boring but necessary jobs with a desire to do something creative and exciting with our lives. He just has a way of expressing it in a more humorous and emotionally honest way. The filmmaking team is a couple who have previously worked only on documentary films. They do a splendid job utilizing a variety of narrative techniques (including documentary footage and animation). Because the real Harvey Pekar is seen within the movie discussing the making of this very film (in addition to delivering the voice-over), it becomes a movie about a character within a comic book within a movie. The directors couldn't have done better than to assign the role of the curmudgeonly Harvey to Paul Giamatti (later seen in the surprise indie hit *Sideways*, 2004), who plays Harvey to perfection. On a September 2005 segment of *Charlie Rose*, novelist Michael Cunningham said, "There are no uninteresting or ordinary lives. There are only inadequate ways of looking at them." *American Splendor* reaches way beyond the adequate into the sublime.

READING THE MOVIE

1. Were you familiar with *American Splendor* comix before you saw the film? If so, how do you think the material transferred to the cinematic medium?

2. In what ways does the film's genre-mixing format manage to maintain a sense of Harvey Pekar's reality?

3. How does the soundtrack both place us in the 1960s, 1970s, and 1980s and give us a sense of Harvey's inner life?

4. What do we learn about Harvey Pekar in the opening scenes, when he is working on the voice-over in the studio? Is this characteristic carried throughout the film? How?

FINDING THE MEANING

5. Why does Harvey say, "Who am I kidding, I'd be lost without my day routine"? (#8, :27:29) Do you feel similarly about your own work schedule?

6. How do the eccentric Harvey and Joyce complement each other? Are they a perfect match? Why or why not? (#11, :45:30).

7. *American Splendor* is a genuinely original biopic. However, it is unusual in that the audience can actually compare the actor who portrays a personality with the person himself, as we, too, can do here. Harvey implored the directors, "Please don't make me into some perfect Hollywood guy with Tom Cruise playing me. I want something real." (*Cineaste*, Fall 2003) How do you think Paul Giamatti compares to the real Harvey Pekar? How close is Hope Davis's portrayal (from what we see) to the real Joyce Brabner Pekar?

8. Harvey discusses with R. Crumb that feeling of being a creative soul trapped in a dead-end job and wanting to express himself, wanting to make some kind of impact on the world or culture. (#4, :15:10) Thanks to the influence of his friend Crumb, comic books happened to be there. But could his creative outlet have been anything, or do you think comics were the best expression for him? Why or why not?

9. Film, by its very nature, inflates its subjects, lending them heroic proportions. How does *American Splendor* avoid turning Harvey into a larger-than-life hero? Harvey's is the story of the working class, the everyman, and the film is careful to maintain that tone. But does it still manage to extract meaning from the mundane and, at the same time, bring the mundane to the extraordinary? If so, how? (#12, :49:20)

10. Harvey Pekar describes himself by saying, "I'm just a gloomy guy, that's all." Could somebody like Harvey ever be really happy? Why or why not?

BONUS QUESTION

In a way, because of the comix and graphic novels, Harvey has become a mythical figure. Harvey observes, "If you think reading comics about your life seems strange, try watching a play about it. God only knows how I'll feel when I see this movie." The play, his appearances on David Letterman, and now the film bring up issues about the nature of storytelling, and the nature of creating a myth or a persona versus the real person. At some point in the film, Harvey comes to the realization that the character he's created is a *character* and might go on without him when he's gone. What other issues about identity does the film touch on?

HE SAID/SHE SAID

Harvey: I will try to be anyone you want me to be.
Joyce: That's a dangerous offer. I'm a notorious reformer.

MEMORABLE QUOTES

Harvey: Right now, I'd be glad to trade some growth for happiness.

Harvey: If you're the kind of person looking for romance or fantasy or escapism, you've got the wrong movie.

Harvey: Life is so sweet and so sad and so hard to let go of in the end.

BEHIND THE SCENES

Although the filmmakers had a bootleg copy of the actual footage of Pekar and David Letterman yelling at each other during Pekar's last appearance on the late-night show, after they edited it, they discovered that viewers were confused because they couldn't make out what the two were saying over their shouting match. Thus the scene is reenacted by actors. (*Cineaste*, Fall 2003)

DID YOU KNOW...?

- Paul Giamatti has a bachelor's degree from Yale and a master's from the Yale Drama School. His father, A. Bartlett Giamatti, is a past president of Yale.

- According to the filmmakers, because Joyce Brabner was often on the set with Harvey, Hope felt intimidated, or she felt that she was being judged. In order to maintain a comfortable environment for the actress, the filmmakers did their best to deter Joyce from watching the monitor during Davis's scenes. (*Cineaste*, Fall 2003)

ABOUT THE DIRECTORS

Husband-and-wife team Robert Pulcini and Shari Springer Berman directed the documentaries *Off the Menu: The Last Days of Chasen's* and *The Young and The Dead*. After making a gigantic splash at the 2003 Sundance Film Festival, *American Splendor* turned out to be one of the big indie success stories of that year. The film made an appearance on numerous critics, "best of" 2003 lists.

STRAIGHT FROM THE DIRECTORS

In an interview with *Cineaste* magazine, directors Berman and Pulcini were asked how they see Harvey Pekar. Robert Pulcini responded, "What's fascinating about Harvey is that he found a way to be heard, he found a medium. He can't draw, but he is an artist, he has a very interesting voice, and he's an unbelievably compelling character. For someone who was trapped in a cubicle, he found a great way to express himself, and it brought him a lot in his life. I think that's admirable. If you can find a way to express yourself, I think there's some redemptive power to expression, and he's a great example of that.... He's leaving behind a very accurate legacy of what it's like for a very common guy to live in his time. All the stuff that people discard or edit out of their lives, that's what he wanted to focus on because sometimes it is the most revealing." (*Cineaste*, Dennis and Joan M. West with Anne Gilbert, Fall 2003)

ABOUT HARVEY PEKAR

In his article the "Pioneer of Autobiographical Comics," Ed Park offers his take on Pekar: "Carved from the pile of lived days, his stories range from the weighty to the evanescent, told with klieg-light honesty or just an ace reporter's ear for talk. Unhampered by his inability to draw, he scripts skeletal storyboards and enlists different illustrators to bring them to life, a self-portrait for four or 40 hands. It's a song of himself he's performed over the past 27 years, and it's a self laden with the techniques and inner-directed impulses of the most exacting of modern authors: self-pity and self-loathing, self-criticism and self-reference, self-consciousness above all." (Ed Park, *The Village Voice*, July 30–August 5, 2003)

MORE INDEPENDENT FILM FAVORITES

Clockwatchers, Glengary Glen Ross, The Good Girl, Mac, Ruby in Paradise, Shattered Glass, Swimming with Sharks

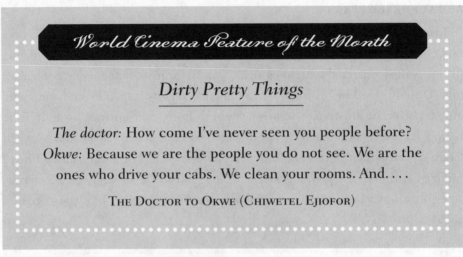

World Cinema Feature of the Month

Dirty Pretty Things

The doctor: How come I've never seen you people before?
Okwe: Because we are the people you do not see. We are the ones who drive your cabs. We clean your rooms. And. . . .

THE DOCTOR TO OKWE (CHIWETEL EJIOFOR)

THE DETAILS

2002, 97M/C; R; DVD. **DIRECTOR:** Stephen Frears. **SCREENWRITER:** Steven Knight. **CINEMATOGRAPHER:** Chris Menges. **AWARDS:** Evening Standard British Film Awards: Best Actor, Chiwetel Ejiofor; Best Film. Humanitas Prize: Feature Film Category. London Critics Circle Film Awards: British Screenwriter of the Year, Steven Knight. American Black Film Festival: Best Performance by an Actor, Chiwetel Ejiofor. Black Reel Awards: Best Actor, Chiwetel Ejiofor. British Independent Film Awards: Best Actor, Chiwetel Ejiofor; Best British Independent Film; Best Director; Best Screenplay. Academy Awards: Nominated: Best Writing, Screenplay Written Directly for the Screen.

THE SETTING

Contemporary London, England.

THE STORY

In the opening scene of *Dirty Pretty Things* Okwe (Chiwetel Ejiofor "chew-ah-tell edge-ee-oh-for") we are plunged into a reality of desperation—someone else's, not our own: the common sight of cabbies pleading for fares. As in life, we either take the ride or not. In either case, our awareness of these distraught drivers ends when we walk away. This gritty film follows the lives of several exiled menial workers and shows us the underbelly of their burdened lives. Okwe, it turns out, was a medical doctor in his native Nigeria. The story revolves around this modest, generous, honorable (but increasingly distressed) man and other illegal immigrant friends and co-workers (Turkish, Russian, Croatian) in his world. Okwe's second job is as a hotel night attendant at the Hotel Baltic, which, although perfectly legitimate during the day, descends into a sort of Dante's Inferno at night. Senay (Audrey Tautou), a hotel maid from Turkey who is hounded by the immigration authorities, allows Okwe to sleep on her couch. He is the only person who offers her kindness, and a genuine affection develops between them. There is also Juliette (Sophie Okonedo from *Hotel Rwanda*), the hotel hooker; Guo Yi (Benedict Wong), Okwe's mortuary attendant friend; and Señor Juan (Sergi López), a diabolical villain running a black market organ business, who offers forged passports for anyone willing to give up a kidney. How *Dirty Pretty Things* renders life in London's immigrant culture is a revelation—not only in terms of what illegal aliens must do to stay in England (let alone stay alive), but the matter-of-factness with which they accept their fate. Degradation is a way of life. The multinational cast in this drama/thriller is outstanding; and you will never again look at an immigrant taxi driver or hotel maid with the same eyes.

READING THE MOVIE

1. To what does the title refer? What was your emotional response to *Dirty Pretty Things*?

2. So much of Chiwetel Ejiofor's performance relies on an internal thought process to appraise other characters' actions, the setting, the plot, and so on. What do you think of his depiction of Okwe? Does Audrey Tatou manage to purge her *Amèlie* gamine quality? What do you think of the other performances of the multicultural cast members?

3. One night the hotel clerk Okwe pulls a human heart from the toilet in Room 512. What is the metaphor here, and how does it play out through the rest of the film?

4. How did you respond to the ending? Is it consistent with the rest of the film or does it change direction? Is it what you expected? What could be an alternate ending?

FINDING THE MEANING

5. Do you think the situation of the immigrants depicted in the film is specific to England or is it relevant to the United States and other countries as well? How? Do you think Senay's life will be much different in New York, as she imagines? (#9, :46:10)

6. Is the story believable? Why does the director use humor with such a serious subject matter? Does it work? Why or why not?

7. The plight of struggling immigrants rarely emerges in the forefront of any Hollywood movie, as it does in *Dirty Pretty Things*. Most of us take for granted meeting the basic tasks and responsibilities of daily life. We are unfamiliar with and desensitized to the hardships that marginalized people must undergo. (#6, :26:32) Were you aware of much of what is exposed in the film?

8. Okwe explains to Senay that the reason they cannot be lovers is because he has a wife back home in Nigeria. "It is an African story," he says simply. Later we find out something different. Why do you think he was untruthful with her? (#13, 1:05:26)

9. Like many films, *Dirty Pretty Things* combines many archetypes—the good man, the villain, the damsel in distress, the comrade, the hooker. Do these archetypal figures diminish or enhance the story? Are they sufficiently well-rounded, or unique, to be believable (is Okwe too good and Senior Juan too corrupt)?

10. In a July 7, 2003, *Rolling Stone*, critic Peter Travers writes about *Dirty Pretty Things*: "Fueled by gripping suspense, dark humor and outraged humanity, the film is a modern horror story that means to shake you." What are other films about the issue of immigration that you have seen? How do they compare with this film in terms of accuracy of subject matter and emotional content? Do you find it informative, entertaining? or both? Why?

BONUS QUESTION

Have you seen other films directed by Stephen Frears? (See the feature"About the Director.") What are they and how do they compare with *Dirty Pretty Things*?

MEMORABLE QUOTES

Guo Yi: There's nothing so dangerous as a virtuous man.
Okwe: For you and I, there is only survival.

DID YOU KNOW...?

- The screenwriter, Steven Knight, is an English television veteran who helped launch the reality show craze when he created the original *Who Wants to Be a Millionaire?*

- Chiwetel Ejiofor was born in England of Nigerian parents. In addition to acting in films, he is a highly regarded stage and Shakespearean actor, who also starred in Woody Allen's *Melinda and Melinda* (2004) and Spike Lee's *She Hate Me* (2004).

- An estimated 15,000 illegal organ transplants have been performed worldwide in recent years. It is usually desperate Third World persons who sell their organs, generally kidneys, for the benefit of wealthy Westerners. (*Cineaste*, Fall 2003)

ABOUT THE DIRECTOR

Other films by British director Stephen Frears include *My Beautiful Laundrette*, 1985; *Sammy and Rosie Get Laid*, 1987; *Prick Up Your Ears*, 1987; *Dangerous Liaisons*, 1988; *The Grifters*, 1990; *The Snapper*, 1993; *Liam*, 2000; and *High Fidelity*, 2000.

STRAIGHT FROM THE DIRECTOR

In an interview featured in *Cineaste* magazine, Stephen Frears discusses his decision to cast an African as the lead actor. "[Chiwetel Ejiofor] very much reminded me of Sidney Poitier. I could see it historically. Only when Sidney Poitier appeared were African-Americans allowed to play leading roles. Now, of course, they play people with faults, people who are human. At the same time, though, you could see that Poitier was the first 'acceptable' heroic black actor. I was quite aware of that and thought there was wisdom in drawing upon that, because, so far as I know, *Dirty Pretty Things* is the first film of substance made in Britain that starred an African actor. There hasn't been a film about an African. The world hasn't become that wonderful all of a sudden." (*Cineaste*, Cynthia Lucia, Fall 2003)

CRITICALLY SPEAKING

David Edelstein, Slate.com, 18 July 2003

Okwe is probably too much of a superhero to be true.... But if *Dirty Pretty Things* is more pretty than dirty, its prettiness is charged with guerrilla wit.... Frears and his great cinematographer, Chris Menges, give the subterranean settings a macabre luster. When Okwe and his Chinese friend play chess in the morgue, they're surrounded by gurneys that are sometimes sterile and sometimes ... not. The whole movie is like that: gleaming, but with a whiff of the charnel house. *Dirty Pretty Things* doesn't quite cut to the bone, but it gets as far as a couple of vital organs.

MORE WORLD CINEMA FAVORITES

All or Nothing, Baran, Distant, The Full Monty, Human Resources, La Promesse, Maria Full of Grace, Meantime, Mondays in the Sun, Time Out

October: Family Fiestas and Holidays

★ ★ ★ ★

It's the whole point of going. We're making a memory.

JIM BURNS (OLIVER PLATT)
PIECES OF APRIL, 2003
DIR. PETER HEDGES

Featuring

CLASSIC MOTION PICTURE: *My Mother's Castle*

CONTEMPORARY MOVIE: *Monsoon Wedding*

INDEPENDENT FILM: *Pieces of April*

WORLD CINEMA FEATURE: *Goodbye, Lenin!*

PREVIEWS

☆ *My Mother's Castle* is the second film based on French film director Marcel Pagnol's memoir of his early-twentieth-century idyllic childhood in Provence. This continuation of *My Father's Glory* finds the Pagnol family taking a holiday and then weekend forays to their heavenly country cottage in the Provencal hills. Marcel, his parents, and their two younger children run into trouble when they try to take a shortcut through their wealthy neighbor's property. This film gets everything right: the family devotion, the sumptuous settings, the French cuisine, and the memories of first love and friendship.

☆ In *Monsoon Wedding*, Aditi is getting married. The groom has been selected, the relatives invited, and the food ordered—but can an arranged marriage really work? And what will she do about her married boyfriend? If this is your first experience of *Monsoon Wedding*, you're in for a real treat. If you've already seen the movie before, this is an opportunity to get all those characters' names and roles straight.

☆ In *Pieces of April*, April Burns (Katie Holmes) invites her estranged family for a Thanksgiving feast in her New York City walk-up apartment. As the reluctant family members, including her prickly mother, who is dying of cancer, are winding their way from some unstated suburb to the big city, April embarks on her own journey through a series of minor catastrophes. Relying on the kindness of her previously unknown neighbors, she learns the real meaning of *thanksgiving*.

☆ Taking place in East Germany prior to and just after the fall of the Berlin Wall in 1989, *Goodbye, Lenin!* tells the story of one loving son's attempt to protect his mother's failing health after she's been in a coma for eight months. During this time their entire world has changed and he fears that, being a devoted Socialist, she may collapse with shock if she learns the truth. The result is a series of often hilarious charades that include restoring furnishings, clothing, and food packaging to those that she will remember. This superbly crafted and nuanced film gives new meaning to the term filial devotion.

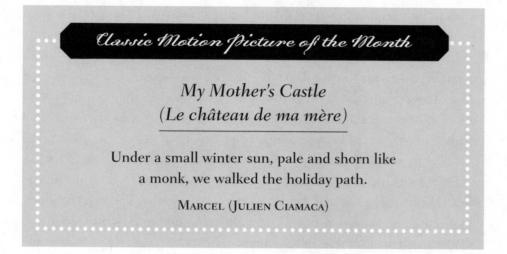

Classic Motion Picture of the Month

My Mother's Castle
(Le château de ma mère)

Under a small winter sun, pale and shorn like
a monk, we walked the holiday path.

MARCEL (JULIEN CIAMACA)

THE DETAILS

1991, 110/C; G; DVD. France (in French with English subtitles). **DIRECTOR:**
Yves Robert. **SCREENWRITER:** Yves Robert (based on the Marcel Pagnol novel).
CINEMATOGRAPHER: Robert Alazraki. **AWARDS:** César Awards, France:
Nominated: Best Costume; Best Music; Best Supporting Actress, Thérèse
Liotard; Most Promising Actor, Philippe Uchan. Seattle International Film
Festival: Best Film.

THE SETTING

Early1900s; Marseille and Provence, France.

THE STORY

In *My Mother's Castle*—the autobiographical companion film to *My Father's
Glory*—we reconnect with Marcel (Julien Ciamaca), the 13-year-old protagonist, whose schoolteacher father takes his family on holiday to a village in turn-
of-the-century southern France. In *My Father's Glory*, Marcel fell in love with
the Provencal countryside during a summer of enchanting outdoor adventures
with his new friend Lilli, and he is heartbroken when the family must pack up
and return to Marseille—and school. The sequel has the family making weekend treks to the glorious cottage. The eight-hour round-trip journey by foot

proves to be a bit much, but, as in all idealized versions of childhood, a time-saving remedy is forthcoming. A former student of father Joseph (Philippe Caubère) is now a caretaker of the canal, along which wealthy estates stand. This young man offers a key to the family that unlocks the gates that separate each estate. This straightway reduces the family's walk to less than one hour. The bulk of the story centers on their interactions with various property owners and guards. But once at the cottage, along with Marcel, we eagerly succumb to the voyeuristic pleasures of a child's-eye view of the world: a table filled with Christmas Eve culinary delights, the pleasures of al fresco dining, and meeting the mysterious, elegant young girl who becomes Marcel's first love. Through the director's attention to sensory detail, we can almost smell the fragrant wild thyme and rosemary growing in the hills, taste the robust olive oil on rustic homemade bread, and feel Marcel's embroidered linen pillowcase upon our own cheek. But, alas, all fairy tales must come to an end. At the bittersweet conclusion to this film about remembrances, the narrator's voice, an adult Marcel, tell us: "Such is the life of man, moments of joy obliterated by unforgettable sorrow, but there's no need to tell children that."

READING THE MOVIE

1. How would you describe the film's sets and costumes?
2. What is most striking about the cinematography?
3. Which elements are repeated to emphasize a point or a perception?
4. What is the point of view of the film?

FINDING THE MEANING

5. Were the characters sufficiently developed so that you could identify with them or did they remain stereotypes?
6. The adult Marcel's remembrance of his childhood seems almost too good to be true. Is it a human quality to remember our past as being happier than it actually was? Does the story bring up any of your own childhood holiday memories? Does it make you nostalgic?

7. The film makes a clear point that Marcel's father, Joseph, is not a "religious" person. How does it do this and what is the purpose? What effect does this seem to have on Marcel? (#5, :15:45)

8. How does the movie convey the importance of work and vocation in human lives? (#19, 1:09:36)

9. What do you most like about this film? How did you feel about the film's ending? (#26, 1:34:30)

10. Is *My Mother's Castle* reminiscent of any American or European films?

ABOUT THE AUTHOR

My Father's Glory and *My Mother's Castle* are linked autobiographical stories by the popular French playwright and filmmaker Marcel Pagnol, who also wrote the two novels *Jean de Florette* and *Manon of the Spring*, which were made into films in the 1980s. His own films, such as the trilogy *Marius, Fanny,* and *Cèsar,* depict the lives of the inhabitants of his beloved hometown Marseille.

CRITICALLY SPEAKING

Janet Maslin, *New York Times*, 26 July 1991
Much of the appeal of [this] seductively scenic film is based on pure charm. . . . Thanks to the rosiness of Pagnol's boyhood memories, and to the great affection with which [the director] presents them, no event of daily life is seen as too trivial to be cause for delight. . . . *My Mother's Castle* . . . all banquets and bouquets, concentrates as fully on life's smaller joys as on its larger ones, and does so with the kind of panache that has already charmed much of France.

Hal Hinson, *Washington Post*, 16 August 1991
If the French Department of Tourism had tried, it couldn't have produced a film more enraptured by its setting, more sensitive to the allure of its way of life or more attuned to its contented rhythms. [The film] makes you want to drop everything, head for Provence and snooze in the velvet shade of its trees. . . . The movie overwhelms us with that after-meal feeling of lazy fullness; it's as pleasing as an afternoon nap, and about as eventful.

MORE CLASSIC MOTION PICTURE FAVORITES
A Day in the Country, Guess Who's Coming to Dinner?
Hannah and Her Sisters, It's a Wonderful Life, Mr. Hulot's Holiday,
The Philadelphia Story, Playtime, Summertime

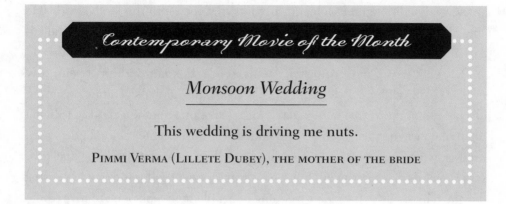

Contemporary Movie of the Month

Monsoon Wedding

This wedding is driving me nuts.

PIMMI VERMA (LILLETE DUBEY), THE MOTHER OF THE BRIDE

THE DETAILS

2001, 114M/C; R; DVD (in English, in Hindi and Punjabi, with English subtitles). **DIRECTOR:** Mira Nair. **SCREENWRITER:** Sabrina Dhawan. **CINEMATOGRAPHER:** Declan Quinn. **AWARDS:** Venice Film Festival: Golden Lion, Mira Nair; Laterna Magica Prize, Mira Nair. British Independent Film Awards: Best Foreign Language Film.

THE SETTING

New Delhi, India.

THE STORY

Monsoon Wedding is a festive and infectious film fairly pulsating with vibrant colors, mutinous music, and rowdy characters. The bride-to-be is gorgeous cosmopolitan Aditi (Vasundhara Das). In the hope of preserving a modicum of tradition amid the American globalization of East Indian culture, her loving upper-middle-class Indian parents, Lalit Verma (Naseeruddin Shan) and his wife, Pimmi (Lillete Dubey), have found the perfect mate for Aditi in Hemant Rai (Parvan Dabas), a young engineer now living in Texas. The fact that the betrothed couple have never met doesn't worry Lalit and Pimmi. After all, their own arranged nuptials worked well for them 25 years ago, didn't they? And then there's that not-so-small matter of love—that Aditi feels for another man. There are several additional relationship subplots that feed into this Bollywood-style comedy (and potential tragedy) of clashing cultures and classes: the young Indian-Aussie Rahul Chadha (Randeep Hooda)—whose vocabulary confounds and annoys Lalit (as do most things, it seems)—is attracted to Aditi's cousin, sexy Ayesha (Neha Dubey); P. K. Dubey (Vijay Raaz), the oddball wedding organizer, has his eye on the Verma family maid, Alice (Tilotama Shome); and Ria (Shefali Shetty), now in her late twenties and unmarried, the daughter of Lalit's deceased brother, whom he has raised since she was a child. *Monsoon Wedding* may possess elements of a soap opera, but it offers an experience of pure joy and sensual delight. There's an extravagant wedding being planned—and you're invited.

READING THE MOVIE

1. How does *Monsoon Wedding* compare to other films (numbering in the dozens) about weddings? Consider *Father of the Bride* (the original, starring Spencer Tracy and Elizabeth Taylor or the remake, with Steve Martin and Diane Keaton); *My Big Fat Greek Wedding; Polish Wedding; Four Weddings and a Funeral; Wedding Crashers* and *The Runaway Bride.*

2. How would you describe what the riotous cinematography by Declan Quinn and the rollicking soundtrack by Mychael Danna (with *bhangra*, Punjabi pop/folk tunes, and *ghazals*, traditional Indian love songs) bring to your enjoyment of the film? What is the symbology of the monsoon rains? What does it represent in the movie?

3. *Monsoon Wedding* invites us into a complexity of cultures and classes. Punjabi and New Delhi subcultures, along with Australian and American diversity, are represented, as is generational and socioeconomic disparity. What are the filmmakers saying about these cultural differences and class issues and the effects of globalization?

4. What are the five interwoven stories? Are there aspects that they all share, are they uniquely distinctive, or are there aspects of both? What do you imagine the filmmakers are pointing out about the nature of romantic relationships?

FINDING THE MEANING

5. What message about arranged marriages do you think that the director is trying to convey? Can you see that there might be beneficial aspects inherent in forgoing the Western notion of romantic love and replacing it with a more judicious approach?

6. We see Dubey, the wedding organizer, in his professional setting: safari work clothes, snooty persona, and self-important cell phone compulsion. But what do we learn about him when the camera follows him home? (#12, 1:16:50) How does being in love with Alice affect Dubey's personality? How does the actor playing Dubey, Vijay Raaz, affect your understanding and acceptance of the character?

7. Salon.com critic Charles Taylor writes, "There's something in *Monsoon Wedding* of the forced, cheery conventionality of MGM in the '50s, the idea that the deepest contentment can be found in the blandest of suburbia, and its optimism rings false for many of the same reasons." Do you agree with his perspective? Why or why not? Do you think director Mira Nair may have intentionally conveyed the sensibilities of MGM in the 1950s, or is she working with another genre that's closer to her own experience? If you are familiar with the genre of cinema called Bollywood, are there any characteristics that the filmmakers incorporate into *Monsoon Wedding*? (#17, 1:46; #18, 1:49:38)

8. Would you say that the characters develop and evolve during the course of the film or are they—and do they remain—more stereotypically conceived portrayals? Why? In either case, are you able to relate to any or all of the characters' circumstances and emotional dilemmas?

9. How does Mira Nair handle Aditi's cousin Ria's childhood secret? Does it add to the overall story or detract from it?

10. Aditi is portrayed as a fairly modern young woman (she's having an affair with a married man). Why do you think she is amenable to her parents' wishes of arranged nuptials for her? (#4, :09:14) And why would Hemant, who has already made a new life in the United States—and seems at least somewhat Americanized (he's stopped

smoking)—seek a wife from India? From what we are told about Aditi and Hemant, do they seem well matched? Why or why not?

BONUS QUESTION

How do other films by director Mira Nair that you may have seen (*Salaam Bombay! Mississippi Masala, Kama Sutra,* and *Vanity Fair*) compare with *Monsoon Wedding*? What are some similarities? Differences?

CULTURAL REFERENCES

India produces 700 films a year. It's the largest film industry in the world. The center is Bombay, hence, "Bollywood." There are four primary elements of this cinema: They are always pageant like musical comedies, they always revolve around a love story, they are lush and beautifully produced, and the films have the element of fantasy. According to Sabrina Dhawan, "Indian films are much more fantastic . . . than films that come out of America. The suspension of disbelief is far, far, far greater in Bollywood than it could ever be in Hollywood. It's developed its own language, because it's so disconnected from world cinema." (*Script* magazine, David Cohen, May/June 2002, Volume 8, #3)

MEMORABLE QUOTES

Ria: I don't think you're ready for marriage.
Aditi: I just want to settle down.
Ria: So what do you do? Get married to some guy selected by Mummy and Daddy? You've barely known him for a couple of weeks!

BEHIND THE SCENES

During the shoot of *Monsoon Wedding*, director Mira Nair repeatedly viewed Fellini's *La Dolce Vita*, "mostly to show my crew how to choreograph madness." (*Filmmaker* magazine, Peter Bowen, Winter 2002, Volume 10, #2)

FROM THE DIRECTOR

No, the visuals in *Monsoon Wedding* are not the psychedelic images of the late 1960s: they are faux Bollywood. Indeed, director Mira Nair explains, "It's a Bollywood film made on my own terms."

In the DVD documentary *The Making of Monsoon Wedding*, Mira Nair says, "While *Monsoon Wedding* is a portrait of modern contemporary India, it is also a very personal story about my kind of people, Punjabi people. It is a community that works hard, parties hard, and has a huge appetite for life."

MORE CONTEMPORARY MOVIE FAVORITES

*Avalon, Meet the Fockers, Mother, My Big Fat Greek Wedding,
What About Bob? What's Cooking?*

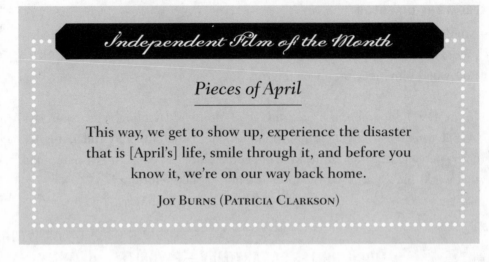

Independent Film of the Month

Pieces of April

This way, we get to show up, experience the disaster that is [April's] life, smile through it, and before you know it, we're on our way back home.

JOY BURNS (PATRICIA CLARKSON)

THE DETAILS

2003, 80M/C; PG-13; DVD. **DIRECTOR/SCREENWRITER:** Peter Hedges. **CINEMATOGRAPHER:** Tami Reiker. **AWARDS:** Sundance Film Festival: Audience Award; Special Jury Prize: Patricia Clarkson. National Society of Film Critics Award: Best Supporting Actress, Patricia Clarkson. National Board of Review: Best Supporting Actress, Patricia Clarkson. Boston Society of Film Critics Awards: Best Supporting Actress, Patricia Clarkson. Academy Awards: Nominated: Best Supporting Actress, Patricia Clarkson.

THE SETTING

Contemporary New York City and an unnamed suburb of New York City.

THE STORY

April Burns (a terrific Katie Holmes), the black sheep of the family, invites her estranged family for a Thanksgiving feast at her bleak Lower East Side walk-up apartment in the tender and touching *Pieces of April*. The reluctant family members, including her feisty mother, Joy (Patricia Clarkson), who is dying from breast cancer; her buoyantly resilient dad, Jim (Oliver Platt), April's sole supporter; her needy, perfectionist sister Beth (Alison Pill); her stoner brother Timmy

(John Gallagher, Jr.); and her senile Grandma Dottie (Alice Drummond), wind their way from some unstated suburb to the big city. They stop occasionally to fill up on Krispy Kremes so that, as Joy says, they won't have to eat April's terrible cooking, and they bury a roadkill with Timmy's memorial service: "We're sorry we didn't know you and we hope you died quickly." Meanwhile, April embarks on her own journey through a series of minor catastrophes, such as trying to cook a turkey with an out-of-commission oven and a bizarre encounter with a vindictive dog lover, Wayne (Sean Hayes), who lives in her building. Relying on the generosity of her African-American boyfriend, Bobby (Derek Luke) and previously unknown ethnic neighbors, she learns the real meaning of gratitude. According to director Peter Hedges, *Pieces of April* is about "the preciousness of time and the importance of making memories."

READING THE MOVIE

1. What does the opening sequence convey about the characters? About the movie?

2. There are long stretches without any music at all. What do you think the director's purpose was in doing that? What role does silence play?

3. What is Jim's role in the family? What is his role in the film? How does his way of looking at life differ from Joy's? What was your emotional response to the film? Did you identify with one of the characters in particular? Did you care about them?

4. What do the various journeys undertaken in the film represent?

FINDING THE MEANING

5. Would you call the Burns family dysfunctional? Would you say this is true for most families or is it more about simple personality differences?

6. We are never directly told what has been the source of the estrangement between April and Joy. (#3, :08:40) What do you think it might be? Is there something in particular about the mother–daughter relationship?

7. At one point, Joy jumps out of the car and refuses to go any farther. What is she really saying? (#14, :53:45) Do you think Joy is an indifferent mother? Is April a disrespectful daughter? Why or why not?

8. In the DVD commentary, the director says, "My job as a dramatist is to find out where these characters want to go, and make it as hard as possible for them to get there." What do you think he means?

9. Do you think that, like the Burns family, many people feel conflicted about spending holidays with their family? Do you? Does the film invite you to think differently about or behave differently toward your own family?

10. Do you think the film was successful in portraying the diversity of American culture? (#17, 1:01) What are the cultural assumptions in *Pieces of April*?

BONUS QUESTION

What other films deal with the mother–daughter relationship? How do they compare to *Pieces of April*?

MEMORABLE QUOTES

April: Once, there was this day . . . this one day when . . . everyone realized they needed each other.

Joy [to her daughter, Beth]: You're just like me, except for your slight weight problem.

BEHIND THE SCENES (from the DVD director's commentary)

- The neighbor who tells April that she is a vegan and can't stand the smell of cooking flesh is director Peter Hedges's wife.
- The turkey salt-and-pepper shakers that Bobby buys for April were bought by Hedges's mother for the film production, who searched them out at Goodwill stores while she was ill. One of the shakers shattered on the set and had to be reassembled and glued back into form.

- The film's title is from a Three Dog Night song, which the director had originally planned to include.
- Peter Hedges says that *Pieces of April* is not an autobiographical rendering, but was affected by the fact that his own mother died from cancer. "It's not about her," he discloses, "but a tribute to her."

DID YOU KNOW...?

- *Pieces of April* is the first original screenplay by writer/director Peter Hedges. His other adapted screenplays are *What's Eating Gilbert Grape* and *About a Boy*. (*FLM* magazine, Peter Hedges, Fall 2003)
- Hedges had an original budget of $3 million dollars, but the deal fell through, and he ended up completing the film for under $200,000. (*Chicago Sun Times*, 24 October 2003). The actors worked for $200 a day, the crew for $100 a day, and a percentage of the box office.

STRAIGHT FROM THE DIRECTOR (on the writing process)

"One of the great pleasures of writing is how empowering it can be. You can punish your enemies, kiss the girl you never got to kiss or ennoble an experience that seems devoid of meaning." (*Script* magazine, Peter Hedges, Volumn 9, Number 5)

MORE INDEPENDENT FILM FAVORITES

Desert Bloom, Everyone Says I Love You, Into the West, Joy Luck Club, Soul Food, The Summer House, Tortilla Soup, The Wedding Banquet

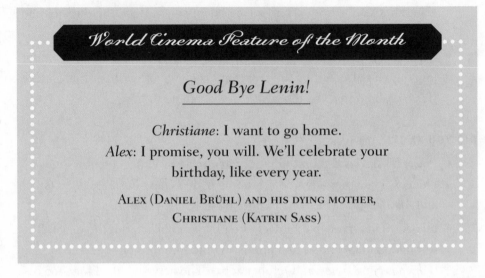

World Cinema Feature of the Month

Good Bye Lenin!

Christiane: I want to go home.
Alex: I promise, you will. We'll celebrate your
birthday, like every year.

ALEX (DANIEL BRÜHL) AND HIS DYING MOTHER,
CHRISTIANE (KATRIN SASS)

THE DETAILS

2003, 121M/C; R; DVD. **DIRECTOR:** Wolfgang Becker. **SCREENWRITERS:** Bernd Lichtenberg and Wolfgang Becker. **CINEMATOGRAPHER:** Martin Kukula. **AWARDS:** Berlin International Film Festival: Best Director. César Awards: Best European Union Film. Goya Awards: Best European Film. London Critics Circle Film Awards: Best Foreign Language Film. German Film Awards: Best German Film; Best Actor, Daniel Brühl; Best: Direction, Editing, Music, Production Design.

THE SETTING

1978–1990; East Germany, before and after the collapse of Communism.

THE STORY

In *Sleeper*, Woody Allen's 1973 fast-moving social satire, Allen's character awakens from a 200-year-long coma to learn of the previously unknown health benefits of hot fudge sundaes, red meat, and smoking, and to find a dictatorial leader running the U.S. government. *Good Bye Lenin!* is a new twist on the Rip Van Winkle legend, except this time the story takes place on the eve of the Communist collapse in 1989 in East Germany, and it is Christiane (Katrin Sass), the mother of our teenaged protagonist, Alexander Kerner (Daniel Brühl), who has been in a coma for eight months. Christiane, a devoted Communist, who has raised her children on her own after her husband defected to West Germany, suffered a heart attack, and any shock or surprise might induce a second, which could be fatal. For her protection, Alex devises an hilarious ruse by pretending that everything remains the same, namely, that the East has not gone West, and the Berlin Wall has not given way to an advancing capitalism. This elaborate plan includes dressing in the old style drab clothes, repackaging pickles and jam in jars with familiar labels, and recording news events that help explain the many subtle mysteries that befuddle Christiane, such as where that colossal Coca-Cola banner on the building opposite her room came from. According to Alex's faux news source, Coke was actually invented in East Germany during the Second World War. Fortunately, all this can be done in a "controlled environment," as Christiane is confined to her bedroom. In this bittersweet comedy about family (and national) politics, the birthday party that Alex and his sister Ariane (Maria Simon) arrange for their bedridden mother (quite possibly her last) is emblematic of their love for her, and of the family's need to carry on as if nothing had changed. However, in a bit of a twist ending, we see that Alex hasn't been the only one living a lie.

READING THE MOVIE

1. What is the film's narrative approach? Is it successful?

2. The film utilizes both home movie clips of the characters' childhoods and historical documentary footage. What's the effect of these images on your understanding of the film? How are flashbacks used?

3. Do you think the tragic and comic elements of the film are true to life? Why or why not? What do you think of the scene where Christiane watches the removal of the statue of Lenin? What emotions is the actress portraying? What do film techniques of camera angle, music, and so on, contribute to the scene? (#18, 1:22:15)

4. How did you respond to Daniel Brühl, the actor playing Alex? If this were an American film, which actor could you imagine playing the role?

FINDING THE MEANING

5. While his mother is in a coma, Alex says, "In her long, deep sleep, she orbited like a satellite around our small planet, and our smaller republic." Why does the director use the metaphor of space travel throughout the film? What does it add to the story?

6. Before seeing the film, what did you already know about life in East Germany prior to the fall of the Berlin Wall? Did you learn anything from the film about politics or social constructions under a socialist regime? If so, what? Did the film cause you to reexamine any assumptions you may have held as truths?

7. When Christiane is in the hospital for the second time (while Alex is with his father), we see Lara telling Christiane the truth about the German Democratic Republic. (#25, 1:45:35) Why do you think she did this? Was it the right thing to do? Why do you think the director doesn't follow through by letting Alex know?

8. In a voice-over, Alex says, "As I stared at the clouds that day, I realized that truth was a rather dubious concept, easily adapted to how Mother saw the world." (#14, 1:05:03) This carries a deeper meaning when we learn the "truth" about Alex and Ariane's father. What do you think of their mother's choice? Did she think it in their best interest? Is there a kind of justice in Alex's deception?

9. Alex recalls, "Mother slept through the relentless triumph of capitalism." What is the director saying about communism? About capitalism? Does he seem to prefer one more than the other?

BONUS QUESTION

What other mother–son relationship films have you seen? (For example, *This Boy's Life, My Life as a Dog, Almost Famous,* and *What's Eating Gilbert Grape.*) Consider how they compare to *Good Bye Lenin!*

BEHIND THE SCENES

The film was primarily shot in the former East Berlin, but because much of the film takes place after the fall of the wall those areas that were filmed needed to be extensively "de-Westernized" by removing ads for Western products and graying many buildings. (imdb.com)

ABOUT THE DIRECTOR

"Forty-nine-year-old . . . Wolfgang Becker was born and raised in the West and claims the distance allows him to see things more clearly. Extensive research into the 'East German state of mind' led him to conclude that, contrary to popular belief, not everyone hated life under state socialism." (*Sight and Sound*, Dina Iordanova, August 2003)

STRAIGHT FROM THE DIRECTOR

Wolfgang Becker, in an interview with Cineuropa (cineuropa.org, 10 February 2003): "The destruction of the family unit is a very important part of the plot and this separation is also a consequence of the division of Germany. Unification did not resolve those problems. Outwardly, nothing remains of the former East Germany except for the little green men on our traffic lights, but the memories are all intact. I really tried to be as truthful to the memories as I could because memories are fundamental for all of us."

CRITICALLY SPEAKING

Ruthe Stein, *San Francisco Chronicle*, 12 March 2004

[T]his deliciously offbeat comedy [is] as wildly inventive as anything Billy Wilder ever conceived. . . . *Good Bye Lenin!* is both a touching story of a son's devotion to his mother and a wry commentary on how not all East Germans were thrilled by the fall of the Berlin Wall. . . . Communism may have been boring and turned believers into Stepford wives, but at least you weren't bombarded with Coca-Cola signs and otherwise prodded to consume. It's a measure of the film's even-handedness that it's been a huge hit all over Germany.

J. Hoberman, *The Village Voice*, 2 April, 2004

Had it been directed by Billy Wilder, *Good Bye Lenin!* could have been a sensational farce—the reverse of *One, Two, Three*.... [It] is overlong and a bit tiresome but it's actually about something—not so much *ostalgie* [nostalgia] as the conditions that create it. That Communism itself was a fake façade makes Alex's imaginary motherland the simulation of a simulation. There's a haunting quality to his bittersweet realization that "the GDR I created for her became the one I would have wished for."

MORE WORLD CINEMA FAVORITES

Eat, Drink, Man, Woman; Enchanted April; Fanny and Alexander;
Like Water for Chocolate; Mama Turns One Hundred; My Father's Glory;
Stealing Beauty; A Sunday in the Country

November: Political Passions

★ ★ ★ ★

Dad always used to say the only causes worth
fighting for were the lost causes.

JEFFERSON SMITH (JAMES STEWART)
MR. SMITH GOES TO WASHINGTON, 1939
DIR. FRANK CAPRA

I think that a guy who's always interested in the
condition of the world and changing it either has
no problems of his own or refuses to face them.

HENRY MILLER, WITNESS OF COMMUNIST WRITER
JOHN REED (WARREN BEATTY)
REDS, 1981
DIR. WARREN BEATTY

Featuring

CLASSIC MOTION PICTURE: *Network*

CONTEMPORARY MOVIE: *The Contender*

INDEPENDENT FILM: *Silver City*

WORLD CINEMA FEATURE: *The Nasty Girl*

PREVIEWS

☆ In *Network*, Howard Beale, the recently widowed news anchor for the
fictional television station UBS, has just been informed that, due to

poor ratings, he's also lost his job. "Mad as hell" at what passes for news these days, Howard, who believes he has nothing to lose, plans to go out with a bang, literally, thereby giving sensation-seeking vampiric viewers what they want. In our celebrity-driven, reality-TV-based world, this visionary classic is ever more timely.

☆ In *The Contender*, after the sudden death of the U.S. Vice President, Senator Laine Hansen has been hand-picked by the president to serve as the first woman vice president. But first she must suffer through a grueling Senate approval hearing. Laine discovers that sometimes, dirty politics and ethical behavior are not mutually exclusive as she fights to maintain her personal dignity and private life. Joan Allen's noble but only slightly nuanced performance makes this political drama a Capraesque crowd pleaser.

☆ *Silver City* is a political thriller/murder mystery that opens with a gubernatorial candidate (indisputably familiar to us), who, while giving an interview, snags a dead body. His devious handler hires a private detective to discover who might have set them up. Along the way, the detective finds out more than he—and they—counted on. The plot may be a bit convoluted, but we meet many interesting characters along the way, and learn that, thanks to John Sayles, political satire is alive and well in the movies.

☆ *The Nasty Girl* is a fictionalized account of a true story about a historian in Germany who risks everything to discover the truth about her hometown and its inhabitants during World War II. We meet Sonja when she is the young darling of her school and celebrated by the entire town. Clever and personable, her life seems charmed . . . until she begins to ask the questions that no one cares to answer. The film's almost whimsical tone belies the serious subject matter of heroism and accountability.

Classic Motion Picture of the Month

Network

I'm as mad as hell, and I'm not going to take this anymore.

HOWARD BEALE (PETER FINCH)

THE DETAILS

1976, 121M/C; R; DVD. **DIRECTOR:** Sidney Lumet. **SCREENWRITER:** Paddy Chayefsky. **AWARDS:** BAFTA (British): Best Original Screenplay. Independent Spirit Awards: Best Screenplay; John Cassavetes Award. Sundance Film Festival: Audience Award; Special Jury Prize: Faye Dunaway. National Society of Film Critics Award. Best Supporting Actress, Faye Dunaway. San Sebastián International Film Festival: Special Jury Prize.

THE SETTING

1975; New York City.

THE STORY

Network opens on a New York City street, where two aging journalist buddies— Max Schumacher (William Holden), a television news producer, and Howard Beale (Peter Finch), a newscaster (who has just learned that, due to low ratings, he's been fired), commiserate about the state of a medium to which they have devoted their lives for more than 20 years. Speaking about the ever-increasing sensational approach to the "news," Max facetiously suggests they create a series entitled *Suicide* or *Execution of the Week*. Getting in the spirit, Howard enthusiastically rejoins, *"Terrorist of the Week."* Max continues: "Suicides, assassinations, mad bombers, Mafia hit men, automobile smash-ups: *The Death Hour*. A great

Sunday night show for the whole family." But the next day, it's no laughing matter when Howard (now sober and all too serious) announces during his broadcast that the following week he plans to commit suicide right on the air. An up-and-coming young female producer named Diana (Faye Dunaway) views Howard as a "latter-day prophet. A magnificent messianic figure inveighing against the hypocrisies of our times." She plans to use Howard's increasing ratings as a stepladder to the corporate top. Important in its day—more than 35 years ago—the social relevance of the issues and ideas brought forth in *Network* has, in the first decade of the twenty-first century, increased to an alarming extent. The pillaging of democracy by greed-driven corporate conglomerates has never been better scrutinized. A worthy pairing with this prophetic classic is the 2004 documentary *Outfoxed: Rupert Murdoch's War on Journalism*. After viewing *Network*, you might even feel compelled to holler out an open window, "I'm as mad as hell and..."

READING THE MOVIE

1. The only music heard in the film comes from commercials and television show themes. What was the director's purpose in doing this? How does it affect your experience of the film?

2. There is a very specific progression in the lighting scheme. It starts out very naturalistic, with very little light, and becomes increasingly more brightly lit and glossy. Why would the director have chosen this technique? What does it bring to your understanding of the film? Of the characters?

3. Is the editing meant to produce certain emotional responses in the viewer? Does it emphasize the world around the characters, or the characters themselves?

4. How does the film make you feel at the end?

FINDING THE MEANING

5. When *Network* was first released, it was considered a comedy-drama. How would you classify it now? Why?

6. Once the network programming division, run by Frank Hackett (Robert Duvall), a power-hungry executive, devours the money-losing news department, how does the news become just another type of entertainment? (#14) Today, how similar or dissimilar are news and entertainment? Why do the networks simultaneously run the same stories? Do sound bites affect our ability to thoroughly examine an idea or issue? If so, how?

7. Long before the advent of "reality television," *Network* was a cautionary story. How was the film prescient at its time of our current state of television? What would Diana (Faye Dunaway) and Max (William Holden) think of talk show hosts such as Geraldo Rivera or Sally Jesse Raphael?

8. What effect did Howard Beale's (Peter Finch) "I'm as mad as hell, and I'm not going to take this anymore" speech have on you? (#15)

9. How did Mr. Jenson's (Ned Beatty) speech to Howard strike you? What statement is Paddy Chayefsky, the scriptwriter, making by including the "Ecumenical Liberation Army" and the character Laureen Hobbs? (#22)

10. The progression of events in *Network* is simultaneously unlikely and terrifying. At what point did you feel that the events had progressed beyond the plausible?

BONUS QUESTION

Compare *Network* to later and more contemporary films about the television culture that you have seen, such as *Being There*, *Videodrom*, *Broadcast News*, *The Truman Show*, *Ed TV*, *To Die For*, *Bruce Almighty*, and *Pleasantville* (see August). What similarities do you find? What differences?

CULTURAL REFERENCES

During the time the movie takes place in (1975), the United States was experiencing high rates of crime, inflation, and unemployment, the latter two precipitated by an Arab oil embargo. The kidnapping of Patricia Hearst, granddaughter of newspaper magnate William Randolph Hearst, by the Symbionese Liberation Army was symptomatic of the cultural anxiety of the time.

MEMORABLE QUOTES

Howard Beale: All human beings are becoming humanoids, all over the world, not just in America. We're just getting there faster, since we're the most advanced country.

DID YOU KNOW...?

According to director Sidney Lumet, actors Gene Hackman and Henry Fonda, and newscasters Walter Cronkite and John Chancellor all passed on the role of anchor Howard Beale, which won Peter Finch (who died at the end of production) a posthumous Academy Award.

ABOUT THE DIRECTOR

Commenting on the assumption at the time of its release that *Network* was a "brilliant satire," Lumet explained 25 years later that he and Paddy Chayefsky always felt, "This isn't satire, it's sheer reportage. We were both brought up in television, so we knew what we were dealing with. But . . . I'm stunned at how prescient it is. A lot of what was hilarious 25 years ago [gets] no laughter [now] because it has all come true. So it hits you with a kind of impact that was not originally intended." (www.dga.org)

CRITICALLY SPEAKING

At the time of its release, many critics praised *Network*'s brilliance, as the following excerpt from Vincent Canby illustrates. But the acclaim was not unanimous, as Pauline Kael suggests.

Vincent Canby, *New York Times*, 15 November 1976

Network can be faulted for going too far and not far enough, but it's also something that very few commercial films are these days. It's alive. This, I suspect, is the Lumet drive. It's also the wit of performers like Mr. Finch, Mr. Holden, and

Miss Dunaway. As the crazy prophet within the film says of himself, *Network* is vivid and flashing. It's connected into life.

Pauline Kael, *The New Yorker*, 20 December 1976
The central gag in *Network*—Howard Beale becomes the first man killed because of lousy ratings—sounds like a good premise for a farce about TV, which has certainly earned farce status.... But in the *Network* script Chayefsky isn't writing a farce: he's telling us a thing or two. And he writes directly to the audience—he soapboxes. He hardly bothers with the characters; the movie is a ventriloquial harangue. He thrashes around in messianic God-love booziness, driving each scene to an emotional peak.

MORE CLASSIC MOTION PICTURE FAVORITES

All the King's Men, All the President's Men, Birth of a Nation, Citizen Kane, Dr. Strangelove, A Face in the Crowd, The Front, The Great McGinty, JFK, The Manchurian Candidate, Modern Times, Mr. Smith Goes to Washington, The Parallax View, Reds, Seven Days in May

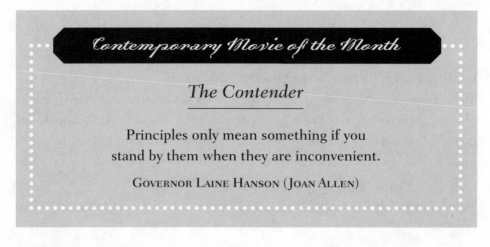

Contemporary Movie of the Month

The Contender

Principles only mean something if you
stand by them when they are inconvenient.

GOVERNOR LAINE HANSON (JOAN ALLEN)

THE DETAILS

2000, 1260M/C; R; DVD. **DIRECTOR/SCREENWRITER:** Rod Lurie.
CINEMATOGRAPHER: Denis Maloney. **AWARDS:** Academy Awards: Nominated:
Best Actress, Joan Allen; Best Supporting Actor, Jeff Bridges. Independent Spirit
Awards: Nominated: Best Female Lead, Joan Allen; Best Supporting Male, Gary
Oldman. Screen Actors Guild Awards: Nominated: Outstanding Performance
by a Female Actor in a Leading Role, Joan Allen. Outstanding Performance by
a Male Actor in a Supporting Role, Jeff Bridges and Gary Oldman.

THE SETTING

Late 1990s; Washington, D.C.

THE STORY

Laine Hanson (Joan Allen) is President Jackson Evans's (Jeff Bridges) second
choice to fill the recent vacancy of the vice president's position. His first choice
is Governor Jack Hathaway (William L. Petersen), but could Hathaway's heroic
attempt to save a drowning woman ironically be turned into a Chappaquiddick-
like tragedy and used against him by the Congressional committee members?
As it turns out, Senator Hanson may have a skeleton in her own closet: a college
group sex indiscretion that the head of the committee, the out-for-blood
Republican Congressman Sheldon Runyon (Gary Oldman), has happened upon.

Whether to abide by the committee's and Runyon's demand to either acknowledge or deny the accusation is the crux of Laine's (and the film's) dilemma. Lurie, the director/writer, uses this question to examine political, social, moral, and gender issues well worth considering. Written during the middle of the Clinton sex scandal, Lurie pondered the question, How would a woman in a position of political power handle this situation? Allen's portrayal of a fearlessly uncompromising woman, a stellar supporting cast, especially Oldman and Sam Elliott as President Evans's top adviser, and a surprising subplot, make *The Contender* worthwhile viewing. And it's most encouraging to see a woman being considered for a top political office, even if it *is* only in the movies.

READING THE MOVIE

1. What does the title mean in relation to the story? Is there a connection to other films?

2. Is the dialogue realistic or consistent with the tone of the film?

3. The scene of President Jackson Evans's (Jeff Bridges) speech to Congress is reminiscent of what classic film?

4. Do you think the director is too concerned with depicting Laine in a positive light? Is she a believable character?

FINDING THE MEANING

5. Do you feel that both sides of political arguments are equally represented? If so, which ones might those be?

6. Does the example of the relationship between sex and politics in *The Contender* accurately epitomize the standard for political moral values? During his impeachment hearing, President Clinton reasoned, "Even presidents have private lives." Do you agree with Laine's claim that sexual behavior is inherently private? Is Laine's claim that the questioning about her sexual history would never be applied to a man accurate? Why or why not? What are the demonstrations of sexism in the film? Is *The Contender* predominantly about the issue of gender? Why or why not?

7. What did you think of the dedication that ends the movie: "For Our Daughters"? Should anyone in public life stand by while people unfairly discredit him or her? Is Laine's silence a kind of compliance?

8. In politics, is there such a thing as political effectiveness at nobody's expense? At one point, the president's adviser, Kermit Newman (Sam Elliott), suggests using a form of blackmail with Representative Runyon. Her response is that they would then be no better than he is. Kermit replies, "We *are* no better than he is!" In the end, what saves Laine, her self-righteous character or President Evans's questionable tactics? (#17, 1:35:19) Is there an irony in this? Does your view of Evans change?

9. Does the plot twist surrounding the revelation of Governor Jack Hathaway (William L. Peterson) seem like a deus ex machina (a contrived solution to a standoff)? (#17, 1:41:30) Is it consistent with what we know about his character or not?

10. Is the character of Congressman Sheldon Runyon believable? Do you see any "cracks" of humanity revealed in Gary Oldman's perceptibly villainous performance? If so, what might they be? (#8, 1:00)

BONUS QUESTION

By giving a voice to controversial issues in a film, it helps elevate discussion. Could a film such as *The Contender* make it easier for a woman to eventually become vice president or president?

MEMORABLE QUOTES

Laine: I just wouldn't be using sex as leverage, if I were you, Sheldon. Because, you know, there's one thing you don't want. It's a woman with her finger on the button who isn't getting laid.

BEHIND THE SCENES

In the service of his characters' development, Jeff Bridges fervently researches all types of material. For this film the director suggested that Bridges study Mario

Cuomo's speech to the Democratic National Convention in 1992 as inspiration for President Jackson Evans's speech before Congress.

DID YOU KNOW...?

In the DVD commentary, Rod Lurie, the director, admits that he was so eager to work with Joan Allen, he wrote the character of Laine Hanson specifically for her.

MORE CONTEMPORARY MOVIE FAVORITES

Bulworth, Dave, Guilty by Suspicion, Mandela, The Manchurian Candidate, Primary Colors, The Quiet American, Richard III, Wag the Dog

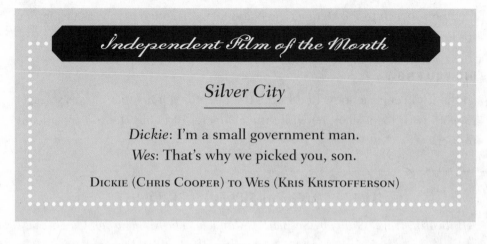

Independent Film of the Month

Silver City

Dickie: I'm a small government man.
Wes: That's why we picked you, son.

DICKIE (CHRIS COOPER) TO WES (KRIS KRISTOFFERSON)

THE DETAILS

2004, 128M/C; R; DVD. **DIRECTOR/SCREENWRITER:** John Sayles.
CINEMATOGRAPHER: Hasell Wexler. **AWARDS:** San Sebastián International Film
Festival: Best Director, John Sayles. Political Film Society Awards: Democracy,
John Sayles.

THE SETTING

Immediately before a gubernatorial election; contemporary Colorado.

THE STORY

Director John Sayles does not shy away from controversial subjects. Most of his
films deal with social and political injustice of some kind, whether it's labor in
Matewan, racism in *The Brother from Another Planet*, baseball in *Eight Men Out*,
or real estate in *Sunshine State*. In an interview, Sayles said, "Our movies are
political in that they deal with how people affect each other, and how governments
affect people and how people affect governments, but they are not ideological.
I would say they just recognize that there are politics involved in a lot of things.
There are politics involved in sports, it may be racial, sexual or economic, but they
are there and they are affected by history and they are changing constantly."
(*Now* interview by David Brancaccio, PBS, 6 August 2004) *Silver City* deals with
a "fictional" gubernatorial race in Colorado. Republican candidate Dickie Pilager

(Chris Cooper in yet another perfectly tuned performance) is the son of Senator Judson Pilager (Michael Murphy), a bought-and-paid-for politician who doesn't have a great deal of faith in his son's abilities to fish, let alone govern a state. And he's not alone in his misgivings. An irate enemy of the candidate refers to Dickie as "a mama's boy, a draft dodger, and a dimwit." But Dickie has been chosen exactly for his malleability. This political thriller/murder mystery drives home the message that politics is in bed with big business and is willing to desecrate the environment (and every human value) for the sake of increasing its already bursting bank account. In a political system that embraces ex-wrestlers, body-builder/movie action heroes, and bungling, frat boy sons of wealthy politicians, *Silver City* sometimes seems more like a docudrama than the feature film it is. But this insightful and well-meaning (if sometimes confusing) satire is the perfect discussion-group film. Don't vote before you see this film.

READING THE MOVIE

1. Does the film employ any consistent symbols, metaphors, or images? If so, what is their purpose?

2. In what ways is the film realistic? In what ways is it unrealistic?

3. *Silver City* garnered mixed responses from critics and viewers. Why do you think this film was polarizing? What is your perspective on it? Does it make you feel hopeful about the political state of the United States government? Why or why not?

4. With the forceful juxtaposition of image and music, the final scene carries an emotional impact. Do you think the statement it makes is accurate or exaggerated or understated? Why?

FINDING THE MEANING

5. In the 1930s, the actor Will Rogers once wisecracked, "We have the best politicians money can buy." How does this quote apply to *Silver City*? Is it still relevant to contemporary politics?

6. What is the point of view of the writer/director? Is he trying to convince you of something? If so, what means does John Sayles use to

convince you of his view: Character? Situations? Humor? Are these mechanisms effective?

7. In an interview, Sayles said that *Silver City* is "part of the conversation. This film is unique . . . in that it's a fiction film. . . . It's a mystery. But in that forum there are things that you can do that make people think. And that's the main thing that I like people to walk away from all of our films [with], just saying, 'Well, how does this apply to my life?'" In what ways might this film apply to your life?

8. How does the movie depict the current state of politics in the U.S. government? Under the veneer of a murder mystery, what are some of the subjects it covers? Does the film offer any resolution? (#11, :56:40)

9. The ensemble cast is, for the most part, composed of well-known actors. However, the lead is a relatively unknown actor, Danny Huston (son of director John). Is he a good choice? Were you able to empathize and identify with him? Why or why not? (#3, :11:40) There are four primary roles for women in *Silver City*: Nora Allardyce (Maria Bello), Danny's former lover; Maddy Pilager (Daryl Hannah), Dickie's renegade sister; Grace Seymour (Mary Kay Place), Danny's boss and the developer's wife; and Lupe Montoya (Alma Delfina), an employee at the investigative agency. What voice does each woman contribute to the film? How do each of them contribute to Danny in some way?

10. What's your opinion on Benteen's proposed Silver City planned community? What is this project really about? (#11, :51:27) What are the film's concerns about the confusion between democracy and capitalism? Do you share these concerns?

BONUS QUESTION

Sayles's *Silver City* was preceded by these earlier films about campaigns: *Bulworth* with Warren Beatty (1998); *Bob Roberts* with Tim Robbins (1992); and *The Candidate* with Robert Redford (1972). How does *Silver City* compare to one or more of these films?

CULTURAL REFERENCES

Disclaimer from director John Sayles: "Any similarities between characters portrayed in *Silver City* and officials of the Bush administration are unavoidable."

MEMORABLE QUOTES

Maddy Pilager: People have lost the ability to be scandalized.

FROM THE DIRECTOR

"The research [for *Silver City*] wasn't hard—every slab of hypocrisy I turned over revealed a thriving colony of rot beneath it, and I decided to base the central metaphor of the story on my own interpretation of the famous Trickle-Down Theory so chipperly (or Gipperly?) introduced by Ronald Reagan. I read a bunch about the methods, historical and present-day, of separating gold and silver from baser materials, about where those toxic leftovers go when the shiny stuff is spirited away, and got to use the word 'lixivlant' in a screenplay." (*FLM* magazine, Summer 2004)

ABOUT THE DIRECTOR

John Sayles (b. 1950) writes, directs, and edits all his films. *Silver City* is his fifteenth feature film. His career started as a novelist and short story writer, and he began working as a screenwriter for Roger Cormans's New World Pictures in 1979. His films include *Return of the Secaucus Seven* (1980), which was made on a mere $40,000 budget and helped launch the independent film movement; *Lianna* (1983); *The Brother from Another Planet* (1984); *Matewan* (1987); *Eight Men Out* (1988); *City of Hope* (1991); *Passion Fish* (1992); *The Secret of Roan Inish* (1994); *Lone Star* (1995); *Men with Guns* (1997); *Limbo* (1999); *Sunshine State* (2002); and *Casa de los babys* (2003).

CRITICALLY SPEAKING

Roger Ebert, *Chicago-Sun Times*, 17 September 2004

Sayles' wisdom of linking a murder mystery to a political satire seems questionable at first, until we see how Sayles uses it, and why. One of his strengths as a writer-director is his willingness to allow uncertainties into his plots. A Sayles movie is not a well-oiled machine rolling inexorably toward its conclusion. . . . Not all problems have a solution, not all wrongs are righted, and sometimes you find an answer and realize it doesn't really answer anything. To solve a small puzzle is not encouraging in a world created to generate larger puzzles.

David Edelstein, Slate.com, 17 September 2004

On its own, the movie takes off into the comic stratosphere in its first sequence and then slowly sinks to Earth, made logy by its noble means and Sayles' increasing inability to shoot anything but fat clots of undramatic talk in the most boring manner imaginable. I know, he's the quintessentially admirable independent filmmaker, but on the evidence of *Silver City*, he has systematically unlearned everything he once knew about how to tell a story onscreen.

Frederic and Mary Ann Brusatt, spiritualityhealth.com

John Sayles has made another sobering, complex, and multidimensional movie about politics and community in America. . . . He is not afraid to paint a broad canvas or to explore subjects viewed as too hot to handle by other less courageous filmmakers. The similarities between President George W. Bush and Dickie Pilager—especially the verbal gaffes when not reading a script—provide needed moments of humor. But Sayles is deadly serious about the dangers that ensue when savvy political operatives such as Raven degrade the language by Orwellian tricks. . . . *Silver City* explores the moral rot that lies behind many of the most intractable problems of our times. This is a film that must be seen and discussed by all concerned citizens.

MORE INDEPENDENT FILM FAVORITES

*Bob Roberts, The Corporation, Death and the Maiden, The Fog of War,
Manufacturing Consent, Matewan, Tanner*

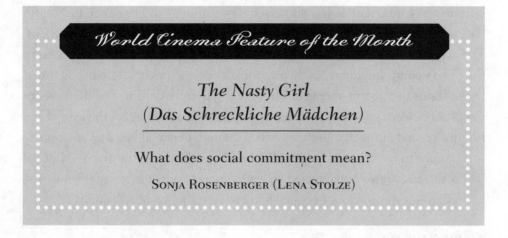

World Cinema Feature of the Month

The Nasty Girl
(Das Schreckliche Mädchen)

What does social commitment mean?

SONJA ROSENBERGER (LENA STOLZE)

THE DETAILS

1990, 90M/C; R; DVD (in German with English subtitles). **DIRECTOR/ SCREENWRITER:** Michael Verhoeven. **CINEMATOGRAPHER:** Axel de Roche. **AWARDS:** BAFTA (British): Best Film Not in English Language. Berlin International Film Festival: Best Film; Best Director. New York Film Critics Circle Award: Best Foreign Film. Academy Awards: Nominated: Best Foreign Film.

THE SETTING

1970s through early 1980s; Pfilzing, Germany.

THE STORY

The Nasty Girl begins with a scene of city workers washing graffiti off buildings in the fictional town of Pfilzing, Germany. The graffiti reads, "Where were you from 1939–45? Where are you now?'" These are questions, we learn, to which many of the townspeople would rather not respond. So when Sonja Rosenberger (Lena Stolze) begins seeking answers, the epithet "nasty girl" is hurled at her like a hunter's spear. Sonja couldn't be more surprised. Having started out as a bright and much-celebrated Catholic schoolgirl, her quest began innocently enough as an entry for a European writing contest. Sonja assumed that her topic "My Home Town in the Third Reich" would corroborate her belief that her fellow citizens were innocent of Jewish persecution through an allegiance to Nazism during the Second World War; and, indeed, had even been heroic in their actions. The contest deadline comes and goes, and, due to her being forbidden access to the town's court and library archives, Sonja's essay is uncompleted. The threat to the status quo seems silenced. But now she is more determined than ever to uncover the town's secrets. In order to do so, Sonja becomes (in the eyes of the filmmaker, and our own) a heroine, who, through personal loss and great physical danger to herself and her family, insists on learning the truth. Michael Verhoeven has written and directed an entertaining film that asks—and answers—important questions about personal and collective political culpability.

READING THE MOVIE

1. What are the pseudo-documentary techniques the director employs?
2. How does the film mix color and black-and-white cinematography to convey different time periods?
3. What does the symbolism of the tree represent to the character? To the town?
4. In what ways does the film hint at the theme of repression, which sets the stage for Sonja's later experience?

FINDING THE MEANING

5. What did you learn from this film? Did anything surprise you? Is the writer-director more concerned with Nazi Germany or its modern-day circumstances?
6. How does the identity of the townspeople change when the system by which they have lived collapses?
7. How does the film invite viewers, through identification with the characters, to enter that world?
8. Is the writer-director's sometimes disturbing use of humor effective? What is his purpose? (#11, :56:40)

9. Do you think Sonja did the right thing by rejecting the town's gift? Why or why not? (#3, :11:40)

10. How do you feel about the film's ending? What is the message it evokes? (#11, :51:27)

MEMORABLE QUOTES

Sonja: I feel that something is being hushed up. If so, what?

DID YOU KNOW

- The movie is based on the experiences of German historian Anja Elizabeth Rosmus, whose research unearthed details of Nazis collaboration in her Bavarian hometown, Passau. During the Third Reich, Hitler lived in a Passau house for a brief period that was later converted to a museum.

- The director names Sonja's town, Pfilzing, after the German verb *filzen*, which means "to be stingy or retentive." The term "Pfilzing Syndrome" means feigned ignorance of the Nazi era.

CRITICALLY SPEAKING

Rita Kempley, *Washington Post*, 7 December 1990

With all its resourcefulness and romp … *The Nasty Girl* is a spunky German cousin of *His Girl Friday*, an energetic, black-comic celebration of a gutsy gal news-gatherer and the high cost of digging for truth. Drawn from the real-life exploits of the historian Anja Rosmus, the movie engrosses us in the minutiae of a small life made grand by persistence and old-fashioned pluck.

MORE WORLD CINEMA FAVORITES

Before the Rain, Bloody Sunday, The Blue Kite, Burnt by the Sun, Danton, Divided We Fall, I Am Cuba, Rosa Luxemburg, Some Mother's Son, Tito and Me, To Live, Z

December: Enduring Bonds

★ ★ ★ ★

As near as I can see, the only thing you can take with you is
the love of your friends.

MARTIN VANDERHOFF (LIONEL BARRYMORE)
YOU CAN'T TAKE IT WITH YOU, 1938
DIR. FRANK CAPRA

Featuring

CLASSIC MOTION PICTURE: *Antonia's Line*
CONTEMPORARY MOVIE: *Finding Neverland*
INDEPENDENT FILM: *You Can Count on Me*
WORLD CINEMA FEATURE: *The Barbarian Invasions*

PREVIEWS

☆ *Antonia's Line* takes place in the Dutch rural farmland and covers a 50-year period in the life of Antonia and her multigenerational, matriarchal family. Antonia, her daughter, granddaughter, and great-granddaughter live independent, productive lives as, respectively, a farmer, an artist, a scholar and musician, and a budding writer. The story unfolds as these women's lives intersect with those in their community and we see them engage in the natural order of birth, sorrow, joy, and death. This delightful "feminist fairy tale" won an Academy Award for Best Foreign Language Film with good reason.

☆ In *Finding Neverland* we meet a charming cast of characters: J. M. Barrie (Johnny Depp), the author of *Peter Pan*; his unhappy wife, Mary; widowed Sylvia Llewelyn Davies (Kate Winslet) and her clan of four lively boys; and Sylvia's mother (played with a fierce protectiveness by the rarely seen in films Julie Christie). Just as they are in the film, the boys were Barrie's real-life inspiration for the Darling children in *Peter Pan*, and we fall for them as quickly as does Barrie. Depp's soulful intensity and our glimpse into the creative mind of a writer make this lyrical film enchanting entertainment.

☆ In *You Can Count on Me*, Sammy, a single working mother, lives in the small town where her parents died in an automobile accident and in which she subsequently raised her estranged younger brother, Terry, a misfit drifter. When he suddenly returns, Sammy has her hands full with a former boyfriend; a new boss; a son, Rudy, who erroneously imagines his unknown father as a hero; and now, a wayward brother. She has been an anchor for him, but his shenanigans stir a crisis. This rewarding Sundance winner supplies quirky characters, gifted acting, and satisfying dialogue.

☆ In the French Canadian film *The Barbarian Invasions,* we meet Rémy, a history professor, whose graceful surrender to life-threatening cancer is supported and even made possible by his estranged son, Sébastien (who truly is more of a capitalist guardian angel), and his former friends and lovers from years earlier. This remarkable Academy Award–winning film knows how to be both intelligent and emotional without being either detached or maudlin. The sentiment and images stay with you long after the final credits have rolled.

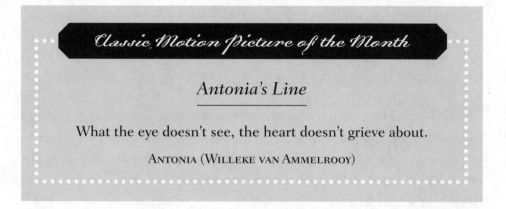

Classic Motion Picture of the Month

Antonia's Line

What the eye doesn't see, the heart doesn't grieve about.

ANTONIA (WILLEKE VAN AMMELROOY)

THE DETAILS

1995, 102M/C; R; DVD (in Dutch with English subtitles). **DIRECTOR/ SCREENWRITER:** Marleen Gorris. **CINEMATOGRAPHER:** Willy Stassen. **AWARDS:** Academy Awards: Best Foreign Language Film. Nederlands Film Festival: Best Director; Best Actress, Willeke van Ammelrooy. Toronto International Film Festival: People's Choice Award, Marleen Gorris.

THE SETTING

Mid-1940s to the mid-1990s; small country village in the Netherlands.

THE STORY

Shortly after the end of World War II, Antonia (Willeke van Ammelrooy) returns to her rural hometown in the Netherlands with her young daughter Danielle (Els Dottermans). Antonia's mother is dying and Antonia will now inherit the family home and farm. As they walk through the town, we see a sign that reads, "Welcome to Our Liberators!" Surely it is for the benefit of the American troops, but in Antonia and Danielle's stride is just the hint of the determined, free-spirited women they will become. Although Antonia appears gruff at times (especially to her gentle suitor, [Farmer Bas—Jan Decleir]), her home, with its very long outdoor dining table, soon becomes a community center to a variety of eccentric neighbors, social misfits, and the mentally challenged. Their names alone pique our curiosity: Crooked Finger, Mad Madonna, Russian Olga, Loony Lips.

Antonia introduces us to each character, and the narrator—her future great-granddaughter, the precocious red-haired Sarah (Thyrza Ravesteijn)—keeps us up to date om their seasonal life changes. Thus we come to know and care about each of them. The director, Marleen Gorris, clearly has a passion for philosophy and understanding the meaning of existence. Crooked Finger, living alone with his cases of books and serving as a mentor to all four generations of Antonia's "line," is the resident philosopher, albeit a dour one, and his musings provide an undercurrent of deeper meaning for the characters' actions and attitudes. But before we know it, 50 years have passed, and Antonia is on her deathbed (where the film opens). Like life, the film is over much too quickly, but what a lovely journey it is.

READING THE MOVIE

1. The writer-director Marleen Gorris has described *Antonia's Line* as a feminist fairy tale. What do you think she means by this?

2. In what ways does the director convey moments of whimsy?

3. What are your favorite scenes in the movie? Why?

4. How does the director convey her feelings about the Catholic Church? (#6, :57:20)

FINDING THE MEANING

5. Do you think a rural village, like the one in which Antonia and her family live, would have been so accepting of unmarried mothers or a lesbian relationship? What is the point the director is trying to make?

6. The character Crooked Finger is the mentor and teacher for Antonia, her daughter, and her granddaughter. (#7, 1:09:30) Therefore, they are all schooled in the philosophy of Schopenhauer, Nietzsche, and Sartre. How does the director incorporate various aspects of these philosophers' theories ("the turning of the will"; freedom and responsibility) into her characters' lives and the meaning of the film?

7. What qualities do you most admire about Antonia, Danielle, Therese, and Sarah? Do the men in the story seem real or too stereotyped? Why?

8. How do the sex scenes organically merge with the overarching themes of the film?

9. Antonia has created "enduring bonds" through her generous sense of hospitality and an inclusive connotation of community. (#5, :47:40) Are there ways in which you are like her or wish to be?

10. How does the film, or specifically Antonia, view death? How has she incorporated that understanding into her view of humanity and life?

MEMORABLE QUOTES

Antonia: Nothing dies forever. Something always remains, from which something new grows. So life begins without knowing where it came from or why it exists.
Sarah: But why?
Antonia: Life wants to live.

ABOUT THE DIRECTOR

Marleen Gorris made her first film, *A Question of Silence,* in 1982 at the age of 30. That and her second film, *Broken Mirrors* (1984), were controversial films that contained feminist themes. In an interview with critic Judy Stone (*Eye on the World: Conversations with International Filmmakers.* Los Angeles: Silman-James Press, 1997) Gorris simply explains about these films, "I wanted to show women's position in society." The 1995 *Antonia's Line* is a much more accessible film, but Gorris warns viewers not to take it too literally and considers that it does not portray real life, rather a tongue-in-cheek version. "Wouldn't it be nice if it had been like that?... It sounds naïve ... but of course, the film is a bit of a fairy tale." Gorris's more recent films were Virginia Woolf's *Mrs. Dalloway* (1997) and *The Luzhin Defence* (2000) with John Turturro.

CRITICALLY SPEAKING

Marjorie Baumgarten, *Austin Chronicle*, 22 March 1996
Antonia's Line is a family saga, and though it bears many of the familiar hallmarks of the form—the village full of colorful characters, the waxing and the

waning of the seasons, and the inevitable conflicts between the needs of the individual and the community—the movie is thoroughly original in its feminist simplicity. Antonia and her "line" of descendants generate a matrilineal heritage and an independence of thought, whose effects extend beyond their immediate blood relations and trickle throughout the community.

Edward Guthmann, *San Francisco Chronicle*, 14 February 1996
The goal of *Antonia's Line*, I'd assume, is to offer an alternative to the standard, male-centered family sagas that reduce women to salty waffle flippers and careworn brood mares. Gorris deconstructs the formula and shows us, over four generations, a line of strong, self-determining icons who humor the occasional man but in general rest easier in the absence of testosterone.

MORE CLASSIC MOTION PICTURE FAVORITES

Antonia and Jane, The Deer Hunter, I Never Sang for My Father

Contemporary Movie of the Month

Finding Neverland

James: She's on every page of your imagination.
You'll always have her there. Always.... She went to Neverland,
and you can visit her there anytime you like.
Peter: How?
James: By believing, Peter. Just believing.

JAMES (JOHNNY DEPP) TO PETER (FREDDIE HIGHMORE)

THE DETAILS

2004, 106M/C; PG; DVD. **DIRECTOR:** Marc Forster. **CINEMATOGRAPHER:** Robert Schefer. **SCREENWRITER:** David Magee (based on the play *The Man Who Was Peter Pan* by Allan Knee). **AWARDS:** Academy Awards: Best Original Score; Nominated: Best Picture; Best Actor, Johnny Depp; Best: Adapted Screenplay, Art Direction, Costume Design, Editing. National Board of Review Awards: Best Picture; Best Film Score. Venice Film Festival: Laterna Magica Prize: Marc Forster.

THE SETTING

Summer of 1903; London, England.

THE STORY

Finding Neverland automatically has two enticements going for it: Johnny Depp and Kate Winslet (good reasons to see *any* movie, actually). This surprisingly moving film is based on the play *The Man Who Was Peter Pan* by Allan Knee. That "man," of course, was Sir James Matthew Barrie (Johnny Depp), a Scotsman, who, we learn, suffered through his own difficult childhood. When Barrie was quite young, his older brother—the family's favorite—unexpectedly died. They then began to call James by his dead brother's name and demanded that he wear the brother's clothes. It seems to have been this extremely disturbing and confusing experience that drew James to the Davies family, including Sylvia (Kate Winslet), and her sons, George, Jack, Michael, and Peter. Their husband and father has recently died of cancer, and they are each dealing with their sorrow in their own ways. Peter (Freddie Highmore) seems particularly at a loss. By the time Barrie meets the Davies family in Kensington Gardens, his last play (*Little Mary*) has flopped and he is anxious to write a successful new one. We see Barrie as creatively innovative, a writer who uses the power of his imagination to confront the constraints of Edwardian London theatregoers, and to heal the hearts of four little boys and their mother. Particularly triumphant are the glimpses the film offers into the writer's creative process and the blending of reality and fantasy: the dancing dog becomes a circus bear; a flying kite inspires the fairy, Tinkerbell; a scolding grandmother prompts an image of a frightening Captain Hook; and the pillow-fighting Davies boys become the "Darling" children of *Peter Pan*. This clever adaptation invites us into a world of joy and humor as well as loss and sadness.

READING THE MOVIE

1. Did the special effects in *Finding Neverland* adeptly transport you to the cinematic make-believe world?

2. One of the criticisms of the film is that it tampers with certain facts (Sylvia's husband and the boys' father was still alive during the first years that Barrie knew them, for instance). Should the filmmakers' compression of reality have been an issue? Does it interfere with your enjoyment of the film?

3. While sitting on a park bench, James first spies the lovely Sylvia Llewelyn Davies (Kate Winslet), an impoverished widow, and her frolicking boys through a square hole in his newspaper—made by a housemaid who thoughtfully excised a withering review of his play. Why did the filmmaker use this image?

4. Do you think the ending of the film enhances or diminishes everything that has come before?

FINDING THE MEANING

5. What do you think the key themes of *Finding Neverland* are? How do you see them portrayed in the film?

6. Why do you think Barrie encourages Peter Llewelyn Davies to start writing? How does this affect Peter?

7. By suggesting that critics have made a "play" serious business, Charles Frohman (a delightfully droll Dustin Hoffman) infers that this spoils the experience. (#3, :16:10) Does thinking critically about a work of art change the way you experience it? If so, in what ways?

8. By the time we are introduced to James and his wife, Mary (Radha Mitchell), their childless marriage already seems in trouble. What appears to be their difficulties? Is either partner more to blame than the other? (#8, :55:50) Is there any hope of saving his marriage while still maintaining his friendship with the Llewelyn Davies family? How is Barrie's relationship with Sylvia different from that with his wife?

9. James tells his friend who alerts him to the gossip about his association with a widow and her sons, 'You find a glimmer of happiness in this world: there's always someone who wants to destroy it." (#5, :34:40) What do you think he means by this statement?

10. Are there ways in which Barrie's relationship with the Llewelyn Davies family was inappropriate? In what ways was it perfectly appropriate?

BONUS QUESTION

In psychology, the *puer,* or Peter Pan Syndrome, is often viewed as an individual's (especially a man's) inability to accept adult responsibilities. What are other films that deal with this subject?

MEMORABLE QUOTES

J. M. Barrie: Young boys should never be sent to bed . . . they always wake up a day older.

Peter Pan: When the first baby laughed for the first time, the laugh broke into a thousand pieces, and they all went skipping about. And that was the beginning of fairies.

FROM THE DIRECTOR

In this stream-of-consciousness piece for *FLM* magazine (Fall, 2004), Marc Forster writes about his experience of finding the imaginal "neverland" of the creative process. "It suddenly made sense to me that everything is always in the process of creation. Creation is the present and the now. . . . The truth was I needed to create a gap in my mind stream by simply directing the focus of my attention into the present. Directing my mind away from any illusory identities, any fictitious identities, or repetitive thought patterns—the identities which move a filmmaker's stories had to surrender, as one's ego is completely dependent on what is happening "next." Directing one's mind is a fable, which needs to be told because it possesses the rare magic to let you see yourself and the world anew."

ABOUT THE AUTHOR

J. M. Barrie's love of children and childhood is not only shown in his play *Peter Pan,* but also throughout the rest of his life. At the time of his death in 1929, the childless Barrie arranged for all the moneys made from the play to be donated to the Great Ormond Street Children's Hospital, which continues to this day. (www.miramax.com)

MORE CONTEMPORARY MOVIE FAVORITES

A Beautiful Mind, The Royal Tennenbaums, Running on Empty

Independent Film of the Month

You Can Count on Me

It's truly good to know that wherever I am and whatever stupid shit I'm doing, that you're back at my home rooting for me.

TERRY PRESCOTT (MARK RUFFALO)

THE DETAILS

2000, 111M/C; R; DVD. **DIRECTOR/SCREENWRITER:** Kenneth Lonergan. **CINEMATOGRAPHER:** Stephen Kazmierski. **AWARDS:** Sundance Film Festival: Grand Jury Prize, Best Film; Waldo Salt Screenwriting Award. Independent Spirit Awards: Best First Feature; Best Screenplay. National Society of Film Critics Award: Best Actress, Laura Linney; Best Screenplay. New York Film Critics Circle Awards: Best Actress, Laura Linney; Best Screenplay. Los Angeles Film Critics Association Awards: Best Screenplay; New Generation Award, Mark Ruffalo. Montréal World Film Festival: Best Actor, Mark Ruffalo; Special Mention, Kenneth Lonergan. Academy Awards: Nominated: Best Actress, Laura Linney. Best Original Screenplay.

THE SETTING

Contemporary Scottsville (Upstate), New York.

THE STORY

The devastating opening of *You Can Count on Me* effectively explains the undercurrent of grief that envelops the two primary characters. Sammy (Laura Linney) is a single mother who lives in her small-town childhood home, raising her eight-year-old son, Rudy (Rory Culkin), while working full-time as a bank loan officer, and still trying to maintain some personal life. Terry (Mark Ruffalo), who was raised by Sammy, is her aimless younger brother, who drifts around the country, working as an odd-jobs construction man. He's been away for more than five years and, needing money and escape from a pregnant girlfriend, decides to return home to visit his sister and nephew. We learn that each sibling has fashioned a different method of coping with his or her early loss. Terry's is more evident in his self-destructive patterns. Sammy's gradually becomes apparent in her dealings with the men in her life. She's a caretaker whose skills transferred naturally from her younger brother to her son and then, more problematically, to her romantic love interests: Bob (Jon Tenney), who wants to marry her, and Brian (Matthew Broderick), her inept, forlorn, married boss at the bank, who is happy to sleep with her. At heart, this film is about the enduring, yet anguished, relationship between siblings. Director Kenneth Lonergan is a master of natural dialogue. His characters simultaneously push forward and pull back in their exchanges with those they love. Laura Linney is winning in her depiction of an open, nurturing, sometimes baffled woman, who does her best to make sense of and peace with her troubled but lovable brother. Mark Ruffalo, who displays a Brando-like vulnerability, is captivating. For all his bravura and cynicism, it's easy to see that the abandoned child who lives within Terry clearly calls all the shots that threaten to obliterate the adult. Still, he's got one thing going for him: Everyone needs someone in his or her corner, and he knows he'll always have Sammy.

READING THE MOVIE

1. How does the film's opening set up the storyline?

2. Director Kenneth Lonergan comes from a stage theatre background. Do you see any evidence of this in *You Can Count on Me*? If so, in which elements?

3. Does Lonergan's dialogue work? Why or why not?

4. Do you think the Bach cello piece and the country western songs contribute to the story? Why or why not?

FINDING THE MEANING

5. Sammy appreciates the safety of living in Scottsville. But to Terry, it represents a dead end. What are the advantages and disadvantages of living in a small town such as Scottsville? Would you want to live there?

6. Do you think Sammy is a good mother? A good sister?

7. Sammy has a fairly established middle-class existence. Terry's life is one of nomadic uncertainty. (#5, :20:10) Which lifestyle suits you?

8. Do you think Terry provides a fatherly presence? What might he have to teach Rudy? (#15, 1:17:50)

9. What do you think of the minister (played by director Kenneth Lonergan)? How would you describe his talk with Terry? Do you think it was helpful to Terry? (#13, 1:08:20)

10. Amy Taubin, a critic for *The Village Voice,* accuses *You Can Count on Me* of being "a conservative film . . . a throwback to the Eisenhower age." (See feature "Critically Speaking"). Do you agree? Why or why not?

MEMORABLE QUOTES

Terry: I don't want to believe in something or not believe in it because I might feel bad. I want to believe in it or not believe in it because I think it's true or not.

DID YOU KNOW...?

Sammy's friend Mabel, who gets in trouble at the bank for using a colorful computer screen saver, is played by Jeanie Smith-Cameron, Kenneth Lonergan's wife.

ABOUT THE DIRECTOR

In an interview for bbc.co.uk, Lonergan answered James Mottram's question, "Your film is deliberately unhip. Did you feel it stood apart from most American independent films?" "The films that I like are much older. The films I grew up watching were 30s, 40s, and 50s films, and the 70s films, which were current when I was a kid. I don't care for the more recent styles as much. Plus, I didn't feel that with so little experience I had any business dabbling in pyrotechnics. I know a little about trying to build a narrative, and characterization and humor, and working with actors. But I didn't know how to shoot the film, so I thought I'd better keep it simple or I'm gonna look like a fool!"

CRITICALLY SPEAKING

David Edelstein, slate.msn.com, 17 November 2000

You Can Count on Me . . . happens to be the best American movie of the year. . . . What the film is "about" can't be summed up in a line: Its themes remain just out of reach, its major conflicts sadly unresolved. But Lonergan writes bottomless dialogue. When his people open their mouths, what comes out is never a definitive expression of character: It's an awkward compromise between how they feel and what they're able to say; or how they feel and what they think they *should* say; or how they feel and what will best conceal how they feel. The common term for this is "subtext," and *You Can Count on Me* has a subtext so powerful that it reaches out and pulls you under. Even when the surface is tranquil, you know in your guts what's at stake.

Amy Taubin, *The Village Voice*, 8–14 November 2000

It's not just the invocation of faith and family that marks *You Can Count on Me* as a conservative film. Its gender politics are thoroughly retrograde. When the inexperienced new manager imposes his absurd rules on the women in his office, they don't even get together to strategize, let alone confront him outright. Not just aesthetically unadventurous, *You Can Count on Me* is, in every way, a throwback to the Eisenhower age.

MORE INDEPENDENT FILM FAVORITES

American Heart, A Home at the End of the World, Waiting for the Moon

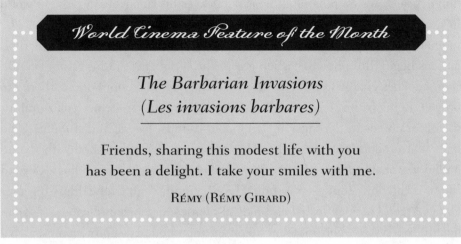

World Cinema Feature of the Month

The Barbarian Invasions
(Les invasions barbares)

Friends, sharing this modest life with you
has been a delight. I take your smiles with me.

RÉMY (RÉMY GIRARD)

THE DETAILS

2003, 99M/C; R; DVD. Canada (In French with English subtitles).
DIRECTOR/SCREENWRITER: Denys Arcand. **CINEMATOGRAPHER:** Guy Dufaux.
AWARDS: Academy Awards: Best Foreign Language Film; Nominated: Best
Original Screenplay. Cannes Film Festival: Best Actress, Marie-Josée Croze;
Best Screenplay. César Awards, France: Best Director; Best Film; Best Original
Screenplay. Genie Awards, Canada: Best Direction; Best Motion Picture; Best
Original Screenplay; Best Actor, Rémy Girard; Best Supporting Actor, Stéphane
Rousseau; Best Supporting Actress, Marie-Josée Croze.

THE SETTING

Contemporary Montreal.

THE STORY

The Barbarian Invasions swims in a complexity of personalities, emotions, and subject matter. Rémy (Rémy Girard) is hospitalized while suffering from the final
stages of cancer. It is left to his ex-wife, Louise (Dorothée Berryman), to arrange
for a reunion with their son Sébastien (Stéphane Rousseau), who, angered by his
father's past marital infidelity and self-centered lifestyle, has not spoken with

him in years. At first reluctant, Sébastien leaves his financial investment world in London to fly to Montreal with his fiancée, Gaëlle (Marina Hands). The moment he walks into his father's crowded hospital room, the mutual recriminations begin. But once Sébastien grasps the seriousness of his father's condition, he takes charge in the best way he can, using his money and authority to provide Rémy with the best medical care and physical and emotional comfort; the latter comes in the form of Rémy's old friends, lovers, and students, who have scattered around the globe. They all arrive at his deathbed with shared memories, libations and white truffles, and philosophical expoundings. Beyond the most obvious topics—mortality, family bonds, and friendship—director Denys Arcand tackles sexual and radical politics, organized religion, Canada's health-care system, corrupt labor unions, sympathetic law enforcement, global terrorism, drugs, and the tabooed, euthanasia. This often humorous drama provides viewers with the awareness that having meaning during one's life also extends to one's demise.

READING THE MOVIE

1. What are the various references to the film's title? Who or what is doing the invading?

2. Why does the film start the way it does?

3. Do any elements of the film strike you as perplexing or unfamiliar?

4. Did you find the characters complex or simplistic? Why? Does the cast of relatively unknown actors to American audiences enhance the film's effectiveness, since there are no familiarity issues to get between the viewer and the characters?

FINDING THE MEANING

5. Although ostensibly about mortality, could the argument be made that *The Barbarian Invasions* is as much about living as it is about dying? How do you respond to the controversial issues of using heroin as a painkiller for Rémy? What would you do in Sébastien's place?

6. Do you think director Arcand is sympathetic to his characters or critical of them? Why? What are the differences between the younger generation in *The Barbarian Invasions* and the older? Which do you think becomes more interesting?

7. Do you think this story of an estranged child reconciling with a dying parent is realistic? Have you had this experience?

8. Rémy recounts his meeting with a Chinese professor, who looked at him in horror when he praised the Cultural Revolution. What does this tell us about Rémy's left-wing politics? (#9, 1:14:50)

9. The bull-headed and lusty Rémy declares, "He's [Sébastien] a puritanical capitalist, I'm a sensual socialist." (#6, :27) Do you think this is true? If so, have his actions somehow contributed to his son's character? Are the lines of distinction between them so easily defined?

10. A question is raised about the relationship between Sébastien and Dominique. Do you think they eventually do marry? Would he find more fulfillment in a relationship with Nathalie (Marie-Josée Croze), the young woman who medicates Rémy? Why or why not? (#10, 1:02:15)

BONUS QUESTION

How does this film's theme of the father/son relationship compare to *Big Fish*?

BEHIND THE SCENES

Director Denys Arcand makes a brief appearance as the union representative who returns Sébastien's laptop to him.

DID YOU KNOW...?

Rémy's son, Sébastien, is played by stand-up comedian Stéphane Rousseau, in his film debut.

FROM THE DIRECTOR

Speaking about his earlier film from 1986, *The Decline of the American Empire*, Denys Arcand observed, "Beyond differences of gender, of age, of sexual orientation, they are all friends. There is a certain gentleness, a certain civility about the characters that counterbalances their cynicism. . . . If the audience does not care about the characters, there is no film." Denys could easily say the same about *The Barbarian Invasion*. (*Sight and Sound*, March 2004)

MOVIE HISTORY

The Barbarian Invasion is a sequel to Denys Arcand's 1986 film, *The Decline of the American Empire*.

MORE WORLD CINEMA FAVORITES

Dear Frankie, The Green Room, Secrets and Lies, The Year My Voice Broke

☆ FILM RESOURCES ☆

Websites Related to Film

The 100 Coolest Film Sites on the Web
(http://www.fadeinonline.com/cage/topfilmsites.html) A film lover's ultimate list.

Academy Awards (www.oscar.com) Official Motion Picture Academy Website
with up-to-date Oscar info.

Ain't It Cool News (www.aintitcool.com) "Cool" movie news, reviews, interviews, and gossip.

All Movie Guide (http://allmovie.com) Historical data about feature films.

American Film Institute (http://www.filmsite.org/afi100films.html) Top 100
Films of All Time Lists.

Apple (www.apple.com/trailers) The best place to view new trailers online.

Asian American Film (www.asianamericanfilm.com) "The latest scoop on
Asian American films and filmmakers."

Asian Movies (http://h.webring.com/hub?ring=asianmovies) "Asian Movies—
The Films, The Stars, The Directors of East Asia, also TV and Video."

Best of Iranian Films (http://www.bestirantravel.com/culture/film.html) A list
and descriptions of the best Iranian films and purchasing info.

The Black Film Center/Archive (www.indiana.edu/-bfca/websites.html) A
great resource for African American film-related Websites.

Bollywood.com (www.bollywood.com) Insider news about upcoming Indian
films and actors.

Critics.com (www.critics.com) Compares the ratings and reviews of recent
releases by 15 prominent critics.

Film Festivals (www.filmfestivals.com) Up-to-date festival information.

Hispanic Film Archives (http://hispanicfilmarchives.blogspot.com) "A portal
for news of Hispanic films and everything relating to them."

Hispano Mundo (http://www.hispanomundo.com/Films.htm) Links to Latin
American film and video sites.

Indiewire (www.indiewire.com) Reviews of and gossip on films and filmmakers of the independent film world.

International Movie Data Base (www.imdb.com) Details about American and international films; find trivia, quotes, plots, info about movies, actors, directors, etc.

Movie List (www.movie-list.com) Teasers, trailers, and "behind-the-scenes" featurettes of your favorite films and new releases.

The Movie Lovers' Club (www.themovieloversclub.com) A continuation of the book *The Movie Lovers' Club*. Check it out for new film and DVD reviews, recipes, insider industry news, and more.

The Movie Quotes Site (www.moviequotes.com) Submit a quote or browse their archive of movie quotes.

Movie Review Query Engine (www.mrqe.com) Articles and reviews span the entire history of cinema.

Movies.com (www.movies.com) "Get movie night right": Find movie times by zip code, as well as info on and reviews of DVDs and "The Buzz" on upcoming films.

Movies Unlimited (www.moviesunlimited.com) "The movie collector's Website": posters, memorabilia, etc.

The Online Film Critics Society (http://ofcs.rottentomatoes.com) Movie reviews by Internet-based film critics and journalists.

Planet Out (http://www.planetout.com/popcornq/fests) An International Directory of Gay and Lesbian Film and Video Festivals.

PopcornQ (www.planetout.com/pno/popcornq) This Lesbian- and Gay-oriented film site has loads of info on what's new in L & G entertainment.

Premiere (www.premiere.com) Information about contemporary films, actors, and directors.

Real Guide (http://movies.real.com) Movie review database with titles beginning in 1998, plus film festivals, awards, and box office data.

Senses of Cinema (http://www.sensesofcinema.com/links.html) This Australian-based site "is an online journal devoted to the serious and eclectic discussion of cinema."

The Silents Majority (www.mdle.com/ClassicFilms) An excellent site for your silent film interests.

The Society for Cinema & Media Studies (www.cmstudies.org). For the American academic film studies conferences and publications.

Yahoo! Movies (http://dir.yahoo.com/Entertainment/Movies and Film) links to 10,000 film sites.

United States and International Film Festivals

AFI Los Angeles International Film Festival (October)

Auckland International Film Festival, Australia (July)

Austin Film Festival, Texas (October)

Berlin International Film Festival, Germany (February)

Cairo International Film Festival, Egypt (December)

Cambridge International Film Festival, England

Cannes International Film Festival, France (May)

Cape Town International Film Festival, South Africa (April)

Chicago International Film Festival (October)

Dublin Film Festival, Ireland (March)

Edinburgh International Film Festival, Scotland (August)

Flanders International Film Festival, Ghent, Belgium (October)

Goteborg Film Festival, Sweden (January)

Hong Kong International Film Festival (April)

International Festival of New Latin American Cinema, Havana, Cuba (December)

International Film Festival of India

Istanbul International Film Festival (April)

Jerusalem Film Festival, Israel (July)

Locarno International Film Festival, Switzerland (August)

London Film Festival, England (November)

Los Angeles Asian Pacific American Film and Video Festival (May)

Mar del Plata International Film Festival, Argentina (November)

Melbourne International Film Festival, Australia (July)

Midnight Sun Film Festival, Sodankyla, Finland (June)

Mill Valley Film Festival, California (October)

Montreal World Film Festival, Canada (September)

Morocco International Film Festival, Casablanca (September)

Moscow International Film Festival, Russia (July)

National Latino Film and Video Festival, New York City

New Directors/New Films, New York City (March)

New York Film Festival (September)

New York Lesbian and Gay Film Festival (June)

Palm Springs International Film Festival, California (January)

Philadelphia Festival of World Cinema, Pennsylvania (April)

Portland International Film Festival, Oregon (February)

Prague International Film Festival, Czech Republic (June)

San Francisco International Film Festival, California (April)

San Francisco Jewish Film Festival (July)

San Sebastian International Film Festival, Spain (September)

Santa Barbara International Film Festival (March)

São Paulo International Film Festival (October)

Seattle International Film Festival, Washington (May)

Shanghai International Film Festival, China (November)

Singapore International Film Festival (April)

Slamdance Film Festival, Park City, Utah (January)

Stockholm International Film Festival, Sweden (November)

St. Petersburg International Film Festival of Festivals (June)

Sundance Film Festival, Park City, Utah (January)

Sydney Film Festival, Australia (June)

Telluride Film Festival, Colorado (Labor Day weekend)

Thessaloniki International Film Festival, Athens, Greece (November)

Tokyo International Film Festival, Japan (October)

Toronto International Film Festival, Canada (September)

Vancouver International Film Festival (September)

Venice Film Festival, Italy (September)

Vienna International Film Festival, Austria (October)

Wine Country Film Festival, Glen Ellen, California (July)

Women in Film International Film Festival, Los Angeles

DVDs for Rentals and Sales

Amazon.com is the largest online retailer. Thousands of DVDs and books on film are available at discounts. It is also the source for countless used DVDs and books on films.

Blockbuster (www.blockbuster.com) One of the world's leading providers of videos and DVDs. The Blockbuster brand enjoys nearly 100 percent recognition among active movie renters in the United States. (rentals and sales)

CafeDVD (www.cafedvd.com) Founded by a group of independent film directors and marketing and engineering professionals in 1999, this site has a wealth of independent, arthouse, foreign, classic, and hard-to-find titles on DVD. (rentals only)

Facets Multi-Media (www.facets.org) This Chicago-based service is the place to rent or purchase those impossible-to-find titles. (rentals and sales)

Film Movement (www.filmmovement.com) A DVD-of-the-month club for award-winning independent and foreign films selected from American and international film festivals.

GreenCine.com (www.greencine.com) A wide selection of "independent, international, documentary, classic films and rare titles." GreenCine is at the forefront of Video-on-Demand: pay-per-view streaming and downloadable movies for PCs. (rentals only)

Ironweed Films (www.ironweedfilms.com) "Films for the curious." A monthly film club featuring award-winning independent films and documentaries. (sales only)

Netflix (www.netflix.com) Netflix refers to itself as "the world's largest online DVD movie rental service, offering more than 3.5 million members access to 50,000 titles." (rentals and some sales of used DVDs)

Olive Films (www.olivefilms.com) An excellent outlet for foreign films. (sales only)

Qwikfliks (www.qwikfliks.com) Qwikfliks' slogan: "Bringing the movies to you is what we truly believe in." Unlike other online rental companies, you need not be a member to browse their site. (rentals only)

Spiritual Cinema Circle (www.spiritualcinemacircle.com) A monthly film club of pre-selected "entertaining, soulful movies."

Film Journals and Magazines (Online and Print)

American Cinematographer (www.theasc.com) Monthly international journal of film and digital production techniques.

Camera Obscura (www.dukeupress.edu/cameraobscura) Duke University Press quarterly; feminist perspectives on film, television, and visual media.

Cineaste: (www.cineaste.com) Quarterly, the art and politics of cinema.

Entertainment Weekly (www.ew.com) Entertainment magazine of popular culture.

Film Comment (www.filmlinc.com/fcm/fcm.htm) Published bimonthly by the Film Society of Lincoln Center, New York City

Filmmaker Magazine (www.filmmaker.com) Trade magazine of independent film.

Film Quarterly (www.filmquarterly.org) University of California Press academic film journal.

Hollywood Reporter (www.hollywoodreporter.com) Premier Hollywood trade publication.

Independent Film Quarterly (www.independentfilmquarterly.com) Information about the independent film community.

Interview Magazine (www.interviewmagazine.com) Entertainment magazine of popular culture.

Moviemaker Magazine (www.moviemaker.com) The art and business of making movies.

Script Magazine (www.scriptmag.com) Covers the craft and business of writing for the movies.

Senses of Cinema (www.sensesofcinema.com) Australian online journal "devoted to the serious and eclectic discussion of cinema."

Sight and Sound (www.bfi.org.uk/sightandsound) Monthly British magazine of world cinema.

Variety (www.variety.com) Entertainment daily or weekly trade paper.

Important Film Terms

ALLUSION A reference (direct or indirect) through an image or slice of dialogue to a person, place, text, another film, or some identifiable cultural concept. (Among many references, Woody Allen alludes to Marshall McLuhan, Kafka, Ingmar Bergman, *Medea*, Billie Holiday, and Sylvia Plath in *Annie Hall*.)

AMBIGUITY "Double meaning" can occur at all levels of a film (plot, narrative, character).

ANGLE (camera angle) The relationship between the camera and its subject. It conveys point-of-view (POV) and may be at eye level or tilted up, down, or oblique, making one character dominant or submissive to another. (Many shots in *Bagdad Café* are intentionally skewed to suggest disorientation.)

ANTAGONIST The primary source of conflict (character, group, nature)—usually referred to as the villain—with the film's hero or protagonist. (In *Respiro* the group of women living in the small village and working in the fish cannery is the collective antagonist of Grazia.)

ANTIHERO A main character or protagonist with whom the audience identifies; lacks the usual characteristics of a typical hero. (Frank Abagnale, Jr., is the perfect anti-hero in *Catch Me If You Can*.)

ARCHETYPE A primary character type that has appeared throughout narrative art forms, such as the hero, villain, mother/father, warrior, or the boy who never grew up. (The hotel manager, Paul Rusesabagina, in *Hotel Rwanda* is a definitive hero archetype.)

ASIDE Called breaking the "fourth wall," this happens when a character looks directly into the camera and addresses the audience (*Annie Hall*, *Nasty Girl*).

ATMOSPHERE The general tone or feeling established in a film, such as the strangeness of Mr. Grey's office in *Secretary*.

BACKLIGHTING When the source of light is behind a subject (usually an actor), which causes it to be cast in shadow or silhouette.

BACK STORY This refers to a character's history or events that happened before the actual story in the film begins. In *Dirty Pretty Things,* for example the back story of Okwe is revealed late in the narrative. However, often the back story is not revealed to the audience, but is primarily a source for actors to better understand the characters they are inhabiting.

BEHIND THE SCENES What goes on off-camera during filmmaking (see the "Behind the Scenes" feature in this book).

BIO-PIC A biographical film of a well-known figure or personality (for example *Henry & June*).

BLACKLIST Refers to the years between the late 1940s and early 1950s in Hollywood when Senator Joseph McCarthy and the House Un-American Activities Committee (HUAC) accused many filmmakers (writers, directors, actors) of being Communists, thus effectively leading to their being "blacklisted," or banned from being hired in the industry. (See sidebars, "Cultural References," under *Julia*.)

BOLLYWOOD This combination of two terms, Bombay and Hollywood, refers to the world's largest film industry found in India. But whereas Hollywood is an actual place, Bollywood is not. (See *Monsoon Wedding*.)

CAMERA MOVEMENT The way in which a cinematographer obtains various camera angles. A tracking or traveling, shot is made while the supported camera is moving. A zoom shot simulates movement toward or away from the subject. A pan shot follows the subject from left to right or right to left, shot from a stationary point. A crane shot is from an overhead panorama. A steadicam is a hand-held camera.

CARICATURE (also Stereotype) A character portrayed in a stereotypical manner without nuance or complexity, such as the candidate figure Dickie Pilager (Chris Cooper) in *Silver City*.

CHICK FLICKS Films primarily about women's issues and attended by women (*Antonia's Line*), which may also be considered highly emotional or oversentimentalized.

CINEASTE French term for a movie lover. Also the name of a film journal.

CINEMATOGRAPHER A film's photographer, also known as "DP" (director of photography).

COMMENTARY A description of the film's action by an unseen source, usually a character. *Good Bye Lenin!* is an example of a protagonist's commentary (also known as voice-over). A second meaning: Many DVDs now offer commentaries from a film's director or actors or from a film historian.

COMPOSITION Just as paintings and photographs contain a composition, a film does, too. This refers to the aesthetically balanced arrangement of colors, figures, shapes, and lighting in any given scene. Because it is based on the life of the painter Vermeer, scenes in *Girl with a Pearl Earring* are especially exquisite compositions that mirror his original paintings.

CONTINUITY It is standard for films to be shot out of narrative sequence. Thus continuity refers to an editor's attempt to make scenes match and the finished product to appear as seamless and natural looking as possible. A second meaning: On the set during filming, it is the job of a specific person to check for the continuity in costume, hairstyle, and props from one day's shooting to the next.

COSTUME Characters' clothing has become of increasing interest to (especially feminist) film theorists and historians as a means of studying genres, contextual fashion, and gender studies. (See *Annie Hall* and *It Happened One Night*.)

CUT This term has many uses: 1) a method of connecting images; 2) different versions of the same film, for example, the "director's cut"; 3) the elimination of scenes during the editing process; and 4) the director's term during filming for concluding a scene.

DEUS EX MACHINA A term from the Greek playwrights, which describes a contrived plot resolution that saves the hero and neatly concludes the story through the unlikely appearance of some external force (god) by some artificial means (machine). (*Big Fish* is a good example of characters being "divinely" lifted out of dangerous or troubling circumstances.)

ENSEMBLE Implies a large cast of characters, usually without any "main character," and several plotlines. (*Thirteen Conversations About One Thing* is a fine example of an ensemble cast.)

EPIPHANY (epiphanic moment) A main character's sudden insight into a personal or collective truth, which usually changes the course of their action or life. For example, in *Norma Rae*, when Norma Rae is promoted at the mill, she is treated like a traitor by her coworkers. The sobering effect of this experience is that she commits to working for unionization.

EXPOSITION Information about characters or events supplied within the narrative. The purpose is to help the audience make better sense of a plot or a character's motivation. (*Y tu mamá también* makes use of this technique.)

GENRE This French word means "type" and refers to different types of films, such as the musical, film noir, thriller, horror, western, gangster, and screwball comedy. A genre film is consistent in its thematic elements and shares enough characteristics that filmmakers and audiences alike easily recognize a film as belonging to a specific group. (*Adam's Rib* is an example of a screwball comedy.)

INDEPENDENT FILMS (indies) Independent filmmakers or small production/distribution companies working outside of the Hollywood studio system. The films they produce are not for mainstream audiences and generally deal with more personal or groundbreaking material. (*The Station Agent*, *Real Women Have Curves*, and *Pieces of April* are independent films.)

LEITMOTIF (motif) An image or piece of music, dialogue, or nonambient sound that is repeated to unify a character's actions or development. (The repeated musical refrain by Franz Liszt in *My Brilliant Career* exemplifies a leitmotif.)

MISE-EN-SCÉNE A French live theatre term that means "staging." It connotes setting, costume, lighting, actors—the arrangement of all elements within the frame of an image.

PACE An audience's subjective sense of how a subject (either information or plot development) is being represented rapidly or slowly to them through action, music, dialogue, or editing. (*Ten* may be an example of a slow-paced film, while *Nasty Girl* might be considered a fast-paced film.)

PERSONA This is the Latin term for "mask" and refers to a film star's on-screen image or identification. The roles that Katharine Hepburn (*Adam's Rib*) played contributed to her "persona" of a sophisticated, intelligent, elegant, and witty woman. Many of the roles that Gregory Peck played (especially *To Kill a Mockingbird*) typified him as a socially conscious and righteous man.

PICTURE WITHIN A PICTURE Federico Fellini's 8½ is an example of this way of telling a story about a filmmaker making a film about the film the viewer is watching.

POINT OF VIEW (POV) Refers to the perspective from which a story is being told. For instance, *American Splendor* is told from the POV of the protagonist, Harvey Pekar.

PREMISE This is the main idea of a movie, usually explainable in a few sentences.

ROAD MOVIE A film in which the main character is on the move, both physically and psychologically; usually involves a metaphoric self-discovery, such as in *About Schmidt* and all four films in June: Traveling Tales.

SCENE A section of narrative that usually takes place in a continuous time period and in the same setting, involving the same characters. An example of a scene in *Pleasantville*: when Betty, the television mom, discovers that she is changing when her lips turn red, Bud takes her makeup compact and tenderly covers it up with gray makeup.

SCREWBALL COMEDY Fast-paced narrative with incongruous situations (*It Happened One Night*) and witty verbal sparring between self-assured, independent female and male costars. Prevalent during the 1930s, the often ribald humor served as escapist fare for audiences during the Great Depression.

SET A constructed place (may represent an interior or exterior locale) where a film is to be shot. A set is distinct from a "location," which is "found," or real; although a location may be altered with lights and props and so on. (*Gosford Park* is an example of a "set"; by contrast, *Hideous Kinky* was filmed "on location.")

SETTING The place (season, geography, social structures, and economic factors) and the period in which the story takes place. (The setting for *Finding Neverland* is the London upper class in the summer of 1903.)

SHOT, SCENE, AND SEQUENCE A "shot" is an uninterrupted run of film, either in the camera or after it is edited. A "scene" is composed of a series of "shots." A series of "scenes" composes a "sequence." An entire film is composed of a series of "sequences."

SOUND This includes all audible aspects of a film: music, dialogue, and sound effects.

SOUND EFFECTS This includes all sounds in a film other than the music or dialogue. Some sound effects might be a barking dog or the screeching brakes of a car.

SPOILER Giving away a character's secrets or a film's plot twists, which might detract from the viewers' pleasure in watching the film. For example, revealing the end of *Dirty Pretty Things* would be a spoiler.

SUBPLOT A secondary, but often complementary, plotline of a story. An example of a subplot in *Invasion of the Barbarians* is the developing relationship between Rémy's son Sébastien and Nathalie.

SUBTEXT This refers to a genuine, but unexpressed, meaning in a character's dialogue or actions. A subtext necessitates the viewer reading into a character's words or reading between the lines. An example of a subtext exists in *Catch Me*

If You Can, in which Carl Hanratty, the FBI agent in pursuit of Frank Abagnale, Jr., becomes a sort of father surrogate.

SYMBOL An object in a film that has meaning beyond its usual implication or function. A word, name, color, sound, object, or person may have a secondary, or symbolic, meaning. Examples of symbols: the E.T. motif (the movie and, later, the doll) in *In America* as a symbol of an "alien" state of mind, and the car in *Ten* as a symbol of one woman's independence and curiosity and caring about the world.

TAG LINE This is a clever phrase, sentence, or sound bite used to market a film on a poster or in a trailer. An example from *About Schmidt*: "Schmidt happens."

THEME The main subject matter or concern in a film. For example, the primary theme of *The Contender* might be the importance of moral integrity or the need for gender equality in politics.

TONE The mood or atmosphere of a film (for example ironic, comic, nostalgic, frightening, or romantic) created as the sum of the film's cinematic techniques are decided upon by the filmmakers. The tone of *Network* is satirical (if not sardonic), while the tone of *My Mother's Castle* is nostalgic.

VOICE-OVER This is the recorded dialogue or commentary of an off-screen source. This narrative can be heard by the viewer but not by the characters, and may take the form of an interior monologue or addressing the viewer directly. The voice-over technique is used in the opening scene and later in *Julia*, when the character Lilly is reflecting on her life.

☆ AUTHOR NOTE ☆

Cathleen would love to hear from you. Please email her at cathleen@ themovieloversclub.com with stories about your Movie Lovers' Club. What works, what doesn't, what are your innovations? What are your favorite films? What topics are you most interested in exploring? And what are your suggestions for future volumes of *The Movie Lovers' Club*?

About the Website:

At www.themovieloversclub.com you can:

- Subscribe to The Monthly Movie Lovers' Newsletter
- Read The Movie Lover's blog
- Find information and reviews on current theatre and DVD releases, including discussion questions.
- Participate in the Readers' Forum at The Cinemania Café
- Learn about Cathleen's Teleclasses and upcoming personal appearances; and how to invite Cathleen to your group's Movie Lovers' Club
- Find out how to attend Movie Lovers' Treks to Film Festivals
- Obtain recipes for your Movie Lovers' Club gathering on The Food Lovers' page
- Enter raffles, and more.

Cathleen wishes you many hours of shared Movie Love enjoyment and meaningful conversation with your family, friends, and new acquaintances.

☆ ACKNOWLEDGMENTS ☆

Since my early childhood, movies have played a significantly tutorial, certainly pivotal, role in my life. I'm not exaggerating when I say that, from the age of three, movies served as my baby-sitters, best friends, teachers, and confidantes. As an only child of divorced parents, I could even say that movies parented me. The cinematic gaze cradled me, enthralled me, and became my eyes. Celluloid magic transmitted hope—and every other conceivable emotion—through its unique way of perceiving the world. Movies "taught" me about the human existential condition, about human drama, about story.

Local movie palaces acted as my weekend companions. My mother dropped me off at 11 a.m. at the Fox Theatre, where I saw one double feature and, afterward, I'd walk down to The Crest or Warner Brothers Theatre, where I'd sit through another double feature. On her days off, we attended The Art House, an unoriginal name for the only foreign film showcase in Fresno, California, where I was raised. Like the town itself, this movie house stood on the outskirts of an accepted social status. Only oddballs attended the "art films" shown in this square, squat stucco building that was painted powder blue on the outside and, like a shaman's cave, black on the inside. In The Art House, I was transported to a world, many worlds, really, that brought one-sided encounters with captivating cultures and heretofore unimaginable human predicaments into the otherwise guileless, uninspired existence of a sheltered child's inexperience. It was here that I saw my first Bergman film when—I was eight.

The summer after graduating from high school, I moved to San Francisco and continued my cinematic education at Mel Novikoff's Surf Theater and the San Francisco International Film Festival, and, later, across the Bay, at Tom Luddy's stellar Pacific Film Archive, near the University of California, Berkeley, campus which I attended. My addresses, lifestyles, and professions have changed several times over the years, but my passion for movies has been a constant.

The Movie Lovers' Club is an opportunity to share my passion with you, and, in turn, for you to share your own Movie Love with your family, friends, and new acquaintances. Even though I formed my first movie club in 1993, the inspiration for this book didn't emerge until 2001. The original book proposal was a very up-and-down venture until, in 2004, Karen Bouris and the staff of Inner Ocean Publishing recognized its potential. I owe my thanks to the collective enthusiasm of Karen, Alma, Ani, and Katie, at IOP, and to their first-rate editing team: Heather, Angela, and Elise.

I am indebted to the valuable advice and insights from friends and readers at various stages in this book's development: Mark Chimsky, Karl and Kateri Alexander, Gail Todaro, Rick Gilbert and Mary McGlynn, Nancy Membrez, Stephanie Palmer, and, especially, Matilda Butler and Bill Paisley.

Attending film festivals is my greatest pleasure and, therefore, I wish to acknowledge two of the world's best which, I regularly attend: The San Francisco International Film Festival and The Telluride Film Festival. It never occurred to me that I might write about films (because I was so busy viewing them), until one day my son asked, "Mom, you like movies so much, why don't you be a film critic?" To those people who published my first writings, I offer my heartfelt gratitude: Laura Shamas at Headline Muse: *The Journal of Psycho-Social Studies*, The International Association for Jungian Studies, in England; Steven Joseph and Dyane Sherwood at *The San Francisco Jung Institute Library Journal*; and, especially, Miguel Pendas, the Creative Director of the San Francisco Film Society and The San Francisco International Film Festival Program Guide. For her encouragement and support, I also thank Ann Martin, of *Film Quarterly*.

While earning my Ph.D. at Pacifica Graduate Institute in Santa Barbara, during a period of seven years, my thinking and writing about films began to deepen and to acquire psychological insight. I am grateful to my professors: the late Dan Noel, Dennis Slattery, Ginette Paris, and Richard Tarnas for their encouragement and assistance with my dissertation: *Technicians of Imagination: Film Directors as Contemporary Shamans*. My thanks to my colleagues and students at the University of California, Santa Cruz, and to Judy Rose, director of Humanities at UCSC Extension, who, for 15 years, has encouraged me to create— and allowed me to teach—nearly two dozen courses including art, women's studies, personal development, creative writing, mythology, and film studies. My special favorite is my course Cinema and Psyche: How the Movies Mirror Our

Minds, which was a precursor to both my dissertation and *The Movie Lovers' Club*.

I appreciate the generosity of spirit that Molly Haskell, Andrew Sarris, and Peter Bogdanovich have shown me, as well as the friendship of Harold Ramis, Erica Mann, and Eliseo Subiela. And thanks to Linda Schierse Leonard for many years of sharing movie-talk and experiences. Her incisive reading of and humanist approach to films, and our shared eclectic tastes, made Linda the ideal movie-going companion.

Heartfelt thanks goes to Dennis St. Peter and Hal and Sidra Stone, for their many years of supportive friendship. And I wish to acknowledge my gratitude to Ellen Levine, the best possible literary agent a writer could have.

Finally, appreciation and affection go to my son, Christian M. Wright, and to my mother, Marilu A. Lindley, and to the legion of friends and associates, too many to name, who have seen me through the long gestation period of this book.

☆ ABOUT THE AUTHOR ☆

Cathleen Rountree, Ph.D., a seventh-generation Californian, is a best-selling author and writing consultant, film analyst and scholar, visual artist and photographer, educator, and cultural mythologist. When she was a child, double features at local movie palaces acted as her weekend baby-sitters, companions, and teachers. Seeing her first Marilyn Monroe movie (*The Seven Year Itch*) at the age of seven, and her first Bergman film (*The Seventh Seal*) at the age of eight, proved to be formative experiences. A life long movie lover, Cathleen researches and writes about the confluence of cinema, psychology, and cultural mythology. Her articles appear in film and psychology journals, and she is the author of nine books, including *The Writer's Mentor: A Guide to Putting Passion on Paper*, which focuses on the art and craft of writing, and the five-volume series of interviews with well-known writers, artists, and public figures—*On Women Turning 30, 40, 50, 60,* and *70*—for which she is often referred to as "the Barbara Walters of interview books." Cathleen regularly speaks at film, writing, and women's conferences throughout the United States and internationally, and teaches writing at the University of California, Santa Cruz. Her consulting service, The Writer's Mentor, provides development and editorial assistance on fiction and nonfiction projects (see www.CathleenRountree.com). She lives with Dios, her Springer Spaniel movie-lover-companion and muse, in a seaside community in Northern California.

☆ INDEX ☆